THE THEOLOGY OF ECUMENISM:

THOMAS AQUINAS AND THE ECUMENICAL IMPERATIVE

THE THEOLOGY OF ECUMENISM

THOMAS AQUINAS AND THE ECUMENICAL IMPERATIVE

Antoninus Wall O.P.

SOLAS Press

2016

COPYRIGHT

All rights reserved Solas Press 2016.

No part of this book may be reproduced in any form, or by any means, electronic or mechanical, including photocopying, recording, or by any information storage and retrieval system, without prior permission, except by a reviewer who may quote brief passages for a review.

ISBN 978-1-893426-06-1

First published as: *The Experience of God in the Community of Man* Dissertatio ad Laurem in Facultate S. Theologia apud Pontificiam Universitatem S. Thomae de Urbe—Roma 1971.

PERMISSIONS info@solaspress.com

Library of Congress Cataloging-in-Publication Data

Names: Wall, Antoninus, 1925

Title: The theology of ecumenism : Thomas Aquinas and the ecumenical imperative / Antoninus Wall, O.P.

Description: First [edition]. | Antioch : Solas Press, 2016 | Includes bibliographical references.

Identifiers: LCCN 2014025546 | ISBN 978-1-893426-06-1

(Paper back) ISBN 978-1-893426-05-4

Subjects: LCSH: Christian union–Catholic Church. | Ecumenical movement. | Catholic Church–Relations. | Thomas, Aquinas, Saint, 1225?-1274.

Classification: LCC BX1785.W35 2016 | DDC 262.001/1–dc23

LC record available at http://lccn.loc.gov/2014025546

TABLE OF CONTENTS

INTRODUCTION..	ix
CHAPTER ONE: ALPHA AND OMEGA..	1
CHAPTER TWO: THE MYSTERY OF GOD AND GODLINESS..	5
CHAPTER THREE: WHAT GOD AND GODLINESS ARE NOT..	11

I. General Statement of Traditional Doctrine

II. Negative Definition of God and Godliness

III. Man's Movement Toward God and Godliness

IV. Application to Ecumenism .

CHAPTER FOUR: WHAT GOD AND GODLINESS ARE..	53

I. Catholic Doctrine on Positive Concepts of God

II. Positive Definition of Godliness

III. Man's Positive Movement Toward God and Godliness

IV. Positive Godliness and Ecumenism

CHAPTER FIVE: FUNDAMENTAL GOD AND RADICAL GODLINESS..	95

I. Fundamental God

II. Radical Godliness in Created Being

III. Radical Godliness in the Doctrine of Aquinas

IV. Radical Godliness and Natural Man

V. Radical Godliness and the Order of Grace

VI. Radical Godliness and Theories of Human Perfectibility

VII. Radical Godliness and Ecumenism

CHAPTER SIX: IMAGE OF GOD BY NATURE..   ..   155

I. Image and Likeness

II. The Evolution of Man as Image of God

III. The Universe as the Womb of God

IV. Freedom as Midwife

V. Image in Community

VI. Flawed Image

CHAPTER SEVEN: IMAGE OF GOD BY GRACE..   ..   209

I. The Message of Christ

II. The Life of Grace

III. Evolution in the Life of Grace

IV. Grace and Nature, the New Life and the Old

V. Image by Grace and Ecumenism

VI. Image by Grace in Community

VII. Image in a Community of Faith

VIII. Image in a Community of Hope

IX. Image in a Community or Charity

X. Summary

CHAPTER EIGHT: CHRIST AND HUMANITY..   ..   253

I. The Incarnation

II. Mission of Christ

III. The Encounter with God Through the Humanity of Christ

IV. The Special Work of Christ

V. Christ and the Church

VI. Christ and the Sacraments

VII. Christ and Humanity—Conclusion

BIBLIOGRAPHY..   311

ABBREVIATIONS

BIBLICIAL ABREVIATIONS

Acts	*Acts of the Apostles*
I Cor.	*1 Corinthians*
II Cor.	*II Corinthians*
Eph.	*Ephesians*
Jn.	*John*
Mt.	*Matthew*
II Pet.	*II Peter*
Phil.	*Philippians*
Rom.	*Romans*

Note: Scriptural quotations are taken from *The Jerusalem Bible,* Garden City, New York NY: Doubleday and Company Inc., 1966

OTHER APPREVIATIONS

Abbott — Walter Abbott, S.J., editor, *The documents of Vatican II*, translation edited by Joseph Gallagher (New York: Guild Press- America Press- Association Press, 1966).

Compendium — Thomas Aquinas, *Compendium of Theology,* translated by Cyrl Vollert, (St Louis: B. Herder Co., 1952).

Contra Gentiles — Thomas Aquinas, *Summa Contra Gentiles*, (Rome: Desclees and Co. - Herder 1934).

De Anima — Thomas Aquinas, *In Aristotelis Librum De Anima Commentarium,* Ed. P. Angelus Pirotta (Roma: Marietti, 1936).

Ethics Thomas Aquinas, *Commentary on the Nicomadaean Ethics,* 2 volume, translated by C. I. Litzinger (Chicago: Henyr Regnery Co., 1964).

Metaphysics Thomas Aquinas, *In Metaphysican Aristotelis Commentaria,* ed. M.R. Cathala (Roma: Marietti, 1935).

NCE *New Catholic Encyclopedia,* 25 volumes (New York: McGraw and Hill Co., 1966).

Summa Thomas Aquinas, *Summa Theologica,* translated by the Fathers of the English Dominican Province (New York: Benzinger Brothers).

PREFACE

This theological investigation is intended to make Catholics and non-Catholics familiar with the deep roots of ecumenical thinking in Saint Thomas Aquinas' understanding of Christianity. Saint Thomas (1225-1274) is a most authoritative exponent of Catholic theology, and therefore, he reveals that the modern interest of the Church in ecumenism is not a temporary, pragmatic adaption to the trends of time. Rather it flows from the deepest and earliest sources of the Church.

Central to Aquinas' ecumenism is the role of the Incarnation in Christ's mission and the life of the Church. In the light of Sacred Scripture he sees the Incarnation as God's loving will to share *Divine* perfections with humans in the fullest way possible.

God could have provided to us his divine perfections as 'manna from heaven;' why then, did God choose to become flesh? Aquinas argues, that had God divinized humans directly we would have shared His perfections, *but not in the radical way they exist in Him.* God's perfections do not come to Him from outside or above; all come from within, out of his very being! Therefore, God willed that humans would share His perfections in the most radical, godlike way—they would come out of human nature as their *proximate source*. This intent is beautifully expressed in the words of Saint Irenaeus (c125-c200), "God became man in order that man may become like God." Aquinas also notes that no one human being is capable of receiving the fullness of divine life present in Jesus. God requires a community of persons to receive this fullness. And it is to the extent that one is open to the fullness of Christ's presence in the entirety of the community that one approaches the encounter with God.

I made this study of ecumenism in the late 1960's. As a professor at the Dominican school of the GTU (Graduate Theological Union) in Berkeley, I was faced with the challenge of preparing Catholic students for the priesthood. At the same time it was essential to make this Catholic tradition intelligible to the non-Catholic intellectual community. The need for this theology that shows ecumenism as a fundamental requirement of human society is greater than ever.

Editor's Note

The first purpose of an editor is to excite in the reader the thoughts and emotions that the author intended. Here the original text, a doctoral thesis, was obviously written for a very specialized group, and so some changes in structure and phraseology were desirable for a broader audience. Also since the 1960's there have been questions about the proper use of gender references in English language usage. For example, in readings from sacred scripture we find "brothers and sisters" often substituted for "brethren." This is an area very much in flux and we have left untouched the masculine forms used as generic references.

Dominic Colvert

INTRODUCTION

1. The sudden emergence of the spirit of ecumenism stands as a major phenomenon in contemporary Christianity. Ecumenism has replaced historical attitudes with a new desire to understand, respect, share and, to the extent possible, to be open to the unifying experience of God's presence in *all* religious communities. This ecumenical thrust has revised the tendency toward mutual animosity, distrust, and even hatred that have dominated most Christian Churches since the Reformation. The practical consequences of the ecumenical spirit has been manifest particularly in the improving relations between many Christian Churches.

Ecumenism in the Catholic Church has not been limited to its relations with other Christian Churches. It also extends to the Church's relations with Jews, Moslems, Eastern Religions, Atheists and, in a word, with the whole human race. This extension of Catholic understanding of ecumenism was explicit in numerous pronouncements of Vatican II (Second Vatican Council October 11th, 1962 to December 8th, 1965). The opening statement of the Council was directed "to all men and nations."[1] In Pope Paul's Christmas message in 1965 he spoke of the concern for all mankind as being the dominant mood of the Council.[2] In the pastoral constitution on the *Church in the Modern World* the Council Fathers speak as follows:

> We also turn our thoughts to all who acknowledge God, and who preserve in their traditions precious elements of religion and humanity. We want frank conversation to compel us to receive the inspirations of the Spirit faithfully and to measure up to them energetically. For our part the desire for such dialogue which can lead to truth through love alone, excludes no one, though an appropriate measure of prudence must undoubtedly be exercised. We include those who cultivate beautiful qualities of the human spirit, but do not yet acknowledge the Source of these qualities. We include those

---

[1] Abbott, "Message to Humanity," p. 3.
[2] *Ibid.*, footnote 7, p. 4.

who oppress the Church and harass her in manifold ways. Since God the Father is the origin and purpose of all men, we are all called to be brothers. Therefore, if we have been summoned to the same destiny, which is both human and divine, we can and should work together without violence and deceit in order to build up this world in genuine peace,[3]

In the *Decree on Ecumenism* the Council Fathers describe the ecumenical movement as follows: "The ecumenical movement means those activities and enterprises which, according to various needs of the Church and opportune occasions, are started and organized for the fostering of unity among Christians."[4] In the mind of the Council Fathers, then, ecumenism would seem to be limited to the work of fostering unity among Christians. However, in reaction to widespread desire for the Council to address itself to the non-Christian world, and taking cognizance of the billions of humans who live outside the Christian community, the Council subsequently issued its *Declaration on the Relationship of the Church to Non-Christian Religions* in which it expressed its desire to foster cordial relations with all men:

> In her task of fostering unity and love among men and even among nations, she [the Church] gives primary consideration in this document to what human beings have in common and to what promotes fellowship among them.
>
> For all people comprise a single community, and have a single origin, since God made the whole race of men dwell over the entire face of the earth (*cf. Acts* 17:26). One also is their final goal: God. His providence, His manifestations of goodness, and His saving designs extend to all men (*cf. Wis.* 8:1; *Acts* 14:17; *Rom.* 2:6-7; 1 *Tim.* 2:40) against the day when the elect will be united in the Holy City ablaze with the splendor of God, where nations will walk in His light (*cf. Apoc.* 21:23).[5]

---

[3] Abbott, "Pastoral Constitution on the Church in the Modern World," n. 92, pp. 306-307.

[4] Abbott, "Decree on Ecumenism," n. 4, p. 347.

[5] Abbott, "Declaration on the Relationship of the Church to Non-Christian Religions," n. 1, p. 660.

Pope Paul VI implemented this Decree by a papal bull issued on May 19, 1964 in which he established the Secretariat for Non-Christians:

> The secretariat's aims are to create a climate of cordiality between Christians and followers of other religions, to dissipate prejudice and ignorance especially among Catholics and to establish fruitful contact with members of other religions concerning questions of common interest.[6]

The purpose motivating the papal bull according to P. Humbertclaude, "is the extending of the ecumenical movement fostered by the establishment of the Secretariat for Promoting Christian Unity to all believers, even the non-baptized."[7] The common ground for this extension is man as the natural image of God. The Secretariat is not designed exclusively for believers in one God, "*qui unum Deum colunt*" (Apostolic letter, April 30, 1964) but is aimed at responding "to the spiritual needs of all men" (reply to Cardinal Tisserant, June 23, 1964).[8] In writing about ecumenism in this thesis, I will be using the term in this broader sense, understanding by it the openness to dialogue with all men as images of God, at least by nature if not by grace.

2. The response of Catholics to this ecumenical development varies. Many Catholics, including clerics, react to it with unequivocal distaste, fearing that it will lead to compromise, dilution of faith, indifferentism, and an amorphous form of humanism and secularism. Some feel that it puts into serious question the traditional mission of the Church to convert men to the one fold of Christ.

Others accept ecumenism as a possible good and qualified blessing, but fail to attribute to it significance beyond that of a phenomenon of secondary importance, representing an accidental development that has little relation to the essentials of Christian life and growth. That is to say, they look upon the grace of ecumenism as a kind of *gratia gratis data*.

---

[6] *Ibid.*, footnote 1, p. 660.
[7] P. Humbertclaude, "Non-Christian Secretariate," *NCE, Vol. 10, p. 488.*
[8] *Ibid.*

Finally, there are those who hold ecumenism to be not only a good, but an essential and primary good of the Christian life. They see it originating in the inner dynamics of grace and forming a necessary condition for the normal development of the spiritual life.

3. The ecumenical impulse was officially recognized and accepted as a genuine manifestation of the workings of the Holy Spirit by Vatican II. This fact can be documented by numerous declarations of the Council. In the Decree on Ecumenism one reads:

> Today, in many parts of the world, under the inspiring grace of the Holy Spirit multiple efforts are being expended through prayer, word, and action to attain that fullness of unity which Jesus Christ desires. This sacred Synod, therefore, exhorts all the Catholic faithful to recognize the signs of the times and to participate skillfully in the work of ecumenism.[9]

In the same Decree one reads:

> Let all Christ's faithful remember that the more purely they strive to live according to the gospel, the more they are fostering and even practicing Christian unity. For they can achieve depth and ease in strengthening mutual brotherhood to the degree that they enjoy profound communion with the Father, the Word, and the Spirit.
>
> This change of heart and holiness of life, along with public prayer for the unity of Christians, should be regarded as the soul of the whole ecumenical movement, and can rightly be called "spiritual ecumenism."[10]

To these quotations many more could be added stating in one form or another that ecumenism is the expression of God's grace at work in human nature.

---

[9] Abbott, "Decree on Ecumenism," *n. 4, p. 347. Footnote 22.* The translation of the Decree from Cardinal Bea's Secretariate (Jan. 1965) expands "skillfully" (*sollerter*) into "take an active and intelligent part" in the work of ecumenism.

[10] Abbott, n. 7, p. 351.

4. Accepting this judgment of Vatican II about the nature and origin of the ecumenical impulse, I propose to examine this thrust in the light of traditional concepts of Catholic doctrine concerning the mystery of God, the Incarnation, the Church, Grace, the Sacraments, the Cross, and the Mission of the Church. My aim will be to determine how ecumenism, as a work of the Holy Spirit, may be fitted into the dynamics of the Christian life as conceived in traditional Catholic thought. Can ecumenism be accepted as something that logically flows from that thought as a natural development and outgrowth of it; or does it represent a phenomenon so new and different that it cannot be comfortably reconciled with and integrated into traditional doctrine?

In making this analysis I will offer the doctrine of Thomas Aquinas as one who represents an authoritative expression of traditional Catholic thought. My intention will not be to critically analyze and reevaluate the traditional doctrine in the light of the development of ecumenism. Rather, I will endeavor to offer a faithful, exact reproduction of the substantial content of that traditional doctrine, and then evaluate the ecumenical development in its light.

In this context I will argue that the ecumenical thrust can not only be reconciled with the substance of traditional Catholic doctrine as expressed in Aquinas, but that it must be seen and accepted as a logical, more explicit development of that tradition, perfectly in harmony with the full implications of the Incarnation. I will argue that the ecumenical impulse is an essential expression of man's growth in godliness, and that it is essential and primary to the ordinary workings of sanctifying grace. I will propose that it proceeds in a particular way from the dynamics of the theological virtues of faith, hope, and charity with a primacy given to charity.

I will further argue for the unity of the grace of ecumenism in the sense that openness to God's presence in Protestants, Jews, Moslems, humanists, atheists, and in the whole of mankind, is inseparable from the openness to God's presence in the community of Catholic believers. While my analysis will touch on a variety of objects and aspects of the Christian life, there will be an underlying formal unity throughout these considerations in so far as the study will at all times be dealing *with the community of man as the point of primary and principal experience of God.*

My intention is to present the material in a way that avoids any effort to persuade or 'convert' the non-Catholic reader, but only to make Catholic tradition intelligible if not digestible. In the same spirit of ecumenism, I will try not only to make the Catholic Church of today intelligible to non-Catholics but, equally important, to make the Catholic Church of yesterday intelligible to the Catholic Church of today.

Finally, part of my motivation in selecting this subject is my conviction that humanism will become increasingly the force of the future. In the American environment in particular this will be due to sociological, economic, and many other reasons. As men become increasingly withdrawn from contact with nature and more preoccupied with themselves and their own humanity, I see that the Church, as never before, will be called upon to assist them to recognize and experience the revealing presence of God primarily in the workings of their own humanity.

CHAPTER ONE

ALPHA AND OMEGA

The traditional Catholic understanding of the relation of God to the universe may be summarized as follows: God is a Father of infinite love who brings all creation into existence as an expression of that love.[1] He imparts to created entities, individually and collectively, a share in His reality so that the actuality of every creature is a derivation of and a created participation in His divine being.[2] To the extent that a creature exists it reflects both in its being and activity the likeness of the divine source.[3]

The dynamics of all creatures express and reveal in their ultimate reality a thrust toward ever greater godliness in accord with the potential for such divine likeness present in their nature.[4] Only by interpreting the actuality and activity of creatures in light of this movement toward greater godliness, can one find an ultimate intelligibility in the mystery of created being.

While a likeness to the divine source is true of the universe at large, it is verified in a special manner of human nature which embodies the highest degree of participated godliness—potential and actual—among visible entities.[5] If any ultimate meaning is to be found in the human mystery,[6] the dynamics of human activity on the individual and collective level must be understood and interpreted in the context of a hunger for, and specific thrust toward, the godliness proper to man's unique participation in divinity.

---

[1] The theological analysis of the essentials of Catholic understanding of the relation between God and the universe as Creator and created, is found in the *Summa*, I, qq. 44-49.

[2] *Cf. Summa*, I, q. 44, a. 1; q. 47, aa. 1,2; *Compendium*, cc. 21. 68. 102.

[3] *Cf. Summa*, I, q. 105, a. 5; q .4, a. 3.

[4] *Cf. Summa*, I, q. 45, a. 4c and ad 3; q. 65, a. 1c; *Compendium*, c.103.

[5] *Cf. Summa*, I, q. 65, a. 1c; q. 93-Man made in the image of God.

[6] *Cf. Summa*, I-II, q. 2, aa. 6,7,8; q. 93, a. 8; *Compendium*, c.104.

In the absence of such an understanding the human situation past, present, and future, individual and collective, remains in the final analysis, an unintelligible, meaningless, frighteningly pointless phenomenon—certainly not the product of a loving Father. In the absence of such an interpretation the universe is the end result of a soul-chilling, impersonal, and chance process. Though the negative views often given of the thrust toward godliness tend to be described through poetic and euphemistic images, they fail to conceal the *dread* in attendance to the lack of discernment of the loving Father of man and the universe.[7]

In the light of the traditional Catholic view, it follows that every facet of the human situation will reveal an ultimate intelligibility only in the context of man's necessary, though often unconscious, groping toward divinity.[8] The nature of man's potential and hunger for, and movement toward godliness, must be reflected upon and in some degree understood, if human life is to provide a real explanation of itself. That is to say, man's hopes and frustrations, loves and hates, intimacies and alienations, wisdom and foolishness, glories and shames, must be studied and evaluated as healthy or diseased strivings after godliness if they are to offer a final meaning.

If God is the final goal of the human thrust, then the truth about God will be the ultimate revealing and controlling principle of the understanding of man.[9] In turn, if God reveals Himself primarily in and through human nature, as Christianity affirms,[10] the deepening insight

---

[7] Jean-Paul Sartre's espousal of existential atheism possesses the special merit of providing an uncompromising statement in dramatic settings of the emptiness of godless reality without any softening of the hard human implications of this life view. For an analysis of Sartre's atheism see James Collins, *The Existentialists,* A Gateway Edition (Chicago: Henry Regnery Co., 1964), pp. 69-87.

[8] *Cf. Summa,* I, q.44, a.4c; q.60, a.5c; I-II, q.7, a.7 ad.2 ; q.1, a.7; II-II, q.26, a.3; *Compendium,* c.104.

[9] *Cf. Summa,* I, q.87, a.1. Since the potential is not Intelligible and since man becomes fully actual only through knowing God (*Ibid.* q.93, a.7), it is man's possession of the truth of God which makes him intelligible to himself.

[10] *Cf. Ibid.,* I-II, q. 1, a. 2c. God reveals Himself primarily through the human nature of Christ, but fully through the rest of humanity in its relation to Christ.

that man acquires into the mystery of his own being becomes the point of most profound revelation of the mystery of God. The two understandings, the one of God and the other of man, will evolve together revealing to man the mystery of his humanity by revealing in that humanity the mystery of divinity.

Now, the primary light will not come from what man discovers about his own humanity, but from what man finds revealed about God in that humanity; or as a more exact expression of the Catholic tradition, from what God chooses to reveal of Himself to man in his humanity. This revelation of divinity that man finds in his own nature becomes the source of light by which man comes to the ultimate understanding of his own being.

Proceeding from this Catholic view I will examine first what it is that Catholic doctrine teaches about the truth of God. I will draw from this teaching some of its implications about godliness in man and about ecumenism. I will then examine in more detail what this same tradition affirms concerning man's potential for, and movement toward, godliness. In the subsequent chapters I will analyze the role of Christ. I will examine his relations to humanity as the link between God and man—the divine and the human—through whom man achieves true godliness. In all of these considerations the focal point of my inquiry will be *human nature as the primary, principal point of contact with, and experience of, God.*

CHAPTER TWO

THE MYSTERY OF GOD AND GODLINESS

Catholic doctrine asserts before all else that God is a mystery absolutely transcending the capacity of the human intellect or any created intelligence, to understand.[1] If one attempts to comprehend the divine reality, he is in fact reducing the infinite Godhead to the strictures of created concepts.[2] Progress in the intellect's endeavor to know the truth about God takes the form of a growing awareness and appreciation of the radical incapacity of human intelligence to accomplish this task.

The closer man comes to the mystery of God the more clearly he recognizes that he does not and cannot know Him. In the intellect's attempt to know, symbols are formed to express what the mind imperfectly grasps about God, only to be discarded as their inadequacy becomes painfully evident and so that other symbols may be substituted.[3] The human mode of advance in this area is represented by a form of progressive demythologizing accompanied by the creation of new, hopefully more adequate myths, to express better the impossibility of the task.

Man's efforts to know God are further complicated by the distress human nature experiences in the presence of the unknown—particularly in the presence of the ultimate unknown.[4] Man's tendency is to reduce all reality, and especially the mystery of God, to a level which permits rational analysis and confident formulations of clear, comfortable concepts. This tendency is itself a distortion of man's desire for godliness in that he endows his finite, inadequate insights with the characteristics of Divine Truth. While this trait will be examined in

---

[1] *Cf. Summa* I,q. 1, a. 1c; q.1, a.12; q.2, a.1c; *Compendium*, c.26.

[2] *Cf. Summa*, I,q.12, a.2; *Compendium*, c.105.

[3] *Cf. Summa*, I, q.1, aa.9, 10, 13.

[4] Since truth is the object and good of the intellect, ignorance is an evil for the intellect. When ignorance involves the ultimate truth which man most loves and desires to possess, the absence of such truth constitutes the most serious evil and an object of fear. *Cf. Summa*, I-II, q. 42, a. 1.

detail later in Chapter Three, it is desirable to mention here that though many accept in theory the Church's doctrine that God is a mystery, in practice they are tempted to make of that same mystery an object that is accessible to rational analysis and understanding.

To the extent that created being shares in divinity, it also participates in the mystery surrounding God. The more a creature attains godliness in being and activity, the more it partakes of the divine mystery. The godliness that human nature aspires to represents the highest degree of participation in divinity among visible creatures.[5] And to the extent that a man evolves in godliness, his development will present to him a growing mystery that defies rational analysis and understanding. To grow in godliness, therefore, is to move into areas of human development that add new obscurities to the human situation that defy facile analysis. It is one thing to assert that the goal of human development is a more intense participation in godliness. It is quite another thing, however, to define and classify the progressive changes involved in this evolution.

As human nature takes on more of the perfections of God, the capacity of the intellect to keep up with and comprehend the nature and dynamics of this change is quickly outrun.[6] Therefore, when I state that human nature must be understood and interpreted in the context of man's thrust toward godliness I do not mean to imply that through such interpretation that human endeavors, experiences, frustrations, history, and existence, can suddenly be neatly fitted into an overall pattern and explained so as to radiate intelligibility and eliminate obscurity. On the contrary, I mean to assert that such an interpretation will more and more affirm a mystery that refuses to respond to pietistic explanations and consoling simplifications. The closer the mind approaches to the reality of true godliness in human nature—as man experiences awe and

---

[5] *Cf. Summa* I, q. 93, aa. 1; 2.

[6] *Cf. Summa*, I-II, q. 68, a.2 Aquinas' argument for the necessity of the Gifts of the Holy Spirit is based on the inadequacy of human intellect to keep up with and control the requirements of the life of grace as it intensifies in the soul.

reels before the reality of God—the more the mind will experience awe before the human miracle.⁷

Just as men shrink from the inscrutability of God and seek a false security by endeavoring to reduce the divine mystery to a consoling level of clear, comfortable, digestible rational insights, so man shrinks from the mystery of godliness in human nature and attempts to bring this phenomenon under control by a simplistic interpretation of it that squeezes out the elements of the unknown and reduces it to a comfortable prop or crutch with which to face life. To those to whom the responsibility is given as teachers and preachers of the Word to assist others in opening themselves to the mystery of God and godliness in their lives, the temptation is always operative to pander to this human desire by reducing the understanding of God and godliness to a convenient, consoling life support from which both obscurity and challenge have been removed.

The fact of the mystery of God and godliness has particular relevance today when so many Christians find themselves confused and hurt both in their understanding of God and in their traditional interpretation of their own lives.⁸ Many wonder whether their churches are not undergoing a corruption of faith, slipping from the comforting security of the past with its clear concepts of God and the meaning of

---

[7] *Cf. Summa*, I-II, q. 110, a.1. Since grace is a formal, though analogous, participation in the divine life, its intrinsic reality transcends the intensity and perfection of being of the natural order. In the view of Aquinas the good of grace in one individual surpasses the good of nature in the entire universe. Also *Cf. Summa*, I-II, q. 113, a. 9, ad. 2.

[8] For an analysis of the crisis in faith today see Karl Rahner, *Theological Investigations*, Vol. VI *Concerning Vatican II, The Man of Today and Religion, (*Baltimore: Helicon Press, 1969), pp. 3-20. Also Karl Rahner, *op.cit.,* Vol. V, *Thoughts on the Possibility of Belief Today,* pp. 3-22. E. Schillibeeckx, *God and Man (*Sheed and Ward, 1969), pp. 18-41. And by the same author, *Secularization and Christian Belief in God* (Sheed and Ward, 1968), pp. 51-90. Robert Gleason, *The Search for God,* (Sheed and Ward, 1964), pp. 5-18, Gustave Weigel, *The Modern God: Faith in a Secular Culture* (New York: The Macmillan Company, 1963), pp. 1-56. Harvey Cox, *The Secular City* (New York: The Macmillan Company, 1966), pp. 1-13.

human existence, into the disturbing doubts of the present where the notions about God and human life become confused. This confused state promises a bleak future which will be even more destructive of the thinking of the past. Now, confusion and doubt in one's sense of God and the presence of the divine in our lives may, in fact, be indicative of a weakening and even loss of faith. According to Christian experience, however, such disturbing spiritual phenomena ought not to be automatically interpreted in this pessimistic sense. They may equally be manifestations of growth rather than degeneration. They can be an expression of man's approaching closer to the mystery of God and godliness in his own humanity—with the accompanying price of obscurity and anxiety which the Gospels and the testimony of mystics inform us is the inescapable condition of this approach.[9]

In either an individual or community, whether we are dealing with growth or degeneracy in the presence of this confusion and doubt will probably best be determined, not by an analysis of the psychological states involved, but by an examination of the practical effects that these states produce in daily performance. This is to apply the criterion of the gospels:

> Make a tree sound and its fruit will be sound; make a tree rotten and its fruit will be rotten. For the tree can be told by its fruit.[10]

When the fruits which not only accompany the confusion and doubt, but actually originate in and grow out of them are godly ones—such as greater wisdom, humility, compassion, love, a deeper sense of the mystery and wonder of life, and gratitude for the gift of life—the pain giving rise to these results should be recognized as signs of growing proximity to God and evolving godliness. It should not be attributed to the loss of God or be judged to be the accompaniment of godlessness. Whereas if the fruits of a warm, comfortable, unchallenging, clear, consoling, seemingly healthy, intimate relation to God are apathy, indifference, self-complacency, arrogance, sustained prejudice and superiority, these should be evaluated as evidence of separation from rather

---

[9] See Antonio Royo and Jordan Aumann, *The Theology of Christian Perfection* (Dubuque: The Priory Press, 1962), pp. 313-317 ; 322, 342.

[10] *Mt.* 12, 33.

than closeness to God. They should be recognized as characteristics of godlessness rather than of godliness—whatever be the external forms of religious expression that may accompany them.

Catholic tradition clearly affirms the essential mystery of God's being. However, as articulated in the theology of Thomas Aquinas, tradition rejects the notion that the human intellect cannot form valid concepts about the divine mystery. Tradition asserts that both negative and positive concepts of varying degrees of adequacy can be formulated about God. That is to say, man can with confidence and clarity affirm what God *is not*, and with less confidence and much obscurity affirm imperfectly by analogy what God *is*.

I will first examine the negative concepts about God, and then the positive concepts which the Catholic tradition offers about the nature of God. After a brief summary of doctrine, I will formulate negative and positive definitions about the nature of man's potential for divinity, and the movement of man toward, and his attainment of God. I will then describe some of the implications of this understanding of godliness in regards to ecumenism.

CHAPTER THREE

WHAT GOD AND GODLINESS ARE NOT

I. GENERAL STATEMENT OF TRADITIONAL DOCTRINE

Catholic doctrine denies of God any element whatever of limitation.[1] This dogma evolved from reflections on the characteristics of created being and Uncreated Being as seen under the light of revelation.

Among the limitations found to be inherent in created being theologians single out composition (intrinsic divisibility of any kind) imperfection, finiteness, restriction in place, changeableness, temporality, and multiplicity. Each of these limiting traits of created being is specifically denied of God by concepts that express more the absence of such limitations in Him than a positive content or presence in the divine essence. Thus God is not composite but Simple;[2] not imperfect but Perfect;[3] not finite but Infinite;[4] not restricted in place but Omnipresent;[5] not changeable but Immutable;[6] not temporal but Eternal;[7] not multiple but One.[8]

For the sake of comparison and doctrinal development, I express in Table 3-1 the limitations of created being under column A, and the concepts expressing the divine essence as specifically stripped of such limitations and existing in an order essentially distinct from and outside of the created order, under column B. In my subsequent analysis, I will

---

[1] The theological basis of this denial proceeds in Aquinas from his proofs for the existence of God in which he argues to an ultimate source of reality which is pure act. Cf. *Summa,* I, q. 2, a. 3.

[2] *Ibid.*, I, q.3.

[3] *Ibid.*, I, q.4

[4] *Ibid.*, I, q.7.

[5] *Ibid.,* I, q.8.

[6] *Ibid.*, I, q. 9.

[7] *Ibid.*, I, q. 10.

[8] *Ibid.*, I, q.11.

employ A as the symbol of created being, and B as the symbol of Uncreated Being.

A-CREATED BEING IS/GOD IS NOT	B-GOD IS/CREATED BEING IS NOT
composite	Simple
imperfect	Perfect
finite	Infinite
restricted in place	Omnipresent
changeable	Immutable
temporal	Eternal
multiple	One
TABLE 3-1	

Each of these limitations and the implications involved in their absence from the divine essence receive lengthy analysis in Catholic doctrine. But for my present purpose this summary suffices as the basis for formulating a general, negative definition of God and godliness.

II. NEGATIVE DEFINITION OF GOD AND GODLINESS

God is B, and man is A—this doctrine presents the possibility of elaborating an imperfect definition of: first, the potential and desire of man for divinity; second, the movement of man toward divinity; and third, the actual attainment by man of divinity:

1. The potential and desire of man for God must involve the capacity and hunger in human nature to transcend the limitations proper to his initial state of creatureliness, and move towards the greatest possible participation in the unrestricted characteristic of Uncreated Being. This implies essentially a movement of A to B—from the conditions of

WHAT GOD AND GODLINESS ARE NOT

created being to those of Uncreated Being; from composition to simplicity; from imperfection to perfection; from finiteness to infinity; from restriction in place to omnipresence; from changeableness to immutability; from time to eternity; from multiplicity to unity.

2. Man's movement toward divinity will consist in the actual transition from the limitations of A to a growing participation in the superior, unrestricted conditions of B.

3. The attainment of divinity by man will be measured by the degree to which he in fact succeeds in evolving beyond the limitations of A with which he begins his existence, and takes on more and more a participated likeness to B.

By way of completing these definitions, I also have in this traditional view of created being and Uncreated Being the basis for an initial definition of godlessness. To the extent that a man by voluntary choice rejects openness and movement to the Simple, Perfect, Infinite, Omnipresent, Immutable, Eternal, and One, and elects rather to close in around and become arrested in transitory, mutable, finite, imperfect, composite and multiple being, seeking to find therein fulfillment of his desire for B, there will be missing from that man's being and activity a godliness the absence of which will be his responsibility.

This analysis as yet offers nothing about the way in which the transition from A to B takes place. Nor does it provide insight into the positive content of God and godliness. The matter of the transition from A to B will be examined immediately, while the second consideration about the positive aspects of God and godliness will be treated in Chapter Four.

III. MAN'S MOVEMENT TOWARD GOD AND GODLINESS

Man's search for divinity which I express as the movement of A to B, tends to work itself out in three general patterns. Pattern I seeks to effect this identity of A and B by the absorption of B into A. Pattern II finds man pursuing B by the rejection of, or independently of A. Pattern III affirms an essential relation between A and B in virtue of which the link to B is found in and through A.

Now these patterns are proposed as umbrella types which cover a variety of different views, and reflect more a practical choice in the way in which A pursues B, than a theoretical exposition of the relation of A to B.

Pattern I

One method by which men seek to satisfy their desire for divinity consists in endowing created being (A) with the characteristics of Uncreated Being (B), thus absorbing B into A. This tendency is manifested in various practical attitudes toward life. For example, we see the tendency of some to endow the "now" with the characteristics of the Eternal, acting as though the present moment were the only moment, outside of which the past, future, and what lies beyond time, for all practical purposes, do not exist. The well known *"now generation"* theme is an expression of this tendency.

Again, one can make the *here* in a practical sense the *everywhere and the omnipresent*, by reducing all life and the meaning of life to the tiny world in which one lives and over which one exercises control. One's immediate sphere of interest and dominion tend to become the whole of reality, so that what lies outside of this immediate world, psychologically and morally does not exist.

And so on with the other obvious expressions of this tendency to expand the limitations of A in a practical, psychological, and spiritual manner into the dimensions of B. We see attempts to make the particular become the universal, the finite good an infinite good, the mutable and transitory object a permanent reality. A common tendency is to make one's self not just one of many humans but the one, supreme, only person, and to act as though part of one's composite being is the whole with indifference towards other aspects and needs of one's nature.

Traditional theology finds the explanation of this human tendency to deify the transitory and finite in the dynamics of man's natural desire for God and godliness.[9] According to Aquinas, man's desire for God in

---

[9] Since God is the universal good, and under this good both man and angel and all creatures are comprised, because every creature in regard to its entire being naturally belongs to God, it follows that from natural love angel and man alike love God before themselves and with a greater love. *Summa*, I, q.

the form of his appetite for Happiness and the Perfect Good is natural and necessary. It is not an acquired and free desire.[10] Freedom enters in only in the choice of the specific object in which man elects to find this perfect fulfillment—which of necessity he seeks.[11] The object of this election is *freely* chosen only because it is not the perfect good or, in the case where God is being considered, it is not presented by *reason* as the perfect good.[12] Since man is motivated in every human act by a final end,[13] and since the true final end for which he is created and which alone can satisfy his natural desire, is the Perfect Good (B),[14] either he in rectitude effectively pursues B, or he seeks his happiness in created being (A). In the latter case he of necessity endows the finite object of his choice with the characteristics of B, thereby deifying it.[15] Aquinas is thinking here of a practical identification of B with A, and not a theoretical one.

One may in *theory* acknowledge the existence of B as essentially distinct from A, and one may recognize that his natural desire for happiness is to be fulfilled only in B. However, in the *practical* order, while agreeing that A objectively cannot function as an adequate alternate to B one can at the same time espouse A as his final goal. When this is done, since he is not free to turn off, so to speak, his desire for complete fulfillment, and since that desire is operative in his embrace of the mutable good, he must project into it a power for rendering fulfillment that it objectively does not possess—thereby endowing it with the properties of B. Practical and irrepressible evidence of the hunger for God in humans is found in the restlessness and

---

61, a. 5c. Also *ibid.*, I, q. 82, a.2; I-II, q.5, a8. For recent theological analysis see Reginald Garrigou-Lagrange, *The One God* (B. Herder Company, 1954), pp. 307-331. Jacques Maritain, *Approaches to God (*Harper, 1954), pp. 109-114. Karl Rahner, *Nature and Grace* (Sheed and Ward), 1963, pp.3-46.

[10] *Summa*, I,q.82, a.1; I-II, q.5, a.8c; I-II, q.10, aa. 1,2.

[11] *Ibid.*, I - II, q.13, aa. 3,5.

[12] *Ibid.*, I, q.61, a. 5 ad 5; I, q.82, a. 2c.

[13] *Ibid.*, I - II, q.1, a.6.

[14] *Ibid.*, I - II, q.3, a. 8.

[15] *Ibid.*, I, q.63, a.1 ad.4; I-II, q.6, a.4 ad. 3; I-II, q.8, a. 1.

dissatisfaction of men with their chosen lot that emerges when the mutable object fails to fulfill the expectations of providing the complete happiness that human nature necessarily pursues.[16]

The impossibility of escaping the desire for God and the possibility of only concealing this desire from one's self, is further manifested by another aspect of created being. Since man by nature is not an actually existing being, but only a potential (contingent) existent of a specific kind, whatever actuality he possesses comes to him not from his essence, but as derived from the actuality of God. Therefore, the actual being, truth, love, life and happiness that man identifies with his true self and loves intensely as his own special possession, does not come to him from his own nature but is a derived participation of the being, truth, love, life and happiness of God.[17]

When a man loves himself and clings to his life, whether he is conscious of the fact or not, he is loving his participation in divinity and the inseparable source of that participation.[18] The atheist who is in fear and sorrow at the approach of death, trembles and weeps not at the prospective loss of existence and life that belongs to his nature, but at the loss of his participation in God's being and life. The death he fears is not the loss of his true self, but the return to his true reality as a potential existent when bereft of the bit of godly actuality that has been given to him.

Since man's desire for B is a natural and necessary one in the form of his desire for perfect happiness, he does not have to be convinced that he should desire the Infinite. Concerning such a desire, he has no choice. The role of the Apostle and preacher is not to convert men from a love of the finite to a love for the Infinite. Conversion consists rather

---

[16] Aquinas makes this restlessness and lack of complete happiness with created goods the criterion by which he determines the object in which man's ultimate end is to be found. *Cf. Summa*, I - II, q.4.

[17] "It must be said that every being in any way existing is from God, for whatever is found in anything by participation, must be caused in it by that to which it essentially belongs, as iron becomes ignited by fire....Therefore all beings apart from God are not their own being, but are beings by participation." *Summa*, I, q. 44, a. 1c.

[18] *Ibid.*, I, q. 60, a. 5; I-II, q.93, a.8 ad 3; II-II, q.26, a.3, q.34, a.1.

in man's turning from a finite good to which he attributes the characteristics of the Infinite, to that reality which objectively is the Infinite.[19]

This understanding of man's motivations has particular significance in the contemporary religious order with regard to the "God is dead" and "religion is irrelevant" themes. The implicit assumption of these positions is that man has the freedom to cut out of his life any specific orientation toward the reality of God. For Aquinas the question is not primarily whether man finds value and relevance in the pursuit of God, but whether man who is pursuing God, always and everywhere, in every conscious act, is aware of the nature of his appetite and the object which alone can satisfy his quest.

The person for whom *God is dead* and *religion is irrelevant*, is not in virtue of this attitude liberated from preoccupations and involvements in the whole area of religion to pursue happiness with unfettered spirit in nature, art, science, love, and in the here-and-now. Such a hypothetical liberation would require a metaphysically impossible work of plastic surgery on his very nature. Rather, he is doomed of necessity to adorn the object of his pursuit in the order of A, with the characteristics of B, thereby merely shifting from one form of religious expression to another, while left to answer the question as to whether he is worshipping at the altar of the true God, or of a false god of his own creation.

In some cases his very freedom from the inhibiting influences of religion may itself become the overriding concern of his life so that its maintenance assumes the role of his final goal. In such a development, man's freedom from religion and the tyranny of God, would become in fact *his religion and his god*—with its own special form of tyranny.

According to Aquinas even when man sins, he is not eliminating B and the desire for B from his action, but he is seeking to find B in A. And so the man who rejects God in order to pursue happiness in the created order, is not free to approach creatures as creatures, but is compelled to approach them on his knees as gods. Such creature-gods are

---

[19] *Cf.* Jean Mouroux, *The Meaning of Man* (Sheed and Ward, 1948), pp.145-6.

not always benign ones. Recent history provides ample evidence of this in the ferocious consequences of the deification of racial and political ideologies.[20]

The danger of secularization is not from the threat that it poses to religion in the form of its elimination because of irrelevance and indifference. The real threat comes to humanity from the compelling, universally relevant, irrepressible, inescapable religious component of human nature that promises to reappear in some new, technologically attractive but diseased expression of creature worship. Man's choice, according to Aquinas, is not between religion and no religion. It is a choice between true religion and false religion, between God and an idol.[21]

The theoretical expressions of the identification of A and B and the justifications for this identification, are multiple. Atheism,[22] of course, simply denies the existence of B, while searching in A for the explanation of the illusory creation of B. For Aquinas, as we have seen, this theoretical denial of B does not succeed in purging from man's actions the practical expression of his necessary desire for B. While B has been denied existence by his judgment, the atheist will of necessity be seeking complete fulfillment in his actions, thereby resurrecting B in various disguises right in the midst of A as its capacity to fulfill his desires will be expanded and adorned with the characteristics of B.

In atheistic humanism[23] the pattern is to seek in man's inner resources (A) the autonomous capacity to effect ideal, full, human development (what traditional doctrine would identify as godliness). This

---

[20] In his introduction to the translated works of Meister Eckhart, Raymond B. Blakney presents a forceful statement on the dangers of false mysticism and the necessity of avoiding the false gods which men destructively erect in the absence of true mysticism. He singles out the Nazi movement in Germany as a recent example of such false mysticism. *Cf.* Meister Eckhart, *Meister Eckhart-A Modern Translation*, tr. by Raymond B. Blakney (Torchbooks - Harper and Row, 1957), pp. 5-10.

[21] See Robert Gleason, *The Search for God* (Sheed and Ward, 1964), pp.19-32.

[22] See J. F.Reid, "Atheism," NCE, Vol. 9, pp. 1000-3.

[23] *Cf.* Karl Rahner, "Atheism and Implicit Christianity," *Theological Digest*, Vol. XVI, No. 4, Fall, 1968, pp.43-56.

is sought independently of the assistance and influence of B, which, of course, does not exist in the first place! When humanism is young and optimistic, one finds attributed to human resources a quality of wisdom, rectitude, and power that suffices to assure an ideal evolution of the human potential. Christian tradition ascribes this quality more to the providence of God than to innate human perfection. It finds in this idealization of human resources the hidden emergence of B in A. Humanism tends to lose optimism and grow cynical as this *godly* factor in man shrinks to the more humble dimensions demanded by the painful experience of man's inadequacies.

In atheistic existentialism[24] one finds the denial of the objective reality of B. But, interestingly, one does not always find the denial of A's desire for B, or of man's appetite for B. Whence comes the sickness resulting from man's encounter with reality if man does not bring to that confrontation an appetite for fulfillment that is frustrated because the object he yearns for, B, is missing? If the appetite for divinity (B) did not exist in man (A) there would be no explanation for man's frustration at the godlessness of reality.

Christian atheism would appear in substance to be atheistic humanism with a Christian twist.[25] While God (B) does not exist, man (A) has the inner resources not only to achieve ideal development of his potential, but as it turns out, he can achieve this perfection after the manner and model of Christ. First, however, the divine element (B) must be removed from the humanity (A) of Christ. Then, one must

---

[24] *Cf.* James Collins, *op. cit.* pp. 40-87.

[25] As an explicit expression of the absorption of God (Uncreated Being) into created reality, with Christ activating and inspiring this absorption, see Thomas J. J. Altizer and William Hamilton, *Radical Theology and the Death of God* (The Bobs-Merrill Company, 1966). Also Thomas J.J. Alitzer, *The Gospel of Christian Atheism* (The Westminster Press, 1967). For a sympathetic survey and study of the development of Radical theology see John Charles Cooper, *The Roots of the Radical Theology* (The Westminster Press, 1967). For a review and critique of recent trends in Christian Atheism see the article by R. F. Aldwinckle, "Did Jesus Christ Believe in God? Some Reflections on Christian Atheism," *New Theology* NO. 5, edited by Martin E. Marty and Dean G. Peerman (The Macmillan Company, 1969), pp. 62-68.

attribute to that humanity of Christ the natural capacity for perfection which traditionally Christians, and Christ himself, have attributed to the action of the Father (B) in him. Then it must be discovered that every human possesses the same inner resources that are found in Christ. And the identification of B with A is complete. Mediated by Christ B is identified in Christ with A. Then the message of Christ, who has long since departed from the human scene, makes it clear to us that we have the same means of development that he enjoyed, and B which is identified with Christ, becomes identified in turn with our humanity.

Other expressions of the theoretical identification of the created and uncreated orders abound. Coomarswamy proposes that the concern of the modern, western man with A to the neglect of B, or obliviousness to B, can best be understood as the aftermath of the post-Renaissance. There we have the development of the empirical, positivistic sciences with the resulting influence they exercised over the mentality of Western civilization.[26]

The empirical man tends to approach reality with a total concentration on the many, the relative, and the changeable. This mentality is alien to the development of metaphysics and mysticism with their concentration on the One, the Absolute, and the Permanent. The only place in Western thought where Coomarswamy encounters the same preoccupation with the One, Absolute and Permanent that typifies the concern of the Eastern sages, is in scholastic thinkers of the middle ages. The influence of the empirical mentality might best explain the recent tendency among some thinkers to make of God a kind of eternally evolving relative or Absolute Relative, which is another expression of the identification of B with A.[27]

---

[26] *Cf.* A. K. Coomaraswamy, *The Transformation of Nature in Art* (Dover: Constable, 1937), pp. 9-16.

[27] *Cf.* E. Baltazer, "God in An Evolving World," *Catholic World*, 211-103-6. June 1970. Also James Collins, "God and Contemporary Philosophy," *Commonweal*, Vol. 85, No. 18, June 1970, pp. 528-534. Eugene Fontinell, "Transcendent Divinity and Process Philosophy," New Theology NO. 7, edited by Martin E. Marthy and Dean G. Peerman (The Macmillan Co. 1970) pp. 172-189.

Lastly, mention should be made of the various forms of pantheism in which this identification of B with A is explicit.[28] One encounters this deification of A into B among many scientists, artists, and poets.

Pattern I has little difficulty in accepting Catholic doctrine on B's use of A as an instrument through which B acts on the created order, since it goes beyond that doctrine by making A not only the instrument of B, but identical with B.

Pattern II

A second general pattern by which man's desire for divinity seeks fulfillment is found among those who, unlike Pattern I, stress a radical difference of Uncreated Being (B) from created being (A). The differences seen will also affirm in varying degrees an *opposition* between A and B so as to deny to A the capacity to function as a point of contact with B.

This pattern may take the extreme form of a theoretical and practical dualism. With this the visible aspects of A are held to have in no way derived from B, and to stand totally opposed to B, so that the way to union with B involves the explicit rejection of A and a movement away from it.[29] Such a dualism has been repeatedly condemned by Christianity and is radically unacceptable for the Christian who must hold that B is the source of A, and that A therefore participates in the goodness of B and stands in a positive relation to it.

While Christians must affirm in theory the positive link between A and B, among many there is a tendency to downgrade this relation. A is treated as a relatively indifferent contributor to contact with B, or in the practical order is seen as an obstacle and deterrent to such contact rather than a positive link with B. In practice, according to this pattern, one must minimize and even reject the temporal and finite if one is to

---

[28] *Cf.* E. R. Naughton, "Pantheism," *NCE*, Vol. 10, pp. 947-950.

[29] *Cf.* Louis Bouyer, "Gnosticism," *Dictionary Of Theology*, tr. by Charles Underhill Quinn (Desclee Co. Inc., 1965), pp. 180-2. G.W. Macrae; "Gnosticism," *NCE*, Vol. 6, pp.523-8. J. Ries; "Manichaeanism" *NCE*, Vol. 9, pp. 153-160; Saint Augustine, *Confessions*, tr. by Vernon J. Bourke (New York: Fathers of the Church, Inc. 1953), pp. 57-75, 103-112.

achieve union with the Eternal and Infinite. One must, in a sense, leap frog over the multiple and imperfect, in order to land in the bosom of the One and Perfect. The less one is living in contact with the multiplicity and diversity of creatures, the more ideal is the basis for his contact with the Simple and Infinite.

Although I am treating of a practical pattern of behavior rather than a theoretical position, I note that theories in support of this practical approach to A emerge in a variety of forms. Thus a modified practical dualism, for example, occurs in the Catholic Church under such forms as Jansenism and Catholic brands of Puritanism.[30] It can be found in certain theories about the religious life that present it as a salutary flight from the world (that is created being or A) into a relatively disembodied environment which is held to be conducive to a more ideal contact with divinity precisely because it is disembodied.

This pattern may also be found at work in the thinking of those who would use the liturgy and the sacraments as unique moments of contact with divinity which are not duplicated in anyway throughout the rest of the created order. Thus denying them as extraordinary exemplifications of the potential for the whole of the created order (A) to be used as the instrument of God's and Christ's sanctifying presence. This pattern tends to emphasize the transcendence of God so much that it removes Him from that intimate presence in the whole of creation that Aquinas, among many other theologians, attributes to Him.[31] Thus contact with

---

[30] *Cf.* L. J. Cogner, "Jansenism," *NCE*, Vol. 7, pp. 81-88. B. Matteucci, "Jansenistic Piety," *NCE*, Vol. 7, pp. 88-92.

[31] "God is in all things; not, indeed, as part of their essence, nor as an accident; but as an agent is present to that upon which it works. For an agent must be joined to that wherein it acts immediately, and touch it by its power; hence it is proved in Physic. vii that the thing moved and the mover must join together. Now since God is very being by His own essence, created being must be His proper effect; as to ignite is the proper effect of fire. Now God causes this effect in things not only when they begin to be, but as long as they are preserved in being; as light is caused in the air by the sun as long as the air remains illuminated. Therefore as long as a thing has being, God must be present to it, according to its mode of being. But being is innermost in each thing and most fundamentally inherent in all things since it is formal in respect of everything found in a thing, as was shown above (Q.7, A.1).

and worship of the Transcendent God takes on the aspects of a totally other-world phenomenon.

Other expressions of this pattern can be found in the radical separation of the temporal and spiritual spheres of life. It can be found in the supposed opposition between the material and the spiritual,[32] and in the withdrawal or minimizing of the Church's concern for the here and now. This attitude has sparked the criticism that the Church and religion are unreal, an opiate of the people, and irrelevant.

Among other Christian churches, this pattern may be seen at work in the rejection of Sacraments conceived as physical causes of grace and constituting a form of blasphemy in which Uncreated Being is

---

Hence it must be that God is in all things, and inner-mostly." *Summa*, I, q. 8, a. 1. *Cf.* also I, q.7, a.1 ad 3; *Compendium*, c.130.

This matter touches on the entire question of the immanence and transcendence of God. It is the variety of viewpoints on this question which provide the point of fundamental divergence between opposing systems of theology. My analysis of the three patterns of approach to created being is based in part on the possible responses to this question. Pattern I represents those who affirm immanence at the threat of transcendence. Pattern II is characteristic of the approach of those who assert the transcendence of God in a way that endangers the divine immanence. Pattern III is the position of those who, as represented by Aquinas, endeavor to preserve both the immanence and transcendence of God. Battista Mondin argues that Aquinas' use of analogy of intrinsic attribution allowed him to express and safeguard both the divine immanence and transcendence. He holds that Tillich's symbolism based on the 'principle of correlation,' expressed the immanence of God in such a way as to endanger the divine transcendence. On the other hand he finds that Barth's 'analogy of faith' while affirming God's transcendence, placed in jeopardy God's immanence in created being. According to Mondin's analysis, then, Tillich would be following Pattern I and Barth, Pattern II, *Cf.* Battista Mondin, *The Principle of Analogy in Protestant and Catholic Theology* (Hague: Martinus Nijhoff, 1963), pp. 174-177.

[32] *Cf.* Karl Rahner, *Theological Investigations*, Vol. VI, *Concerning Vatican Council II* (Baltimore: Helicon Press, 1969), pp. 153-178.

lowered to the level of the created order.³³ In the theoretical sphere it surfaces as a rejection of the capacity of created being to provide any basis whatever of insight into the mystery of God, since creatures can in no way reflect a likeness of the Creator.³⁴ The use of analogy for some is a form of intellectual blasphemy, comparable in its own way to the downgrading of God in ritual worship since it asserts that the ineffable mystery of God can be expressed in the finite concepts of the human intellect.³⁵

Many Churches reject the Catholic doctrine which affirms not only the positive link of A with B as effect with its cause, but also teaches that B elevates A beyond its natural confines, grafting onto it the perfections of activity of Uncreated Being. This doctrine of the instrumental elevation of A by B underlies the Catholic understanding of the mysteries of the Incarnation, the Church, the Sacraments, and the Priesthood. The rejection of these traditional doctrines emerges from a pattern in which A is so radically disassociated from B as to exclude the possibility of B using A as an active instrument. Thus some Word of God theologians tend to remove from created truth the potential to be elevated by Uncreated Truth as the instrument of Truth's revelation of itself in the created order.³⁶ Others, in denying the reality of sacramental marriage or the sacrament of penance, are rejecting the notion that created love can be the instrument of Divine Love, and that a human act of forgiveness can be made the instrument of Divine Forgiveness.

One of the difficulties that must be confronted in this pattern of disassociation of A from B, or minimizing A's potential for providing contact with B, arises from the fact that the Christian himself is, and remains, an inescapable part of A. In whatever activities he engages, he brings with him the composition, imperfection, limitation in space and time, multiplicity and finiteness of his created state. He cannot, so to speak, jump out of his own skin, as the condition for union with B. In

---

[33] *Cf.* Louis Bouyer, *The Spirit and Forms of Protestantism*, tr. by A.V. Littledale (The Newman Press, 1956), pp. 148-158.

[34] *Ibid.*, pp. 151-155.

[35] *Ibid.*, pp. 160-161.

[36] *Summa*, I, q.1, a.8 ad 2; q.1, a.10; q.12, a.13.

WHAT GOD AND GODLINESS ARE NOT

trying to move away from A psychologically, intellectually, and spiritually, in order to dispose himself for the encounter with B, he is endeavoring to move away from himself. Whether he succeeds in this remains the question. It is seemingly an impossible chore, or succeeds only in weakening his contact with reality in the state of A and thereupon deifies a washed out expression of the periphery of A as a mystical identification with B, duplicating in a less rich manner what is in fact the same identification of B with A found in Pattern I.

If a man's contact in this life with God takes place through the medium of created effects, it would appear that the withdrawal from the effects is not a movement closer to the cause, but a retreat into a vacuum which is then adorned with the identity of the cause.[37] It would appear also that Pattern I has this advantage over Pattern II, that while both are liable to deify A, the reality so deified in Pattern I is richer in being content (godliness) than the vacuous type of being deified in Pattern II.

Pattern III

The third pattern of pursuit of Uncreated Being (B) by man (A) is found among those who affirm that A is derived from B as the effect comes from its cause.[38] It affirms that A is the likeness of B and is revelatory of B, as every effect is the likeness and revelation of its cause;[39] that A therefore, is contained in B and provides the point of contact with B, as every effect is contained in, and offers a point of contact with its cause.[40] And just as the more perfect effect reflects more fully

---

[37] *Ibid.*, I, q. 2, a.2 ; q.4, a.2.

[38] *Ibid.*, I, q. 44, a.1.

[39] *Ibid.*, I, q. 2, a.2 ad 3 ; q.93, aa.1, 2.

[40] "Although corporeal things are said to be in another as in that which contains them, nevertheless spiritual things contain those things in which they are; as the soul contains the body. Hence also God is in things, containing them: nevertheless by a certain similitude to corporeal things, it is said that all things are in God; in as much as they are contained by Him." *Summa*, I, q. 8, a. 1 ad. 2.

"Now it is plain that the effect pre-exists virtually in the efficient cause; and although to pre-exist in the potentiality of a material cause is to pre-exist in a

the being of the cause and is more conducive to contact with the cause, so the more perfect A is, the more it reflects B and the more conducive it is to contact with B.[41]

Catholic doctrine adds one more dimension to the relation of A to B by asserting that B acts in an extraordinary manner through A as its instrument, endowing A precisely as an instrument with an extraordinary participation in the perfection of B so that A is not only the means to B, but becomes the point of immediate experience of B. Under certain circumstances when one experiences A, he is experiencing more B than A in so far as the actions of an instrumental cause belong more to the principal cause than to the instrument.[42]

To set forth the meaning of this pattern in a more concrete manner, we can consider time as derived from Eternity as an effect comes from its cause.[43] Time, therefore, exists in Eternity and is sustained by Eter-

---

more imperfect way, since matter as such is imperfect, and an agent as such is perfect" *Ibid.*, I, q. 44, a.1."still to pre-exist virtually in the efficient cause is to pre-exist not in a more imperfect, but in a more perfect way. Since therefore God is the first effective cause of things, the perfections of all things must pre-exist in God in a more eminent way." *Ibid.*, I, q.4, a.2.

[41] *Ibid.*, I, q.47, a.1.

[42] *Ibid.*, I, q.47, a.1. "We must therefore say that an efficient cause is twofold, principal and instrumental. The principal cause works by the power of its form, to which form the effect is likened; just as fire by its own heat makes something hot. In this way none but God can cause grace: since grace is nothing else than a participated likeness of the Divine Nature.... But the instrumental cause works not by the power of its form, but only by the motion whereby it is moved by the principal agent: so that the effect is not likened to the instrument but to the principal agent: for instance, the couch is not like the axe, but like the art which is in the craftsman's mind. And it is thus that the sacraments of the New Law cause grace: for they are instituted by God to be employed for the purpose of conferring grace." *Summa*, III, q. 62, a. 1.

[43] "We can know with the certitude of ocular vision that Socrates is sitting while he is seated. With like certitude God knows, in His eternity, all that takes place throughout the course of time. For His eternity is in present contact with the whole course of time, and even passes beyond time. We may fancy that God knows the flight of time in His eternity, in the way that a

nity, and is the point of contact with Eternity, as the effect exists in, is sustained by, and is the point of contact with its cause.[44] The more fully and profoundly time is experienced, the closer one comes to the fullness of the presence of Eternity expressed in time.[45] The more one is open to the experience of the fullness of time, the more he is open to the full experience of Eternity. And so it is with the other forms of created being.

The multiple originates in the One, is present in the One, reflects the One, and is the point of contact with the One.[46] The more fully and profoundly one experiences the totality of multiple being, the more disposed is he for the experience of the One present in each multiple being and in all multiple beings.[47] A similar relation holds between the finite and the Infinite, the composite and the Simple, the here and the Omnipresent, the imperfect and the Perfect, the changeable and the Immutable.

An artistic model

This understanding of the relation of A to B comes from the traditional Catholic view of the work of creation and the relation of the created effect to the Creator. In analyzing this work of creation, Aquinas utilizes the model of the artist's relation to his artistic effects as the classic analogy for illuminating the mystery of divine Creation.[48]

---

person standing on top of a watchtower embraces in a single glance a whole caravan of passing travelers." *Compendium.* C. 133.

[44] *Summa*, I, q. 10, a. 1; q. 14, a.13; q. 86, a. 4.

[45] *Ibid.*, I, q. 47, a. 1 ; q. 115, a. 3.

[46] *Ibid.*, I , q. 13, a.5 ad 3; q.47, a.3.

[47] *Ibid.*, I , q. 47, a.1.

[48] "It has also been shown (Q.14,AA.6,11) that God knows all things, both universal and particular. And since His knowledge may be compared to the things themselves, as the knowledge of art to the objects of art, all things must of necessity come under His ordering; as all things wrought by art are subject to the ordering of art". *Summa*, I, q.22, a.2c.

I will develop the model of the artist as the basis for explaining the workings of Pattern III. My development will proceed with some detail since I will refer to this model frequently.

In analyzing the relation of the artist to his work, the following points may be proposed as matters of common sense experience and reflection:

1. The true artist expresses himself in his work—his inner thoughts, feelings, aesthetic insights, and life. A work of art is the incarnation of the inner life of the artist, giving palpable, visible, audible expression to the impalpable, invisible, inaudible creative stirrings of his inner being. This inner reality of the artist is present in his work, and his work enjoys a certain presence in that inner reality.

The person who contemplates the creative work, is marveling not so much at the sounds, colors, and shapes, as he is marveling at the inner life of the artist which is made sensibly present to him in the work. And through the work the contemplator is introduced into the inner life of the artist from which it emerged.

2. When the artist chooses to express the fullness of his inner life, he confronts a problem in the fact that his materials are not equal to the task of receiving and expressing in any single work the total richness of his inner resources. Since they are of an inferior order to the vitality of his conscious life, sound, color and shape lack the potential for the unrestricted possession of the being found in the spiritual reality of the artist's nature.

"Although creatures do not attain to a natural likeness to God according to similitude of species, as a man begotten is like to the man begetting, still they do attain to likeness to Him, forasmuch as they represent the divine idea, as a material house is like to the house in the Architect's mind." *Ibid.*, I,q.44,a.3 ad.1.

"Whatever is irregular in a work of art, is unnatural to the art which produced that work. Now the eternal law is compared to the order of human reason, as art to a work of art. Therefore it amounts to the same thing that vice and sin are against the order of human reason, and that they are contrary to the eternal law." *Ibid.*, I-II, q. 71, a. 2 ad 4.

WHAT GOD AND GODLINESS ARE NOT

The artist can partially overcome the limitations of his materials by multiplying and diversifying his artistic output, giving to each different work some special, partial expression of the various facets of his aesthetic insights. In this collectivity of works he would be able to express more fully what he could not put into any solitary creation. In this case, while each work could reveal something of the artist to us and offer a point of contact with him, no one work would convey the fullness of his being. The more perfect works would reveal more of his inner life and offer the means of more perfect contact with him.

While any one work, even in isolation, could be the point of contact with, and experience of the artist, if I were to seek the maximum experience of, and contact with him, I would be obliged to study as broadly and deeply as possible the full range of his artistic production. The broader and deeper my contact is with the full collection of his work, the more intimate and complete would be my contact with him.

3. If the artist chooses not only to produce a variety of works revealing different facets of his inner life, but so orders these works one to another that their very relations to each other are themselves works of art and reveal things about the artist that the works in isolation do not express, I would then be required not only to experience all the various works in order to know the full revelation of the artist, but to experience these works in their organization and dynamic relations. Only in this way would the maximum encounter with the artist be effected.

4. If the artist so orders his works that each relates to the others as parts of one unified whole, like the pieces in a mosaic, and he arranges that the more perfect radically illuminate the less perfect so as to elevate intrinsically their inner perfection and capacity to express him, I would need to experience his works in their collective ordering both to know the wholeness which they express in their union and to gain the new insight into the less perfect works which is imparted to them by the more perfect.

If the whole under the unifying influence of the most perfect works, provides a special illumination and reveals the full meaning of each part, when I contemplate the parts in the light of the whole, I would be contemplating the whole present in each part, and each part would take on the perfection of the whole.

5. If the work emanates from the artist in a continuing manner as a kind of dynamic unfolding or unraveling, so as to require the artist's creating presence not only to initiate but also to sustain and complete its artistic expression, then the living presence of the artist in his work and our communion with him through that work, would possess an immediacy and intimacy beyond that quality of contact that would be experienced in works which can exist independently of the artist's presence.

Let us consider two distinct experiences of an artist's mode of presence in his work, that provide two different possibilities of intimate contact with the artist through that work. In the first experience we find ourselves listening to a piece of music composed by Beethoven some two hundred years ago. Since Beethoven expressed himself in that work as we listen to it, his presence is revealed to us and we enter into a kind of communion with him. However, since the composer has long departed from our midst, our contact is not with his personal, living presence, but with the music's participation in the inner life of the absent Beethoven. Contact with him takes place through a medium that can sustain his artistry even in his absence.

In the second experience we find ourselves hypothetically enjoying the privilege of listening to the music of Beethoven which he is in the very act of creating as he sits at the piano and extemporizes. The artistic effect in this case demands his immediate, creating presence since the work in this state cannot be imparted to an independently existing instrumentality to be executed. As the music flows from his fingers, Beethoven is present in it, and through it, he becomes present to us with the added immediacy and intimacy that contact with a person in the very act of creating brings. Our communion with the composer in this second experience would surpass substantially the quality of contact and union possible in the first example.

6. Let us suppose, finally, that the music flowing from Beethoven's fingers is of such subtlety and depth that we lack the sensitivity and perception necessary to experience its full richness of aesthetic content. There is not enough of the Beethoven in our inner perceptiveness to experience fully the Beethoven in his work. Then the composer, as he creates, commences to explain to us the composition, directing our attention, heightening our awareness, preparing our sensitivities for what is to come, working as effectively and creatively on us from within to elevate our perceptions to the level of his work, as he is working

on the music from without. As Beethoven takes possession of our faculties, and we become the willing instruments of his living presence in us, we begin to perceive and experience his presence in his music in a way that otherwise would have been impossible.

Now we find that both the piano and our inner consciousness are functioning as instrumentalities of Beethoven, the piano as an inanimate instrument, and ourselves as vital, voluntary instruments. As Beethoven in us experiences Beethoven in the music, through the complementary operations of the two instrumentalities, we would be led into communion with the inner life of the composer. Such an experience would provide the possibility of the most intimate communing with an artist in and through his work.

It is after an analogy of the model of the artist that Aquinas, reflecting the traditional doctrine of the Catholic faith concerning the work of creation, presents the relation of created being to Uncreated Being. He presents the model in such a way as to find all created effects present in, revealing of, and points of communing with the Creator. His doctrine, in summary, is as follows:

1. All created reality (A) proceeds from God (B) as the finite expression of His divine being. Whatever actuality is present in creatures (A) is a participation of B, and possesses a likeness to B. Whatever being, good, truth, and life is found in A is derived from the Being,[49] Truth,[50] Good,[51] and Life[52] of B. B is intimately present in every aspect of A, both in His own substance and by reason of A's participation in B.[53] Therefore each created effect, even in isolation, is a potential point of contact with B.

2. Since no single work of creation is capable of fully sharing and expressing the goodness of God, and since He seeks to impart to the

---

[49] *Summa*, I, q. 44, a.1.

[50] *Ibid.*, I, q. 7, a. 4

[51] *Ibid.*, I, q. 16, a. 6.

[52] *Ibid.*, I, q. 18, a. 4.

[53] *Ibid.*, I, q. 8, aa. 1, 3.

created order the fullest possible participation in that goodness, God compensates for the limitations of created being by multiplying and diversifying His effects so that the collection of created beings provide a fuller expression of divine goodness than any isolated part.[54] The higher created effects will contain and reveal more of the perfection of their Source than the lower, so as to function as more ideal points of contact with divinity.[55] But the totality of effects will surpass the power of even the highest single created effect to reveal God and provide access to the experience of the divine.[56] Therefore, the more I experience created reality in the fullness of its diversity and multiplicity, the more I encounter the fullness of God's presence in the created order, and the more ideal is my point of contact with Him.

3. God not only creates a variety and multiplicity of beings, but He orders them to each other in a such a way that this ordering constitutes a revelation of divine goodness which is not to be found in the parts in

---

[54] "Hence we must say that the distinction and multitude of things come from the intention of the first agent, who is God. For He brought things into being in order that His goodness might be communicated to creatures, and be represented by them; and because His goodness could not adequately be represented by one creature alone. He produced many and diverse creatures, so that what was wanting to one in the representation of the divine goodness might be supplied by another. For goodness, which in God is simple and uniform, in creatures is manifold and divided; and hence the whole universe together participates in the divine goodness more perfectly, and represents it better than any single creature whatever." *Summa*, I, q. 47, a.2.

[55] *Ibid.*, I q. 47, a. 2.

[56] "Likewise the good of many is better than the good of an individual, and so is more representative of the divine goodness, which is the good of the whole universe. If a higher creature which receives more abundant goodness from God, did not cooperate in procuring the good of lower creatures, that abundance of goodness would be confined to one individual. But it becomes common to many by the fact that the more richly endowed creature cooperates in procuring the good of many. Hence the divine goodness requires that God should rule lower creatures by higher creatures." *Compendium* c. 124.

"For goodness, which in God is simple and uniform, in creatures is manifold and divided; and hence the whole universe together participates in the divine goodness more perfectly, and represents it better than any single creature whatever." *Summa*, I, q.47, a.1.

WHAT GOD AND GODLINESS ARE NOT

isolation. Therefore, to experience the fullness of the divine presence in created being, one must perceive the order by which they are related one to another, with the unity therein radiating from their very diversity.[57] To experience created effects in isolation and disparately, is to fail significantly in experiencing fully the divine goodness that is present in them.

4. God so orders all created effects as parts of a unified whole that the lower are illuminated by the higher, and acquire new meaning and reveal their full reality only when seen in the light of the higher and in the context of the whole. While higher works elevate and perfect the lower works of creation, the lower, in their own way contribute to the perfection of the higher by making it possible for them to give full expression to their participation in divine causality.[58] Both the lower and the higher must be experienced in their mutual relation of perfecting and perfected, if the fullness of divinity in them is to be revealed.

For example, when human nature is studied in the illuminating reflection of the humanity of Christ, an entirely new revelation of divinity is found present in humanity beyond that which is found in our knowledge of man apart from the historical reality of Christ. At the same time, Christ is not fully revealed for the godliness present in his humanity until his human nature has exercised its perfecting power upon the rest of human nature.

To study each independently of the other is to miss the fullness of the divine present in both. So man needs Christ to fully understand himself, and Christ needs humanity to realize fully the divine powers present in His assumed humanity. When the part is understood in the light of the whole, and the less perfect in the light of the most perfect, then the whole and the perfect become present in their special way in the part, and each part becomes in a sense the whole.[59]

---

[57] *Ibid.*, I, q. 47, a.3; q. 65, a. 2.

[58] *Ibid.*, I, q. 65, a.2; q. 103, a. 6 ; q. 105, a. 5.

[59] "Some creatures are said to be higher, because they are more perfect in goodness. Creatures receive their order of goodness from God in so far as they are under His rule. Consequently higher creatures have a greater share

THE THEOLOGY OF ECUMENISM

5. The relation of B to A has a unique characteristic. Since the human artist is a secondary and partial cause, the materials that he uses in his artistic endeavor, have an existence of their own, independently of his causality. Therefore they continue to exist when his creative activity has come to an end and he has departed. Unlike the human artist, God is the universal cause, and the total being of the effect depends upon His causality.[60] And so God must not only initiate the existence of His

---

in the order of divine government than lower creatures. But what has a greater share in any perfection is related to what has a smaller share in the perfection as act is related to potency, and agent to patient. Therefore the higher creatures are related to lower creatures in the order of divine providence as agent is related to patient. Accordingly lower creatures are governed by higher creatures.

"Divine goodness has this characteristic, that it communicates a likeness of itself to creatures. The perfection of divine goodness entails the double truth that God is good in Himself, and that he leads other beings to goodness. He communicates goodness to creatures under both aspects: they are good in themselves and they lead others to goodness In this way God brings some creatures to goodness through others. The latter must be higher creatures; for what receives a likeness of both form and action from some agent is more perfect than what receives a likeness of form but not of action." Thus the moon which not only glows with light but also illumines other bodies, receives light from the sun more perfectly than do opaque bodies which are merely illuminated but do not illuminate. Accordingly God governs lower creatures by higher creatures.

"Likewise the good of many is better than the good of an individual, and so is more representative of the divine goodness, which is the good of the whole universe. If a higher creature which receives more abundant goodness from God, did not cooperate in procuring the good of lower creatures, that abundance of goodness would be confined to one individual. But it becomes common to many by the fact that the more richly endowed creature cooperates in procuring the good of many. Hence the divine goodness requires that God should rule lower creatures by higher creatures." *Compendium.* c. 124.

[60] "Not only the action of secondary agents but their very existence is caused by God. However, we are not to suppose that the existence of things is caused by God in the same way that the existence of a house is caused by the builder. When the builder departs the house still remains standing. For the builder causes the existence of the house only in the sense that he works for the house as a house. Such activity is, indeed, the construction of the house,

WHAT GOD AND GODLINESS ARE NOT

effects, but he must continue to sustain them in their existence. Aquinas offers the example of the light in the air emanating from the sun that ceases to exist as soon as the sun is removed, as expressing analogously the dependency of created being upon the sustaining causality of God.[61] Thus A is not only derived from B, but it cannot continue to exist without the sustaining action of B.[62]

Aquinas therefore conceives the relation of creature to Creator after the manner of the artistic effect depending on the sustaining creative activity of the artist which we described in our example of Beethoven composing on the piano in our presence. Aquinas also conceives created being to be proceeding from this sustaining activity of God in a continuously unfolding or unraveling process involving multiple and diverse expressions of that which exists with an inner unity and simultaneity within the divine essence.[63]

---

and thus the builder is directly the cause of the becoming of the house, a process that ceases when he desists from his labors.

"But God is directly, by Himself, the cause of the very existence, and communicates existence to all things just as the sun communicates light to the air and to whatever else is illumined by the sun. The continuous shining of the sun is required for the preservation of light in the air; similarly God must unceasingly confer existence on things if they are to persevere in existence. Thus all things are related to God as an object made is to its maker, and this not only so far as they begin to exist, but so far as they continue to exist.

"But a maker and an object must be simultaneous, just as in the case of a mover and the object moved. Hence God is necessarily present to all things to the extent that they have existence. But existence is that which is the most intimately present in all things. Therefore God must be in all things." *Compendium*, c. 130. Cf. also *Summa*, I, 45, a. 1.

[61] *Ibid.*, I. Q. 104, a. 1.

[62] *Ibid.*, I. Q. 104, a. 2.

[63] "The fact that God produces things by His will clearly shows that He can produce new things without any change in Himself. The difference between a natural agent and a voluntary agent is this: a natural agent acts consistently in the same manner as long as it is in the same condition. Such as it is thus does it act. But a voluntary agent acts as He wills. Accordingly it may well

Thus our contact with created being that comes from, is sustained by, and demands, the living, active presence of the Creator, and exists in the Creator as an effect in its cause, is our point of immediate and intimate contact with Him. This model, in Aquinas' view, is valid with regards to the revelation of divinity which is to be found through the natural insights of the human intellect throughout the whole of the created order.[64]

6. Catholic doctrine adds another dimension to this relation of A to B when it teaches that God is not only present in the natural reality of A, but that He chooses to use A as an instrument of His activity in the created order. This doctrine also affirms that God elevates human nature as a vital instrument, disposing man to perceive aspects of His presence in A which man's natural powers of perception do not allow him to discern.[65] This elevation by God of the created order and human nature to the level of instruments, thereby providing man with more ideal access to communion with His divinity, is conceived as analogous to our model of Beethoven acting in us as vital instruments to assist our experiencing fully his presence in his work.

Relation of time to eternity

To indicate in a more concrete form the implications of this doctrine when applied to the relations of some specific aspects of created being to Uncreated Being, I will examine Aquinas' thinking concerning the relation of time to eternity:

1. Time is the measure of changeable being.[66] Since changeable being is derived from unchangeable being, whatever reality is present in any moment of time is a limited participation and expression of Unchange-

---

be that, without any change in himself, he wishes to act now and not previously. For there is nothing to prevent a person from willing to perform an action later, even though he is not doing it now; and this without any change in Himself. Thus it can happen without any change in God, that God, although He is eternal, did not bring things into existence from eternity." *Compendium*, C. 97.

[64] *Ibid.*, I, q. 2, a. 2.

[65] *Ibid.*, I, q.12, a. 3.

[66] *Ibid.*, I, q. 10, a.4 ad 3.

able Being.[67] The "now" of time, then, is caused by the Eternal, and is present in the Eternal, and is revealing of Eternity. Each "now" presents a point of contact with Eternity. The more profoundly I experience and go to the depths of the "now," the closer I am to the Eternal source of the "now."

2. The combined being present in many "nows" is a fuller expression of Eternity than the being which is found in any isolated "now." The creation of many "nows" is the Eternal's way of overcoming the limitations of created being and communicating a fuller participation in divine being than could be given in a single "now." The successive stages of being contained in the many moments of time (past, present, and future) are derived from the unchangeable being of the Eternal which is free of the division, opposition and succession of stages found in the unraveling of changeable being. Each moment of time expresses some aspects of divine being, and even in isolation provides the means of contact with the Eternal.

The more perfect moments of time that contain and reveal more of the divine goodness, provide a more ideal basis for contact with the Eternal. Since the totality of "nows" contains and expresses divine goodness more fully than any isolated "now," to experience the fullness of time, that is all "nows" in breadth and depth, is to achieve the most exhaustive contact with the effect and thereby come closest to the Eternal as cause. By way of opposition, the withdrawal from the fullness of time is a withdrawal from the Eternal.

3. The multiple and diverse effects of God reveal Him not only in their isolated reality, but also and with a new dimension of revelation, in their order to each other as parts of a whole. So also while each moment of time constitutes a revelation of Eternity; the very order of these moments of time are further expressions of the Eternal. Thus to experience the fullness of time as the point of contact with the Eternal, one must experience not only all the moments and periods of time, but

---

[67] *Ibid.*, I, q.115, a.3.

also the ordering of these moments among one another, the plan of their unfolding, and the dynamics of the evolutionary process involved.[68]

4. All moments of time are ordered to each other and to the entire of created reality as parts to a whole. The more perfect moments and periods of time which contain a fuller participation in divinity. They illuminate and perfect the presence of the Eternal in the less perfect moments where that participated presence is less intense—at least when those moments are experienced in isolation.

Thus when each moment and period of time is seen not in its isolated reality, but in the light of those moments in which the presence of the Eternal is most perfectly manifested, then the presence of the Eternal in each moment is made to be more fully manifested. When the part is seen through the whole, when the "now" is seen through the fulness of time and the Eternal, then the "now" reflects and radiates the Eternal.

5. The Eternal is intimately present in the unfolding of time. Eternity does not create time and depart.[69] What is always present in God, is revealed to us in successive stages.[70] As I witness the unfolding of reality, it is as if I am witnessing God in His living presence unfolding His divine being, facet by facet, successively offering me insights into the various aspects of His being that in Him exist in perfect unity. Since the Eternal is the first and universal cause of time in that the Unchangeable Being is the total cause of changeable being, time depends on the Eternal to sustain its existence as well as to initiate its being. While time is a participation of the Eternal, the Eternal is also substantially present to time holding it in existence.

6. Not only is the Eternal present to time and expressed partially in time, but, in Catholic belief, the Eternal also takes an extraordinary possession of man living in time, and endows his consciousness and affective powers with the ability to discern and respond to the presence

---

[68] As an example of such an ordering of time in which lesser periods are ordained to more perfect ones Aquinas offers the moment at which Christ, the Creator and Master of time, chose to be born. See *Summa*, III, q. 35, a. 8. *Was Christ born at a fitting time?*

[69] *Ibid.*, I, q. 104, a.1; *Compendium*, c. 103.

[70] *Compendium*, c. 97.

of eternity both in the full sweep of time and in each "now" of time. According to this doctrine, it is the presence of the Eternal in man that permits him to experience the Eternal in time.[71]

Time and eternity for adults

In order to carry this analysis to its final stage, let us consider the relation of time and eternity in a man who has reached his fiftieth year. Behind him lie years of wide and varied experience, starting from his infancy and running into adolescence and adulthood. Throughout this time life was in constant flux, both within him and all around him. Reviewing his present situation in relation to his past and seen in the fullness of time, we can make the following observations:

1. Each moment and each experience of his life contains and reveals on the created level, something of the reality of God, and offers him a point of possible contact with God. While some experiences and moments were happy and others sad, whatever being, truth, good, and life was present in them reveals their ultimate source and God is present in each of them. The more profoundly this man lives the fullness of each moment and period of his life, the more he is in contact with God present in that moment and period.

2. Since no single moment or period of his life contains and expresses the full richness of God's presence, this man requires many different moments with many diverse experiences, gradually unfolding, to think all the thoughts, see all places, know all the persons, savor all the aspects of reality, necessary to achieve a full encounter with created being, the effect, and thereby broaden his contact with the source of this effect. If this man, could, in a single moment, imbibe the full variety and richness of life both without and within, this unraveling of created being would not be necessary for his development. However, if the fullness of man's contact with created reality is the condition determining his contact with divinity, then this unfolding of the richness of created being through multiple and diverse experiences of life is indispensable for man's encounter with God. Therefore, the more in-

---

[71] *Summa*, II-II, q.1 , a.1 ad.1. See also Saint Augustine *op. cit.* pp. 180 ff.

tensely this man lives and experiences every moment of his life to the depths, and retains possession of the past, the more he is in contact with the fullness of created being, and through this medium with Uncreated Being.

If this man were, for any reason, to ignore or run away from any period of his past, he would be running away from his encounter with created being, and running away from himself. And he would also be thereby running away from his point of contact with the Eternal's revelation of Himself under the different aspects present in those abandoned segments of his life. In so running, this man would lack a kind of essential ecumenism toward his own past since he would be denying in practice that God's wisdom and love were the controlling principles operative in those rejected periods.

Those segments of his life will remain points of potential, unrealized contacts with divinity that continue to cry out for him to enter into an ecumenical dialogue with the presence of God to be found there. All things being equal, the longer a person lives and the more varied and multiple his experience of the created order is, the more profound should be his contact with God. A man of fifty years, who enjoys twenty more years of experience of life over the man of thirty, should find in these twenty additional years of experience, the basis for a substantially more intense and profound union with God present to, and revealing Himself in, those years.

3. Since each moment of his life follows upon the other in an orderly sequence, the man must recognize that the order which holds between the different periods of his life, is itself an effect of the creative action of providence. He cannot search for the experience of God only in the disparate moments of his existence. The very ordering of these experiences adds a new revelation of divinity over and above that which is to be found in the moments contemplated in isolation. There is an order, for example, that he must discover between the good periods of his life and the difficult ones, between his Mount Tabors and his Calvarys. Neither can be fully understood without the other.

The difficult moments fail to reveal fully the divine presence in them unless they are seen in their essential contribution to the good moments. The good periods cannot be appreciated in their full revelation of divinity, unless they are contemplated in the light of the difficult ones. The gratuitousness of the good moments, the fullness of the good in them, and their very existence as good, can often be appreciated only when they are contrasted with the evil times. Since each moment is part of a whole, it cannot be possessed and appreciated fully except when it is seen and lived in relation to that whole.

Consider the illusory character and futility of desire in the man who intends to forget the past and live only and fully in the present. Since his present is the summation of his past, and not only contains the past but is the past as seen at this moment, it cannot be possessed and lived except with his complete openness to that past. He cannot understand, control and be in contact with his present reality unless he sees himself clearly as the product of the previous fifty years with all the experiences, hardships, successes, and failures of that entire life span. His relations with his parents and family, his rivalries and disappointments as well as his friendships and triumphs, all go to form his present reality.

The more fully he has lived and continues to live that past in the present moment—not just selected parts of it but the whole of it—the more intimate will be his possession of himself in the here and now, and the more open he will be to the further development of himself in the future. To the degree in which he lives in conscious possession of the whole of his own being, he can live in conscious possession of created reality and live in conscious contact with Uncreated Being revealed in that reality.

4. Not every moment of this man's life will reveal with equal clarity the presence of God The more perfect moments, where the fullness of the divine presence radiates through with greater intensity, will serve to illuminate that same presence in the moments where it is obscure. We will be able to distinguish many "nows" in his life. Each will be rooted in a larger "now" which is finally rooted in, and emerges from, the Eternal Now. There is, first of all, his most circumscribed "now" which is the present moment out of which the potential "now" of his future will grow. His present "now" is the latest growth of the "now" of his entire past that is rooted in the "now" of his generation. This latter "now" comes out of the "now" of human history that is ordered to the "now" of Christ as part to the whole, the imperfect to the perfect. It is

when this man views his present "now" in the light of his past, and his generation and the whole of history, as contemplated in the illuminating, finalizing "now" of Christ, that he finds, in that otherwise constricted present moment, the revelation of the presence of the Eternal Now.

Aquinas emphasizes in this regard the importance of the gift of memory by which a man transcends the limitations of the present moment and possesses the past so as to illuminate that present with the revelations of divinity found in that past. Aquinas finds this possession of the past to be essential to spiritual growth. The recollection of past failures and sins is necessary to the development of humility. The memory of past favors enkindles a greater gratitude toward the benevolence of providence. Prudence cannot mature in us without the contribution of recalled experiences.[72] It would not be an exaggeration to state that, according to Aquinas, one of the normal requirements for sanctity is a past and a good memory of it.[73]

5. If our middle-aged example is growing in the awareness of God's presence in his life, he will recognize that the wisdom and order reflected in the continuing flux of his life and of life around him, is not the effect of a cause that has prepackaged this unfolding plan and then departed from the scene. He will affirm the immediate, living presence of God, sustaining this unraveling of stage upon stage of created being in a series of restricted self-revelations which permit his limited awareness to keep up with and digest the disclosures. Just as we found in the flow of music coming from Beethoven's extemporizing a medium of immediate communion with the inner vital unity from which the flow proceeded, so this man will find in the ordered flow of created events, an invitation to enter into an immediate union with the living, sustaining presence of the Unchangeable Being from Whom this ordered flux emanates.

6. If the life of our adult example is seen as unfolding in the Catholic tradition, he will be confident not only of the Eternal's presence in every moment, endowing each "now" with a significance that transcends its surface limitations so as to contain and express Eternity. He

---

[72] *Summa*, II-II, q. 49, a.1.

[73] Saint Augustine, *op. cit.* pp. 263-326.

WHAT GOD AND GODLINESS ARE NOT

will also acknowledge both the mystery of that presence and the inadequacy of his natural resources to experience it fully. Thus he will open his mind and heart to be possessed by Eternity so as to become the willing instrument of the Eternal's illuminating presence. In the light of that presence he will then examine each moment of his temporal existence with a new power to move over the full range of his life, discerning in the various stages and periods divinity ordering each "now" into a unified expression of the fullness of the Eternal's presence.

The classic example of the man in his middle years who encounters the presence of the Eternal in each stage of his temporal existence, is presented to us in the *Confessions* of Saint Augustine.[74] Augustine in the light of grace came to recognize God's presence in the whole of his life. He found in each moment and in all moments in their relation to each other, his contact with the Eternal. With the indispensable assistance of memory, he searched in his temporality for Eternity. Not content to go back only to his adolescence, or even to infancy, he returns to the very moment of his conception, and moves from there to the Eternity from which this conceiving moment is derived.

From the fuller presence of God in the "now" of his later years, he relived and experienced God's presence in those earlier moments of his past. In his earlier life divinity was in him and all around him, but then he was not so possessed by the Eternal as to experience *His* presence.

As it was with Augustine so it has proven to be with the other great mystics of the Christian life. All share the conviction that God is present throughout their lives. All constantly strive to relive and experience each moment of the past anew. They become as willing instruments of the illuminating inner presence of the Eternal, searching in the depths of every moment for the presence of Eternal. Their movement is not, as Pattern I would have it, one that is arrested in the present

---

[74] *The Confessions of A Sinner,* Saint Augustine, are the expression and fruit of a man who has found Eternity in time. According to the testimony of Augustine himself, he did not succeed in discovering the revealing presence of Eternity in time until he first found Eternity in his heart.

"now" (which is identified with the Eternal). Nor is it a movement that takes them away from and out of time as a means of encountering Eternal after the manner of Pattern II. Rather their movement is into the depths of the "now" which, when seen in the light of the fullness of time, reveals the presence of the Eternal out of which it has come.

A similar analysis based on the doctrine of Aquinas can be made of the other limiting aspects of created being (A) in their relation to Uncreated Being (B). A summary of such an analysis would be the following: composite, imperfect, finite, localized, changeable, multiple being is caused by, sustained by, imperfectly similar to, and present in the Simple, Perfect, Infinite, Omnipresent, Immutable, One, which in turn is substantially present to, but not identical with, nor fully expressed in, each expression of created being.

Every manifestation of A, even in isolation, reflects something of the reality of B, and can be a point of contact with B. All expressions of A are ordered one to another as parts to a unified whole in which the less perfect are illuminated by, and manifest their full reality in, the light of the more perfect and the whole. Therefore the whole participates in B more fully than any part, and more adequately reveals B. When each part is seen in the light of the whole, then it more fully participates in and reflects B, and becomes more ideally the point of contact with B. Therefore, the more fully A is experienced in breadth and in depth, with its parts seen as related to a unified whole, and each part seen in the light of the whole the more perfectly one is in contact with the living presence of B at the source of A.

Some persons espousing Pattern II may object that the mutable, finite good is an obstacle to Uncreated Being. Others may object that love for A embraced in Pattern III rather than a link to B is in fact the object and cause of sin. To those Aquinas answers that no created good of itself is an obstacle to the Creator.[75] It is the distortion that man pro-

---

[75] "Creatures of themselves do not withdraw us from God, but lead us to Him; for the 'invisible things of God are clearly seen, being understood by the things that are made.' (Rom. 1, 20). If, then, they withdraw men from God, it is the fault of those who use them foolishly. Thus it is said (Wis. xiv. 11): 'Creatures are turned into a snare to the feet of the unwise.' The very fact

WHAT GOD AND GODLINESS ARE NOT

jects into the mutable good, making it function as the Immutable Good, which cuts one off from God. The sickness is in the sinner and not in the created reality.

The cure is precisely a correction of the inordinate desire whereby the sinner's love for the created good is not to be suppressed but *purified* so that he may come to love it as it is truly lovable in its relation to the Immutable Good. It is by coming to love A for what is really lovable in A, that one comes to possess B. The man who sees the finite good as the cause of sin, and flees from it, carries the disease with him and further compounds the evil. The disease might well re-emerge in the form of deifying with the characteristics of Health and Life his sick flight from the created good.

IV. APPLICATIONS TO ECUMENISM

The relation of godliness to ecumenism even when examined in this negative aspect, is evident. If ecumenism is the openness to the presence and revelation of divinity in the full range of humanity, this openness is identical with godliness as understood in terms of traditional Catholic theology. To the extent in which a man transcends the limitations of his initial state of creatureliness and expands into the unrestricted conditions of Uncreated Being, to that same extent he becomes ecumenical. To be godly is to be ecumenical.

In so far as he falls short of the ideal participation in the unrestricted characteristics of Uncreated Being, he is closed to the full expression of divinity in humanity. Godlessness and the absence of an ecumenical posture are inseparable.

Whatever works to close one off to the full experience of divinity present in the created order also closes one off to ecumenism. We find the basic modes of behavior that are inimical to ecumenism in the manner of relating created being to Uncreated Being espoused in Patterns I and II.

---

that they can thus withdraw us from God proves that they came from Him for 'they cannot lead the foolish away from God except by the allurements of some good that they have from Him.' " *Summa*, I, q. 65, a.1 ad. 3.

THE THEOLOGY OF ECUMENISM

Pattern I in which the characteristics of Uncreated Being are projected into created being, represents, perhaps, the more universal form that the opposition to ecumenism takes. The tendency to expand the particular into the universal, the finite into the infinite, the imperfect into the perfect, the here and now into the everywhere and eternal, cuts one off in the practical sphere both from the Transcendent present in created being and from the full experience of created being itself.

As an example of this form of opposition to true ecumenism it might be illuminating to consider one of the very first breakdowns of ecumenism recorded in the Christian Church. Saint Paul writes of the divisions that separate some of the first Christian communities, indicating the cause of these divisions.[76] One community claims superiority over all the others because it was evangelized by Peter. A second community argues its preeminence on the basis of having been evangelized by Apollos. Still a third claims this honor because it was preached to by Paul. To the extent that each community extols and magnifies itself, it downgrades the others. Paul rejects this deifying attitude in these communities whereby they have projected into the instruments of the Spirit the prestige of the Spirit Himself. Paul reminds them that it is the One Spirit who has worked in all of them through diverse instrumentalities, and he orders them to seek their glory in the Spirit who unites them and not in distorted glorifications of instruments which divide them.

Paul does not deny that the Spirit has worked fruitfully in these communities and that they offer valid expressions of that divine presence. But he does deny that each community represents the fullest, most ideal expression of divinity, thereby having no need of further, complementary expressions of other Christian communities to fill out the revelation of divinity in them. He encourages them to go to the depths of their experience where they will encounter the spirit's unifying presence as He works in diverse ages, places, and ways. Since the communities had chosen to rest in a superficial, prideful interpretation of the grace they had received, and had projected into this genuine but limited manifestation of God's action on them their natural

---

[76] I Cor. 1, 10 ff.

desire for complete fulfillment here and "now," the grace received which should have united them, became the occasion of their division.

This scandal of division against which Paul cried out, typifies a classic pattern which, in one form or another, continued to occur throughout the history of Church so as to lead to the accusation that religion historically has been more divisive of human beings than it has been unifying. Over the centuries history records how different Christian ages, races, cultures, social classes, communities, religious orders, and other religious groupings, have tended to glorify themselves as the highest expression of godliness to the downgrading of other Christian and non-Christian groups. The pattern continues in the contemporary scene and will continue to express itself wherever Christians expand their limited experience of divinity beyond its objective boundaries and endeavor to make their partial expression of divinity become the whole revelation.

Today we find one group of Christians canonizing the presence and revelation of God in the past while denigrating the activity of the Spirit in the present. Another group glorifies and exaggerates the workings of the Spirit in the contemporary age while rejecting the manifestations of God's presence in the past or minimizing the significance of that presence. Both look to the future not for what it will offer in the way of more explicit, complementary expressions of divinity, but only for confirmation of their special deifications of their particular experiences as the whole and perfect experience. As we hear one group claim supeiority because it is of the twentieth century while another claims this preeminence in its identification with the thirteenth century, and a third seeks its superiority as reincarnation of the first century, we also hear in these words the re-echoing of Saint Paul's time, "we were evangelized by Peter, we by Apollos, we by Paul." And from Paul himself we would hear again, "It is the one Spirit who works in the first century, and in the thirteenth, and in the twentieth.".

The divisions in Christianity have arisen not between good Christians and bad ones, between saints and sinners, believers and non-believers, followers of Christ and enemies of Christ, but between Christians and believers of mediocre virtue and talents who have grafted onto the valid workings of God's grace in them, their own natural desire for instant fulfillment, instant redemption, and instant divinity, thereby creating new, Christian creature-gods in whom the subtle blending of a bit of grace and much flawed human nature obscures the idolatrous component that dominates.

It is in this idolatrous, godless component whereby Christians worship some facet of their humanity which has been imperceptibly interwoven with and identified with divinity, that one finds the constricting, localizing, dividing, negating godlessness adorned with the external garb of religion, which gives birth to, nourishes, and sustains, the tensions and divisions among Christians. It is the elevation of created limited experiences of divinity that have taken place in human nature (A) to the level of divinity itself (B) which underlies many of the divisions that separate Christians (that is Pattern I). It is not the God of Christians that divides, but the godlessness of Christians.

Pattern II is, in a sense, more opposed to ecumenism than Pattern I which at least looks for the godliness present in the created order. The failure of Pattern I stems not from its neglect to search for expressions of divinity in created reality (A), but from its tendency to equate these created, finite participations in divinity with divinity itself (B). In Pattern II, the tendency to affirm an opposition between A and B results in the failure to discover and commune with the presence of divinity that is to be found in and through creatures. In separating God (B) entirely from the created order (A), this pattern excludes openness to the experience of God in creatures, making of ecumenism a dangerous, questionable and even blasphemous form of behavior.

The approach of Pattern III to created being (A) as positively related to Uncreated Being (B), whereby B is asserted to be present to A and revealed in A, is identical with the approach to the created order operative in ecumenism. According to this pattern, one must affirm the presence of the Eternal in and throughout the whole of time, and be open to the experience of Eternal which may be undergone in the past, present and future.

In affirming that multiple being is derived from the One a man must accept himself as only one of many humans. He must be open to the diverse, complementary expressions of the mystery of human life revealed fully only in the totality of human beings, and find in this experience of the whole of human life, his contact with the Unity out of which it came.

A man must accept the fact that no one person, or community, or racial and cultural grouping, can fully express or exhaust the seemingly infinite variety possible to human existence. Much less can one person, community or any social grouping, fully contain and express the actual infinity of Uncreated Being. Thus Pattern III requires that a man seek the broadest and deepest contact with all forms of human existence, and perceive the order by which men are related to each other as parts to a whole, if he is to experience the fullness and unity of human nature, and the fullness of divinity revealed in human nature.

This approach to created being of Pattern III whereby one is to be open to the presence of the Eternal in time, the presence of the One in multiple being, and the presence of the Infinite, Perfect, Immutable and Simple, in the finite, imperfect, changeable, and composite, is identical with the approach of ecumenism to the created order. Therefore, the godliness in man which develops from this approach and the ecumenical impulse are similarly identical.

Man's approach to, and contact with, the created order (A) follows upon his approach to, and experience of himself (part of A). Since the encounter with the rest of created being filters through man's experience of himself, ecumenism begins, and possibly ends with a person's manner of approach to his own reality. If he is open to the presence of divinity in the full range of his own life, he will be open to divinity's presence in the full sweep of the created order. To the extent that he remains closed to the presence of God in his own life, he will remain closed to that presence in created being.

For example, the man who is ecumenical towards himself in the dimension of time, as was Augustine, will search confidently through the entire sequence of his temporal existence for the Eternal's presence in each moment and in all moments in their relation to each other as parts to the whole. Only one so open to himself, will be able to approach every aspect of the temporal being of creatures with a similar openness to the presence of divinity there.

If, on the contrary, he fears to relive and re-experience any segment of his own past since he is convinced that there is no good (B) to be mined in such painful, dark, and shameful moments (A), he will be equally closed to the presence of God in similar periods in the lives of other men. If he has not in fact learned from his own past how God uses weakness to impart strength, foolishness to give wisdom, hatefulness to bring alive love, failure to inculcate humility and gratitude, and sorrow to give joy, he will not be open to the presence and workings of divinity in the weakness, foolishness, lovelessness, failure, and sorrow of others.

Again, if his openness to God's presence in his own life is limited to only those moments of such clarity as the sunsets and the more spectacular beauties of nature provide—at which even the atheist feels his denied share in divinity within stir at divinity's radiant presence without—but does not extend to garbage cans and the debris of his past failures, then his openness to God's presence in the rest of humanity will be restricted to the most obvious and superficial manifestations of that presence. In this latter instance, he would be operating according to the mode of Pattern II where one finds only isolated parts of A offering positive contact with B.

It is the person who follows Pattern III by living in close contact with his entire life, ignoring nothing, neglecting nothing, running from nothing, but searching in the corners and dark spots as well as in the sun-lit and flower-filled areas for that presence of divinity that he knows is there. This is the man alone who can approach the whole of created being confident of finding in each and every part of A, and more perfectly in the whole made up of all the parts, the presence and revelation of B.

The man who closes doors and windows on his own being and withdraws from any part of himself, is the one who necessarily closes doors and windows and withdraws from God's presence in the whole of created being. The skeletons in his closet which, if brought into the light of day could come alive with a divine vitality, stay firmly locked up and remain skeletons, while the greater part of the created order for him continues to exist as a vast cemetery of dust and bones, lacking the vivifying presence of God.

From this negative definition of godliness and ecumenism it is possible to propose a concrete model of the manner in which the godly, ecumenical man approaches divinity, basing our example on Aquinas' comparison of the artist to the Creator. The godly, ecumenical man will approach God as revealing Himself in His created effects in the way that one would approach an artist who reveals himself in his artistic productions.

The godly, ecumenical man, in a word, approaches the whole of created being on his knees, finding himself in the presence of a unified work of divine art. He approaches in the confidence that in every aspect of created being he will encounter both a revelation of God and God Himself. He will be convinced of the organic unity and cohesiveness of the whole in which the Source is totally present to every part, and each part reveals a different, complementary aspect of its Source. He will approach in the knowledge that the whole of this work reveals its Source more perfectly than does any one part, and that as each part is approached in the context of the whole, the Unifying Presence out of which the parts have unfolded and are unfolding to form the whole, will be revealed in His fullness.

Finally, the godly, ecumenical man will not believe that the movement toward created being is a movement away from the Source of created being, nor a movement in which one is arrested on the surface of created being. Rather he will believe that the movement toward created being is one that penetrates to the depths, the core, the Source of created being.

CHAPTER FOUR

WHAT GOD AND GODLINESS ARE

I. CATHOLIC DOCTRINE ON POSITIVE CONCEPTS OF GOD

In our analysis up to this point, nothing has been said about the positive reality that constitutes the actual being of the Simple, Infinite, Perfect, Eternal, Immutable, One. Consequently, no positive analysis has been offered about the actual contents of godliness in man. Nor, therefore, has any proposal been made about the positive aspects of ecumenism indicating the nature of that divinity present in creatures to which ecumenism is open.

In what follows I propose to comment briefly on what Catholic tradition affirms about the positive perfections of God. From this summary of traditional doctrine, I will draw the principal implications concerning positive aspects of godliness and ecumenism.

Affirming always the mystery of God and the inability of created intelligence to penetrate into that mystery, Catholic doctrine at the same time asserts the possibility of man's acquiring imperfect knowledge and expressing valid, though radically limited, positive concepts about God by way of analogy.[1] This position reflects Saint Paul's teaching that, "ever since God created the world His everlasting power and deity—however invisible—have been there for the mind to see in the things He has made."[2] In substance this tradition asserts that the human intelligence can proceed to a certain positive knowledge of God as cause, from His revelation found in the created universe as effect.[3]

---

[1] For an analysis of Aquinas' understanding and use of analogy see Battista Mondin, *op.cit.* pp. 1-102. Also by the same author, "Analogy, Theological Use of," *NCE*, Vol. 1, pp. 465-468. Also P. Klubertanz, "Analogy*,*" *Ibid.*, pp. 465-8; in the *Summa* Aquinas deals directly with the matter of analogy in theology in Part I, QQ. 12 and 13.

[2] *Rom.* 1. 20.

[3] *Summa*, I, q. 4, a.3; q.13, a.4c and ad 1.

Among positive characteristics of created being theologians distinguish two types of perfections. One class of perfections involves being which is of its nature inherently limited, such as vegetative and sensitive life, or corporal being. Such perfections are called *mixed*, and are attributed to God, not as actually existing in Him, but in so far as He possesses the perfection and power to produce them. Their presence in God is termed virtual.

A second class of perfections are those that of their nature imply no element of limitation whatever, although they are experienced by us in a limited state in the created order owing to the finite capacity of creatures to receive and participate in them. These are called by theologians *simple perfections*.[4] Among them are classified being, knowing, loving, living, efficiently causing, and rejoicing. All *simple perfections* are attributed to God as actually present in the divine essence with the qualification that their manner of existence in Him is essentially distinct from the existence that they enjoy in the created order.[5] In God these simple perfections are present as identical with the divine essence, perfectly united and free of any limitation.[6] Thus one does not

---

[4] "There are some names which signify these perfections flowing from God to creatures in such a way that the imperfect way in which creatures receive the divine perfection is part of the very signification of the name itself as *stone* signifies a material being, and names of this kind can be applied to God only in a metaphorical sense. Other names, however, express these perfections absolutely, without any such mode of participation being part of their signification, as the words *being, good, living*, and the like, and such names can be literally applied to God." *Ibid.* I, q.13, a.3 ad 1.

[5] "Thus whatever is said of God and creatures, is said according to the relation of a creature to God as its principle and cause, wherein all perfections of things pre-exist excellently. Now this mode of community of idea is a mean between pure equivocation and simple univocation. For in analogies the idea is not, as it is in univocals, one and the same, yet it is not totally diverse as in equivocals: but a term which is thus used in a multiple sense signifies various proportions to some one thing; thus *healthy* applied to urine signifies the sign of animal health, and applied to medicine signifies the cause of the same health." *Ibid.* I, q.13, a.5.

[6] "The perfect unity of God requires that what are manifold and divided in others should exist in Him simply and unitedly. Thus it comes about that He is one in reality, and yet multiple in idea, because our intellect apprehends Him in a manifold manner, as things represent Him." *Ibid.* I, q.13, a.4 ad3.

say that God has being, truth, love and life; but rather that God is Being, Truth, Love and Life, essentially, personally, unchangeably, infinitely, and eternally.

Since these perfections as found in their created and uncreated form are essentially distinct, our knowledge of them on the created level cannot lead to direct understanding of the divine essence. For example, because created love is essentially different from Divine Love, it cannot provide the basis for grasping the nature of Divine Love. However, Catholic doctrine holds that there is an imperfect, non-essential, similarity between created love and Divine Love which offers a limited foothold onto some knowledge of Divine Love. This foothold consists basically in the truth that whatever being and perfection are found in created love as an effect, are derived from, and present in Divine Love as its cause. Therefore, since a cause cannot give being which it does not itself possess, whatever being and perfection is present in created love, must be possessed by Divine Love, though possessed in a higher form which involves the absence of any limitation.[7]

What that *higher form* is and what shape *unlimited love* assumes, we do not know. This, however, we do know, that Divine love is *more* and not *less* than created love and that all limitation is excluded from it.[8]

---

[7] "Therefore the aforesaid names signify the divine substance, but in an imperfect manner, even as creatures represent it imperfectly. So when we say 'God is good' the meaning is not, 'God is the cause of goodness,' or, 'God is not evil;' but the meaning is, 'Whatever good we attribute to creatures, prexists in God,' and in a more excellent and higher way. Hence it does not follow that God is good, because He causes goodness; but rather, on the contrary, He causes goodness in things because He is good; according to what Augustine says, 'Because He is good, we are.' *Ibid.*, I, q. 13, a.2.

[8] "Now it is plain that the effect pre-exist virtually in the efficient cause: and although to pre-exist in the potentiality of a material cause is to pre-exist in a more imperfect way, since matter as such is imperfect, and an agent as such is perfect; still to pre-exist virtually in the efficient cause is to pre-exist not in a more imperfect, but in a more perfect way. Since therefore God is the first effective cause of things, the perfections of all things must pre-exist in God in a more eminent way." *Ibid.*, I, q. 4, a.2.

THE THEOLOGY OF ECUMENISM

Therefore if one were to make Divine Love less than created love, or to attribute to Divine Love any element of finiteness, limitation in place and time, changeableness, or restriction of any kind, Catholic tradition would immediately and with certitude reject such an understanding of divinity. However, if one were to probe for the positive, essential contents of Divine Love, this tradition would in essence respond that it is all that created love is and *more*, free of any limitation. Beyond this admittedly inadequate insight into Divine Love, Catholic doctrine would not presume to go.[9]

While affirming the essential mystery of God, the possibility of analogous knowledge of God can be seen in that a cause is known in and through its effects. In order to understand the traditional doctrine it would be profitable to return to our model of knowing the artist through his work as exemplifying our mode of approach to God through creatures. Let me offer a situation in which a painting of an unknown artist is presented to me for scrutiny. It is a small painting, simply executed, with little sophistication. Since the artist reveals himself in this work, I can validly form a concept of his ability as an artist. And since the work is a simple one, I confidently picture in my mind his level of artistic insight and technical mastery.

Then a second painting of his is shown to me that significantly surpasses the first in its perfection and revelation of the artist's ability. Now I must immediately expand and raise my judgment of the artist so as to incorporate this new evidence of his creativity that the work provides. There then follows a series of encounters with other works produced by him. Each new painting substantially surpasses the previous ones in its manifestation of the talent of the artist. At each experience of his work I find myself forced to alter and expand my judgment of his ability as an artist. After witnessing a number of his works, it finally becomes clear to me that I am in the presence of a true genius. From that moment onward, I cease trying to understand and define the richness of his creative powers.

---

[9] "Because His essence is above all that we understand about God and signify in word." *Ibid.*, I, q. 13, a.1 ad. 1.

WHAT GOD AND GODLINESS ARE

When asked by others to explain him in response I simply affirm the mystery of his giftedness with my "How do you explain genius?" And yet, if someone were to deny of his inner creativity a quality of aesthetic insight or technical mastery which is clearly evidenced in his work, making him in this sense artistically inferior to his own creations, I would immediately reject this position as being patently contradicted by his actual achievements. As I continue to study the new works that flow from him, and expand my capacity to appreciate his accomplishments, my awareness of the quality of his genius would grow together with an ever increasing appreciation of the mystery of that genius, and the inadequacy of my intelligence to cope with it.

According to traditional Catholic thought an analogous situation applies to our knowledge and experience of God through the medium of creation. Our initial experience of created being presents it to us under its most limited, superficial, simple aspects. From this encounter we formulate clear, comfortable concepts of God, endowing Him with qualities necessary to produce such effects.

As our experience of created reality as an effect grows and its complexity and richness becomes more manifest to us, we must keep expanding our concept of God to endow Him with proportions sufficient to explain His contribution to the created order as its ultimate cause. When finally we find ourselves confounded by the mystery of created being itself, we are forced likewise to acknowledge the essential mystery of its Source and the inadequacy of human intelligence to grasp the nature of that Source.

And so our knowledge assumes the form of a growing awareness more of our inability to know God than of actual knowledge of the divine essence. But this does not mean that we acquire no insight whatever into His being. We know that whatever simple perfections are experienced in His effects, must preexist in Him as the cause, although they possess an essentially higher form in Him. Therefore, if someone asks us to define God, our answer necessarily is that He is a mystery and defies being defined. But if that person denies of God perfections which are present in His work or ascribes to Him any element of limitation, this we immediately reject.

THE THEOLOGY OF ECUMENISM

The most common error about God that one encounters is not the error of those who deny His existence. Such a denial is relatively rare. What is common and almost universal is the error of those who, while affirming God's existence, deny to Him in one way or another the very perfections evident everywhere in His created work and in themselves, thereby conceiving God to be inferior to His work and to themselves.

The person who questions whether God is a personal being while glorying in his own reality as a conscious, free individual so as to be quickly moved to anger by anyone who dares to treat him as less than a person, is questioning whether His creator is inferior in this aspect of being to himself. The woman who doubts that God loves her while certain of the love that she has for herself, is doubting whether the Source of her love is lacking in the very love that He has imparted to her. Again, the man who is concerned out of genuine love about the suffering plight of humans, and wonders if God has an equally intense, personal concern for humanity, attributes to himself a perfection that he is prepared to deny to God. At the root of every person's anxiety about himself and his future is the fear that God does not have the love for him that he has for himself, thereby making God, at least in this area of concern, inferior to himself.

A similar analysis, according to Catholic thought, is applicable to the other perfections of the created order. Whatever perfection of being, truth, life, power, and causality is found in creatures, must preexist in their Source, and in an essentially higher and pure form. As my contact with the full richness of created being, truth, life, power, and causality expands and deepens, I must expand my concept and understanding of the Source. The more I grow in positive knowledge of created being, the greater will be my appreciation both of the richness of the simple perfections as found in their Source and of my radical inability to grasp their nature in that unified existence in the Source. And yet, if anyone presents God, the Source to me as inferior to His work, or projects into Him any limitations notwithstanding my ignorance of His essential mystery I with certitude will reject such an understanding as contradicted by His work.

This analogous attribution of perfections found in the created order to God has been challenged by non-Catholic and Catholic theologians alike.[10] It is not my purpose here to attempt a critical evaluation of this use of analogy nor to defend its application in theology against the critics. It suffices for me to note the historical fact that this is the mode of expressing positive concepts about God which Catholic tradition has utilized. This will serve for permitting me to set forth the substance of this doctrine in order to draw out its implications in regards to godliness and ecumenism.

Theologians, reflecting on the perfections of created and Uncreated Being as seen under the light of revelation, single out in the created order as principal examples of *simple perfections*, being, truth, love, life, happiness, power, justice, mercy, and efficient causality. These perfections as found in the created order, are immersed in the composition, finiteness, changeableness, temporality, and other limitations which are common to created being. They exist as accidents of the creatures possessing them. These same perfections are attributed to God as actually in Him, stripped of all limitations and identical with and united in the divine essence. God does not have being, truth, love and life, but God *is* Being,[11] Truth,[12] Love,[13] Life,[14] Happiness,[15]

---

[10] For recent criticism from Catholic sources of this traditional doctrine expressed in Aquinas, see Leslie Dewart, *The Future of Belief* (London: Burns and Oates, 1966), pp. 171-215. And by the same author, "God and the Supernatural," *New Theology* No. 5, pp. 62-68. For a critique of L. Dewart's work see Bernard J. F. Lonergan, "The Dehellenization of Dogma," *Ibid.* pp. 156-177. For further comments see Justus George Lawler, "The Future of Belief Debate," *ibid.*, 178-190. For criticism from another Catholic scholar see the article of Eugene Fontinell which has already been cited. For a comparison of the Thomistic concept of Analogy with the Symbolism of Tillich, see B. Mondin, *op.cit.*, pp. 118-146. For a comparison with the Analogy of Faith of Barth, see the same work, pp. 147-173. Also Cf Jerome Hammer, *Karl Barth* (Newman Press, 1962), pp. 69-73. J.L. Murphy, "Analogy of Faith," *NCE*, Vol. 1, pp. 468-469. Louis Bouyer, *op. cit.* pp. 151-161. For a criticism of Theistic theology in more general terms see John Robinson, *Honest to God* (London:SCM Press, 1963", pp. 29-44. *The Honest to God Debate*, edited by David Edwards (The Westminster Press, 1963).

[11] *Summa* I, q.2, a.2.

[12] *Ibid.*, I, q. 14, a. 4.

Omnipotent,[16] Just,[17] Merciful,[18] and the First Cause,[19] under the conditions proper to Uncreated Being which is to say, simple, perfect, infinite, and omnipresent, immutable, eternal and one.

Once again, for the sake of comparison and doctrinal development, I will express these perfections attributed to God, in comparison with their presence in human nature, by the following schema of Table 4-1. I will now use A to symbolize created being under both its negative and positive aspects, and similarly use B to express the negative and positive reality of God. Also, when I write of the simple perfections as present in the divine essence, I will use an initial capital letter (for example, Love) to distinguish these perfections from those in the created order which will be written with a small initial letter (for example, love).

Each of these analogous concepts of positive perfections as applied to creatures and to the Creator require and receive detailed study from Catholic theologians. However, their summary here without detailed analysis suffices to provide a basis for drawing some of their implications with respect to godliness in human nature and with regards to ecumenism.

II. POSITIVE DEFINITION OF GODLINESS

In this doctrine concerning the simple perfections attributed to God, keeping always in mind the analogical nature of this attribution, a positive description can be offered of: first, man's potential and desire for divinity; second, man's movement toward divinity; and third, man's attainment of divinity.

---

[13] *Ibid.*, I, q. 20, a. 1.

[14] *Ibid.*, I, q. 18, a. 3.

[15] *Ibid.*, I, q. 21, a. 1

[16] *Ibid.*, I, q. 25, aa. 1,2,3.

[17] *Ibid.*, I, q. 21, a. 2.

[18] *Ibid,.* I, q. 21 , a. 3.

[19] *Ibid.*, I, q. 2, a. 2 ; q. 45, a.5.

WHAT GOD AND GODLINESS ARE

1. The potential and desire (natural and not acquired, necessary and not free) of human nature for God is the potential and desire to achieve the

A-Man Has:	**B-God IS:**
being	Being
truth	Truth
love	Love
life	Life
happiness	Happiness
power	Omnipotent
justice	Justice
mercy	Mercy
efficient causality	First Cause
Which perfections in man are composite, imperfect, simple, finite, changeable, localized, temporal, and multiple.	Which perfections in God are perfect, infinite, immutable, omnipresent, eternal, and one.
TABLE 4-1	

maximum union possible to man's nature with Being, Truth, Love, Life, Happiness, Omnipotence, Justice, Mercy and First Causality, in its personal, essential, pure, ultimate reality. Man does not, therefore, desire the infinite, eternal, immutable in a vacuum, but he desires Being, Truth, Love and Life, which is infinite, eternal, and immutable. The capacity of human nature for union with, and the experience of God, is the capacity of man's created being, truth, love, and life, to expand, evolve, intensify, and attain a state of real union with Being, Truth, Love and Life. To desire God, therefore, is to desire Life in its purest, essential, personal, unrestricted reality.

This means also that one desires to come alive in one's self in the maximum degree in which human nature can be alive. To love God is to love Love, and to want to possess and be possessed by infinite, personal Love. It is to hunger also to love in union with Love in the most intense and all-inclusive manner that human nature is radically capable of loving. To want God is to thirst for contact with living, eternal Truth, and to have one's mind expanded in union with Truth to the deepest, broadest, clearest consciousness of all reality in the intuition of the Source of reality. To hunger for God is to hunger for Being and Actuality, to be able to reach out and embrace and possess and become the totality of existence in union with the living, personal Existent present to every being and from Whom all being is derived.

2. Man's movement toward God will involve a transition from the limited perfections of his created being (A) to growing likeness and increasing participation in the unlimited simple perfections of Uncreated Being (B). It will be a movement toward Being, Truth, Love, Life, Happiness, Omnipotence, Justice, Mercy, and the First Cause with all that is implied in such a movement.

As man's being intensifies and his consciousness expands and deepens, and as his love embraces more and more of the good in greater and greater depth, and as he becomes more profoundly, fully alive, the movement toward divinity will be progressing. As his joy increases in the conscious possession of his own being and of the good divinity will be evolving in him. As his mastery over his own life and his ability to influence and enrich life around him develops—and the need in him grows to treat as sacred every creature with an awareness of its specific nature and function in the totality of things—divinity will be evolving in him. As the tendency to perfect and enrich the poverty of created being, wherever he encounters such poverty, becomes the dominating thrust in his response to reality, divinity will be evolving in him.

3. The attainment of God and godliness will consist in the full actualization of the human potential for being, truth, love, life, and happiness, in man's union with the Source from Whom these perfections proceed. The godly man will be the one whose humanity is perm-

WHAT GOD AND GODLINESS ARE

eated with and radiates the perfection of divinity. For Christians, of course, the supreme model of godliness will be found in the historical reality of the person of Christ in whose human nature one finds the very incarnation of Being, Truth, Love, Life, Happiness, Omnipotence, Justice, Mercy and Divine Causality.

This same doctrine about the positive reality of God permits one also to elaborate a statement about godlessness in man. Since all men necessarily seek the Perfect Good and Happiness the godless man is not the one who does not desire God. Rather, the godless man is the person who chooses to arrest his necessary movement toward divinity in his embrace of a limited object in which he endeavors to find the unlimitedness and purity of being, truth, love, life, power, rectitude, and creativity which is to be found only in God.[20] To the degree in which his chosen finite object is an actuality and, therefore, possesses a limited expression of divinity, it will have the power to expand his being, cause awareness and love, stir the potential for life in him, bring power, rightness, and fruitful creativity to his relations with himself and the world about him.[21] However, to the degree to which this finite object falls short of the unlimited richness of the Being, Truth, Love, Life, Happiness, Omnipotence, Justice, Mercy, and Causality which is God, it will fail in this expansion and enrichment of his being.

Poverty of being, a low level of consciousness, rigidity of affective responses, paralysis and death of spirit, inability to master one's own being and one's surroundings, impotence, sterility, indifference to the deficiencies of creatures which cry out for succor, these are the measurements, signs, and effects of man's separation from God. They constitute the vacuum and emptiness in which goodlessness consists. It

---

[20] *Summa*, I-II, q. 91, a. 7, ad. 1.

[21] "Creatures of themselves do not withdraw us from God, but lead us to Him.... If then they withdraw men from God, it is the fault of those who use them foolishly.... And the very fact that they can thus withdraw us from God proves that they came from Him, for they cannot lead the foolish away from God except by the allurements of some good that they have from Him." *Ibid.*, I, q. 65. a.1 ad3.

is of this void in man that one can truly and objectively speak of a kind of *"death of God."*

III. MAN'S POSITIVE MOVEMENT TOWARD GOD AND GODLINESS

This analysis of man's search for union with God leaves unanswered the question of the precise manner in which the movement toward divinity actually takes place. Experience reveals that in practice man's quest for union with God follows the same three general patterns already proposed, namely Pattern I in which man tends to identify and absorb Uncreated Being (B) into created being (A), Pattern II according to which man seeks contact with B independently of A, and Pattern III in which man finds in A his point of union with B.[22]

Pattern I.

According to my analysis of this first pattern man's positive movement toward God will work itself out in the tendency of many to endow the simple perfections of created being (A) with the characteristics of Uncreated Being (B), so that being, truth, love, life, happiness, power and causality, become adorned with the qualities of Being, Truth, Love, Life, Happiness, Omnipotence, and First Causality. I have already ofered Aquinas' explanation of the dynamics underlying this identification of B with A.[23] The concrete expression of this tendency assumes various forms. Among the more common of these may be found the following:

1. My finite being, which is only one of the many limited existents, becomes for me The One, Central, Primary Being, at least in the psychological and practical order. Although I am prompt to acknowledge in theory that I am not God, the First Being, in practice I tend to keep a candle lit before the shrine of my actuality ascribing to it a centrality and priority which belongs to Being and not to my being.[24]

2. I attribute to my limited, faulty insights into myself, and to my flawed understanding of life or to the more refined scientific, phil-

---

[22] *Cf.* Chapter 3, Section III.
[23] *Cf.* Chapter 3, Section III.
[24] *Summa*, I-II, q. 77, a. 5.

osophical, theological ideology that I espouse, a certainty, necessity, universality, clarity, infallibility, and finality that belongs more to Truth than to my hold on truths.

3. To this love in my life is attributed a permanence and power of fulfillment, a significance and priority over other affections, which is owed more to Love than to my poor love.

4. The created life that I prize and tenaciously cling to in the face of inevitable death, rebelling against the assertion of control over it made by the Author of that life, becomes for me the unique source of my being and the key to happiness, receiving a veneration and dependence from me that is owed to Life and not to life.

5. The mutable good of my choice, around which I organize my life and affections, is endowed with a promise and power of complete satisfaction which objectively can be found only in the Perfect Good and Uncreated Happiness.

6. My vacillating and generally inept power to regulate my life and to control my surroundings and future destiny, is looked upon as possessing a wisdom and efficaciousness that is to be found in Omnipotence and not in created power. And so on the expressions of this tendency to deify created perfections go, assuming as many different forms as there are distinct created goods around which one can build his dreams of perfect happiness.[25]

The limitations inherent in simple perfections found in the created order result in their carrying in themselves a kind of time bomb that will be triggered at the inevitable revelation that time and experience bring of the illusory character of their deifications. The closer one comes to genuine encounter with created beings, the more clearly these limitations are confronted, and the more difficult becomes the task of rationalizing and shoring up the illusions essential to their pursuit as ultimate goals. In moments of striking revelation, when the mutable object of election as one's final end radically fails in its assigned task of fulfillment, we find either a crisis of conversion or a renewed conscious

---

[25] *Ibid.*, I-II, q. 2.

descent into an emergency salvaging effort to reconstruct from the debris another revamped promise of total fulfillment. Our new god then arises out of the ashes of the old, made in the image of likeness of our dreams and desperation.

This descent into the hell of illusion is not necessarily accompanied by the shrinking of the created good in which one seeks to find perfect fulfillment. Sometimes this descent occurs with, and because of a substantial growth in the possession of the mutable good. It is the illusion of the power of the finite good to fulfill, in a way that objectively it cannot, that shrinks. With this shrinking there occurs the growing desperation to reconstitute anew the conviction that such a good can still produce as the Perfect Good. The materialist's bank account may be increasing substantially at the very time that the illusions of the happiness which he was convinced his money could purchase, start to fade into the background. He then either alters his pursuit of happiness, or comes up with a face-saving reason on the conditions under which the money can, after all, still fulfill its promise of providing perfect happiness.[26]

Interestingly enough in projecting powers of fulfillment into finite goods that make them instruments of our desire and dream of perfect happiness—and thereby elevate them to a level of goodness and performance beyond their objective limitations—we duplicate exactly the pattern whereby God endows finite goods with physical properties of divine goodness and creativity. In this way, according to Catholic doctrine, God makes them instruments of His love and will for our fulfillment. The difference between the two patterns is found in the inefficaciousness of human desire to elevate the finite good as opposed to the effectiveness of the divine will in transforming the power of created good to fulfill. In this first case, the enlarged power of finite good is purely subjective and not objective—an illusion and not a reality. That is, love is not Love and truth does not contain and convey Truth. In the second case, the enlarged power of the finite good to fulfill as the instrument of the Infinite Good, is reality and not illusion. That is, love and truth as instruments of Love and Truth contain and

---

[26] *Ibid.*, I-II q. 30, a. 4.

convey the divine perfections, and become points of immediate contact with divinity.[27]

Pattern II

The second general pattern [28] of relating created being (A) to Uncreated Being (B) in the case of the positive perfections of both orders, assumes the form of placing being, truth, love, life, happiness, power, and causality, in radical opposition to Being, Truth, Love, Life, Happiness, Omnipotence, and Prime Causality. Or of so relating them as to make created perfections more an obstacle than an aid to union with Uncreated Being. Thus, for example, the strain of anti-intellectualism which surfaces among Christians tends to downgrade the value of truth as a point of contact with Truth, objectively because there is little or no positive relation between them, and subjectively because truth inflates the ego and renders one less docile to Truth. The Jansenistic, puritanical side of Christians sees love and happiness as detrimental to union with Love and Happiness, and encourages the suppression or severe restriction of the former as a price that the experience of the latter extorts. The claims of life must be rejected in order that Life may be embraced. You cannot cling to life and to Life at the same time! This is the meaning of Calvary—life must be surrendered in order to gain Life?

Remnants of Manichaeism tend to deny to being, especially material being, a positive link with Being. Thus the use of materials in liturgical worship such as light, fire, breath, water, and oil, as points of contact with divinity (that is, Light, Love, Spirit, and Life), is seen as a form of blasphemy. This pattern either rejects entirely the use of such material beings, or makes their use isolated instances of contact with divinity rather than symbols of the contact with God present potentially throughout the whole of creation.

Just as created being objectively does not offer points of effective contact with Uncreated Being, so God will not use created perfections

---

[27] *Ibid.*, III, q. 62, a. 1.

[28] *Cf.* Chapter 3, Section III, Pattern II.

as instruments through which He acts on the created order. Thus Truth does not act through truth, elevating and perfecting the power of created truth so that it becomes the vehicle of the revelation and power of Uncreated Truth. Also, Love, Life, Omnipotence, and First Causality, do not, and cannot, act in and through love, life, power, and created causality, endowing as instruments these created perfections with the physical properties of the simple perfections as found in their uncreated state in the divine essence. Much less does God use material beings (fire, light, air, water, oil, bread, and wine) as instruments through which He acts upon humans in a special manner so as to offer man in his contact with these instrumentalities a point of immediate, extraordinary experience of Uncreated Being.

Pattern III

According to our analysis of this third pattern [29] it follows that the simple perfections found in the limited conditions of created being (A) are derivations, participations, and revelations of the essentially distinct kind of existence that these simple perfections possess in Uncreated Being (B). Therefore the simple perfections of A are contained in B as the effect is in its cause, and B is present to them so that the possession of A is the point of potential union with B. Further, according to Catholic doctrine, B can and does use A as an instrument through which He acts on human nature and communicates His perfections in an extraordinary manner, thus making A when assumed as an instrument the point of special experience of and union with B.

To understand this position, it is necessary to reflect further on the relation of created being to the Creator as expressed in the analogous model of the relation of the artistic effect to the artist[30] Aquinas' doctrine on this relation of simple perfections of the created order to the same perfections present in God is as follows: Whatever being, truth, love, life, beatitude, power, and causality is found in creatures, is derived from, sustained by, revealing of, and present in, though distinct from, the Being, Truth, Love, Life, Beatitude, Omnipotence and Causality, which is God.

---

[29] *Cf.* Chapter 3, Section III, Pattern III.
[30] *Cf.* Chapter 3, Section III, Pattern III.

WHAT GOD AND GODLINESS ARE

The motive operative in the act of creation is—Divine Love willing to impart to the created order an ideal participation in Divine Goodness. Since no one creature can receive the fullness of Being, Truth, Love and the other divine perfections, God creates a variety of beings on which He bestows different, complementary, finite expressions of His infinite being. And He so orders each to the other, the lower to the higher, the part to the whole, that the collectivity and totality of created beings more fully contain and express His Being, Truth, Love, Life, Beatitude, Omnipotence, Justice, Mercy, and Causality than does any single creature or segment of creation.

God not only creates the perfections of A, He is intimately present to each part of A and to the whole of A, so that Truth is present to truth, causing and sustaining it, and is partially, imperfectly expressed in it. So, also, Being is present to being, Love to love, Life to life, Beatitude to beatitude, Omnipotence to power, and Causality to causality. Therefore, the more fully I experience and possess the participated divinity present in the totality of the created order the closer I am to the source from whence that participated perfection is derived, by which it is sustained, and which is substantially present to it.

My experience and possession of created being may come about through a speculative and/or practical mode of activity. Speculatively, I may acquire and expand an abstract knowledge of love, life, power, beatitude, and virtue while finding myself in the concrete condition of one who is lacking in affection, weak, dying, miserable, and a sinner. My encounter with created being is a practical and existential one when I experience both in myself and in others through affective union, the presence and fullness of life, love, power, beatitude, and virtue. For example, I may not be able to define compassion but I am a compassionate person and therefore I experience the practical, concrete effects of the presence and dynamics of that virtue.[31] Again, I ex-

---

[31] "Now the rectitude of judgment is twofold: first, on account of perfect use of reason, secondly, on account of a certain connaturality with the matter about which one has to judge. Thus, about matters of chastity, a man after inquiring with his reason forms a right judgment, if he has learnt the science

perience the fullness of life by becoming more and more alive and responding to the intensity of life around me, even though I cannot offer an adequate description of life in the abstract. Now each mode of activity, the speculative and the practical, provides me with a partial experience and possession of created being. It is the combination of the two which offers me the fullest access to created being.

This access to and possession of created being in its totality is essential to my experience of the fullness of divinity present in each part of the created order. For while God is totally present to every creature, though only partially revealed in each creature, it is only when I experience each being as part of the whole of creation and see it in the light of the whole that I am disposed to experience the fullness of divinity's presence in it. But since everything is received according to the mode of the recipient it is only when I approach a creature as one who has identified with, and become in himself, the whole of created being that I can know and experience this creature in and through the whole of created reality; and thereby experience fully divinity present in it. Therefore, the more I take upon myself the perfections of the whole of created being, and approach each segment of the created order in the light of that whole which I have become, the more I can experience divinity present in each part.

But how can man, a minute fragment of the whole of creation, become in any sense that whole, taking on the fullness of the whole when human nature is itself and remains only a part? How can man transcend his own radical limitations so as to become in a sense the universe, taking on the fullness of created being, truth, love, life, beatitude, power, and causality, so as to experience in each part of creation and in the whole of creation the presence of Being, Truth, Love, Life, Beatitude, Omnipotence and Causality?

Being

As one expression of created being among multiple, created existents, I find in my being only a microscopic revelation of the fullness of divinity present in the total, accumulative being of all created effects. To

---

of morals, while he who has the habit of chastity judges of such matters by a kind of connaturality." *Summa*, II-II, q. 45, a. 2.

WHAT GOD AND GODLINESS ARE

the extent that I can transcend the limitations of my individual existence and take on the being of other created effects, to that same extent my being will expand, evolve, intensify, and move towards the fullness of participated divinity contained in the being of the entire created order, and thereby move into the encounter with the fullness of Being.

Since each created entity is a partial, complementary expression of Being, to the[32] extent that I take on the reality of every being I fill out my participation in Being; and come closer to the full experience of Being. I cannot separate my openness to being from my openness to Being. Nor can I isolate my movement toward Being from my movement toward being. The more I pull back from, and close myself off to being in the created order for whatever reasons, the more I will be pulling back from and closing myself off to Being. My movement toward Being originates in my own, initial, radically restricted hold on being. From there it expands outward to the embrace of and identification with all being; and then penetrates to the depths of my being and all being to the encounter with the Being from which all being proceeds. The question remains as to how I am able, if I am able, to transcend the limitations of my being, and to take on, identify with, and become the being of the entire created order. How can man, a part, become in any sense the whole, the universe ?

Truth

Truth is a property of being.[33] To the extent that an object has being, it is intelligible and can cause awareness of itself in the intellect, since the act of knowing is basically the possession of the form or actuality of the object known by the mind of the knower.[34] The more being an object possesses, the greater is its truth, its intelligibility, its power to cause

---

[32] *Ibid.*, I, q. 47, a. 3.
[33] *Ibid.*, I, q. 16. A. 3.
[34] *Ibid.*, I, q. 84, aa. 1, 2 ; q. 16, a.1 ad. 3.

awareness.[35] In the act of knowing I take unto myself, in a sense, the being of the object known and I become the object known. So as my knowledge of created being expands in breadth and depth, my being expands proportionately. Through knowledge, therefore, I transcend the limitations of my restricted being and become all that I know.[36]

The insatiable hunger in man for truth is the expression of his equally insatiable hunger for being, his desire to identify with, possess, and become one with the whole of reality. It is in this sense that Aristotle states, and Aquinas repeats after him, that man is microcosm.[37] More than this, the truth in created being is derived from, and participates in the Truth of God.[38] Man's hunger for truth, therefore, is also the expression and revelation of his hunger for Truth—God.[39] The biologist searching for truth under his microscope and the astronomer searching for truth in the stars, are in their own way expressing the

---

[35] "Since everything is knowable according as it is actual, God, Who is pure act without any admixture of potentiality, is in Himself supremely knowable." *Ibid.*, I, q. 12, a.1.

[36] "But in those things which have knowledge, each one is determined to its own natural being by its natural form, in such a manner, that it is nevertheless receptive of the species of other things: for example, sense receives the species of all things sensible, and the intellect of all things intelligible, so that the soul of man is, in a way, all things by sense and intellect: and thereby those things that have knowledge, in a way approach to a likeness to God 'In Whom all things pre-exist,' as Dionysius says (Div. Nom. V)." *Ibid.*,q. 80, a.

[37] " Now everything, in so far as it has being, so far is it knowable. Wherefore it is said in *De Anima* that 'the soul is in some manner all things,' through the senses and the intellect. And therefore, as good is controvertible with being, so is the true." *Ibid.*, I, q. 16, a. 4.

[38] *Ibid.*, q. 16, a. 6.

[39] "If therefore the human intellect, knowing the essence of some created effect, knows no more of God than 'that he is,' the perfection of that intellect does not yet reach simply the First Cause, but there remains in it the natural desire to seek the cause. Wherefore it is not yet perfectly happy. Consequently, for perfect happiness the intellect needs to reach the very Essence of the first Cause. And thus it will have its perfections through union with God as with that object, in which alone man's happiness consists." *Ibid.*, I-II, q. 3, a. 8.

same hunger for God (Truth) that is revealed in the ponderings of the theologian and the prayers of the mystic. As one's mind expands with reality it is in possession of the truth of created being; it is growing also in the participation of the truth of God and it is entering into union with that Truth out of which all creation proceeds.

I cannot separate my openness to truth from my openness to Truth. Nor can I isolate my movement toward Truth from my movement toward truth. The more I pull back from, and close myself off to, truth in the created order the more I will be pulling back from and closing myself off to Truth. The more I embrace the full richness of truth in created being, the more I will be embracing Truth. My movement towards truth originates in my initial, naked potential for truth with which I come into existence. It moves outward from there to the embrace and possession of the truth of created being, and then downward the movement continues to the depths of truth to that Truth out of which all truth proceeds.

Now the object known exists in the knower according to the manner of the recipient, and not as it exists in the objective order. The movement in knowing is from the object known inward to the inner possession of the form by the knower. The being of the object known enters into, and is possessed by the knower only in so far as its form is present to the knower in the sense that the knower becomes that form. The concrete objective existence of the object known outside the mind of the knower, with the full range of its power to enrich and intensify, is still not fully possessed. The dietitian's knowledge of the nutritional value of a hamburger, his hunger to know, and speculative possession of the truth of a hamburger, cannot alone do for him what a different kind of desire for and possession of a hamburger can do in the mouth of a hungry man.[40]

---

[40] "The act of a cognitive power is completed by the thing known being in the knower, whereas the act of an appetitive power consists in the appetite being inclined towards the thing itself. Hence is follows that the movement of the appetitive power is towards things in respect of their own condition, whereas the act of a cognitive power follows the mode of the knower." *Summa*, II-II, q. 27, a.4c. Cf. also II-II, q.26, a.6.

Love

To the extent that an object has being, it can enrich with its actuality the being of others, thereby intensifying their actuality and fulfilling in them their capacity and hunger for maximum being.[41] Hence to the extent that an object has being, it is desirable or good. Goodness, therefore, like truth, is also a property of being. The more being an object possesses, the greater will be its desirableness and goodness.[42] Since God alone is infinite being, He alone is infinitely good and desirable.[43] Just as the being of creatures is derived from Divine Being, so also the goodness present in every created being is a derivation of and participation in the goodness of God.[44] And just as the totality of creatures participates more fully in the being of God than any individual being or segment of created being, so the totality of created beings participate more fully in divine goodness than does any individual or segment of the created order. At the origin of created goodness is Divine Love willing to communicate to the created order this participation in divine goodness.[45]

The attraction of an entity toward the good is called love. In intellectual beings, this appetite for the good follows upon the activity of the intellect. In man, therefore, love is a conscious attraction toward the good, a movement toward some being recognized as desirable by the intellect.[46] The more man discovers the goodness present in being

---

[41] *Ibid.*, I-II, a. 1.

[42] "Goodness and being are really the same, and differ only in idea; which is clear from the following argument. The essence of goodness consists in this, that it is in some way desirable. Hence the Philosopher says (*Ethics* i) 'Goodness is what all desire.' Now it is clear that a thing is desirable only in so far as it is perfect; for all desire their own perfection. But everything is perfect so far as it is actual. Therefore it is clear that a thing is perfect so far as it exists; for it is existence that makes all things actual, as is clear from the foregoing (Q.3, a.4; Q.4; A.1). Hence it is clear that goodness and being are the same really." *Ibid.*, I, q.5 a.1c.

[43] *Ibid.*, I, q. 7, aa 1, 2, 3.

[44] *Ibid.*, I, q. 7, a. 4.

[45] *Ibid.*, I, q. 47, a. 1.

[46] *Ibid.*, I., q. 20, a. 1.

or the desirableness of being, the more he is stirred in will to the pursuit and possession of such good.[47] Love always has its object, the good, with the implicit confrontation with reality, being, that the good entails. One cannot develop his capacity to love by withdrawing from reality into a vacuum where he muscles forth from himself more intense and profound acts of love. Rather, one grows in the capacity to love by opening himself to, and savoring the goodness of reality while allowing being to exercise its inevitable and irresistible attraction on a healthy organism.

Since the good of created being is a participation in the goodness of God, man cannot separate his openness to Divine Goodness from his openness to created good, nor can he isolate his movement toward, and responsiveness to Divine Goodness from his movement toward and responsiveness to created good. That is to say, man cannot love God and not love God's work, or truly love created being and not at the same time love God. The two loves go together. The more profoundly, intensely, and fully man loves the full range of goodness of created being, the more he will love Divine Goodness of which created goodness is a participation and derivation and without which created good could not exist. The more a person pulls back from, and closes himself off to a true love of the created good, the more he is pulling back from, and closing himself off to the love of Divine Goodness.[48] Also, since God is Love, it is as a man loves more intensely, profoundly, universally, and unrestrictedly that he approaches to, and experiences Love in his love. Since all created good is derived from and expresses Divine Love, it is only as a man comes fully alive in love to the breadth and depth of good present in the created order that he comes alive to love itself and to Love.

---

[47] *Ibid.*, I-II, q. 27, a. 2.

[48] "For since our neighbor is more visible to us, he is the first lovable object we meet with, because 'the soul learns, from those things it knows, to love what it knows not,' as Gregory says in a homily. Hence it can be argued that, if any man loves not his neighbor, neither does he love God, not because his neighbor is more lovable, but because he is the first thing to demand our love, and God is more lovable by reason of His greater goodness." *Ibid.*, II-II, q. 26, a. 2 ad 1.

Love in man is another expression, together with truth, of his hunger for maximum being. Man's *affective* attachment to being under its aspect of good, complements his speculative possession of being under its aspects of truth. It is primarily through the dual, complementary activities of knowing and loving that man transcends his individual limitations of being, and takes upon himself the perfections of the created order thereby becoming in a sense the universe.[49] And as his being expands and intensifies through a knowing and loving that embraces the truth and goodness of all created being, he moves into deeper union with the Being, Truth and Love out of which the created order's participation in divinity proceeds.

Life

Vital activity is identical with immanent activity. Those creatures are said to live that possess the power of self-movement and self-determination, that is, those that contain their own inner principle of activity originating and terminating within themselves.[50] The more the immanent activity of a creature is self-contained the higher is the expression of life in it and, therefore, the more alive it is said to be. Since knowing and loving are not only immanent activities, but are more perfectly self-contained than vegetative and sensitive forms of vital operations, intellectual beings constitute a higher form of life than vegetative and sensitive beings. And since God is that Being whose act of knowing and loving is identical with His very nature, God not only has

---

[49] "Now love being twofold, viz., love of concupiscence, and love of friendship; each of these arises from a kind of apprehension of the oneness of the thing loved with the lover. For when we love a thing, by desiring it, we apprehend it as belonging to our well being. In like manner when a man loves another with the love of friendship, he wills good to him, just as he wills good to himself: wherefore he apprehends him as his other-self, in so far, to wit, as he wills good to him as to himself." *Ibid.*, I-II, q. 28, a. 1

[50] "Whereby it is clear that those things are properly called living that move themselves by some kind of movement.... Accordingly, all things are said to be alive that determine themselves to movement or operations of any kind: whereas those things that cannot by their nature do so, cannot be called living unless by a similitude." *Ibid.*, I, q. 18, a. 1c.

WHAT GOD AND GODLINESS ARE

life in the highest degree, but God is Life.[51] And since all creation proceeds from the knowing, loving act of the living God, created being is the expression of that Divine Life.

Some creatures are themselves living expressions of the Divine Life, and both the life in them and their power to awaken life in others is a participation in and revelation of the Life from which they are derived. Other creatures are inanimate, but the being, truth, and goodness which constitute their reality is an expression of Divine Life. The power of their inanimate being, truth, and goodness to awaken knowledge and love, and intensify the being of living creatures, is a further participation in the Divine Life from which they come.[52]

Since God is Life, the movement toward God is a movement toward Life in its purest and highest form, and the process of salvation is literally a process of coming fully alive. Man's hunger for and love of life, and his capacity for the experience of life in its purest form, is identical with man's hunger for, love of, and capacity to experience God (Life). Man's coming alive to God is inseparable from his coming alive to created being in which he finds the participated expression of Divine Life.

The more a man is open and alive to the full breadth and depth of the expression of Divine Life in created being, the more he is open and alive to Life. To the extent that he withdraws from or closes himself off to the fullest, deepest vital experience of created being, to that same extent he is dead to the experience of God (Life). With justification the New Testament presents as symbols of sin either impaired life (para-

---

[51] "Life is in the highest degree properly in God. In proof of which it must be considered that since a thing is said to love in so far as it operates of itself and not as moved by another, the more perfectly this power is found in anything, the more perfect is the life of that thing.... Wherefore that being whose act of understanding is its very nature, and which, in what it naturally possesses, is not determined by another, must have life in the most perfect degree. Such is God; hence in Him principally is life." *Ibid.*, I, q. 18, a. 3.

[52] *Ibid.*, I, q. 18, a. 4.

lysis,⁵³ blindness,⁵⁴ disease,⁵⁵) or death.⁵⁶ It is the participated divinity of the being, truth, love, and life of created being that brings man fully alive. And through this experience of the fullness of life in him, he comes to experience Life. Just as a person who contemplates (comes alive to) the work of an artist is led into communion with the inner thoughts, affective movements, aesthetic feelings, and life itself of the artist, so the man who is stirred to life by the participation (ordinary and extraordinary) of Divine Life in the whole of creation, is brought alive to Life and enters into communion with the Life out of which being springs.

Beatitude

Happiness is the conscious possession of good. Perfect happiness (beatitude) is the conscious possession of the perfect good. The degrees of happiness are determined by the perfection of the good possessed and the quality of its possession. The more perfect the good and the more controlled its possession, the more complete is the fulfillment of one's desire for maximum being and the greater is one's happiness. Man's desire for happiness is a further expression of his desire for being under the aspect of the good. Man's desire for perfect happiness, which is operative in every human act, is identical with his desire for maximum being, the perfect good—God.⁵⁷ Since God is the perfect good and intelligent by nature, His conscious possession of Himself as the Supreme Good is identical with His nature. Therefore God not only has perfect happiness, but He is Beatitude.⁵⁸ The power of created being to

---

[53] *Ibid., Mt.* 9,5.

[54] *Ibid., Mt.* 15.14.

[55] *Ibid., Mt.* 9.2.

[56] *Ibid., Mt.* 23.27.

[57] *Ibid.,* I, q. 2, a.1 ad 1.

[58] "Beatitude belongs to God in a very special manner. For nothing else is understood to be meant by the term beatitude than the perfect good of an intellectual nature: which is capable of knowing that it has a sufficiency of the good which it possesses, to which it is competent that good or ill may befall, and which can control its own actions. All of these things belong in a most excellent manner to God—namely, to be perfect, and to possess intelligence. Whence beatitude belongs to God in the highest degree." *Ibid.,* I, q. 26, a. 1.

fulfill desire and to provide limited happiness is a participation in the Beatitude which is God.[59]

Since the totality of creatures participates more fully in the beatitude of God than any *part* of creation, the more one experiences the total participated beatitude of all created being and controls his possession of this beatitude, the more one approaches and savors the Beatitude of God. Since God is Beatitude, the movement toward God is a movement toward happiness in its purest, highest form. This movement toward Beatitude cannot be separate from, or take place independently of one's growing capacity to experience the participated beatitude of created being. The more one is dead to the joys of created being, the more one is dead to the absolute joy of Uncreated Being. The more one develops the capacity to experience the full breadth and depth of beatitude in created being, the closer one comes to the experience of Divine Beatitude from whence created happiness is derived and of which it is a pale, pale reflection and foretaste.

Power

Active power follows upon perfection of being. The more in act and perfect a being is, the more it is the active principle of something. Since God is pure act and infinitely perfect by nature, His active power is infinite and He is omnipotent.[60] God's power regulates and controls the whole of reality. The very efforts of rebellious men to withdraw from His control, fall under God's power. All things are ordained to His purposes.[61] Therefore active power and godliness are identical, as are impotence and godlessness.[62] One is godly to the extent that he masters and controls his own being and his surroundings, his past and future as

---

[59] "Whatever is desirable in whatsoever beatitude, whether true or false, pre-exist wholly and in a more eminent degree in the divine beatitude." *Ibid.*, I, q. 26, a. 4.

[60] *Ibid.*, I, q. 25, aa. 1, 2, 3.

[61] *Ibid.*, I, q. 103, a. 3.

[62] "For it is manifest that everything, according as it is in act and is perfect, is the active principle of something: whereas everything is passive according as it is deficient and imperfect." *Ibid.*, I, q. 25, a. 1c.

well as his present. To the degree that one is lacking in such mastery, he is lacking in godliness. The desire of man to control his life and his destiny is another expression of his desire for perfect being—God.[63]

The active power of created being is a derivation of and participation in the omnipotence of God. Man's movement toward the perfect control proper to God cannot be separated from his movement toward control of the forces of created being which are derived from the power of God. To the degree that a man withdraws from active involvement in regulating and controlling the forces of created being, he withdraws from the movement toward the godliness of participated divine power. Therefore, when a man abandons his effort to regulate and control the forces of created being, he abandons the struggle toward God.

Since all creation exists and operates under the unified direction of the Divine Will, it is only as a man grows in the knowledge and love of created being, grasps the natures of things, sees their relation to each other as parts to a whole, and comes alive to the plan of providence according to which they function and by which their power is determined that he can act in harmony with that plan and participate in the divine power controlling the forces and movement of creation. This conforming of man's timorous, vacillating, largely impotent *fiat* to the Omnipotent Divine *Fiat* takes place through the mediation of that Divine *Fiat*'s expression of will found in created being.[64]

Man must discover and want in the created order what God wills for it and for himself, with all the implications of a true, total, unqualified embrace of, and active involvement in that divine plan at work in the created order, if the union of the human and divine wills is to be effected.[65] There is no way that a man can approach union with the

---

[63] *Ibid.*, I, q. 96, aa 1, 2.

[64] *Ibid.*, I, q. 19, aa 4, 5.

[65] "But a man's will is not right in willing a particular good, unless he refer it to the common good as an end: since even the natural appetite of each part is ordained to the common good of the whole. Now it is the end that supplies the formal reason, as it were, of willing whatever is directed to the end. Consequently, in order that a man will some particular good with a right will, he must will that particular good materially, and the Divine and universal good, formally. Therefore the human will is bound to be conformed to the Divine will, as to that which is willed formally, for it is

divine will apart from his marriage to that will as revealed in created being. At the moment his human *fiat* espouses the Divine *Fiat* as revealed in the reality of created being, he achieves an active participation in the divine power that regulates and controls all being[66] Through his conformity of will and instrumental participation in divine power, he enters into union with the Divine Omnipotence from which all power and all forces and all activity and all being proceed.

Causality

To the extent that a being exists, it can communicate its actuality to others through the exercise of efficient causality.[67] To the degree in which a reality has being it is good, and, therefore, actually tends to communicate its being to others.[68] Since God is Being by nature and the Perfect Good, it is uniquely proper to Him to communicate being in the most universal and primary manner through the act of creation.[69] Whatever being exists apart from God, is being by participation and derives from the essential being of God. Participation in godliness involves participation in divine causality.[70] In the degree in which a creature approaches the divine likeness, it will manifest a tendency to

---

bound to will the Divine and universal good...." *Ibid.*, I-II, q. 19, a.10 c. *Cf.* Also *Ibid.*, III, q. 47, a. 3; q. 18, a.5.

[66] "The human will cannot be conformed to the will of God so as to equal it, but only so as to imitate it. In like manner human knowledge is conformed to the divine knowledge in so far as it is becoming to the agent: - and this by way of imitation, not by way of equality." *Ibid.*, I - II, q. 19, a. 10, ad. 1.

[67] *Ibid.*, I, q. 25, a. 1.

[68] *Ibid.*, I, q. 5, a. 5; III, q. 1, a. 1c.

[69] *Ibid.*, I, q. 44, aa.1, 2.

[70] "But since things which are governed should be brought to perfection by government, this government will be so much better in the degree the things governed are brought to perfection. Now it is a greater for a thing to be good in itself and also the cause of goodness in others, than only to be good in itself. Therefore God so governs things that He makes some of them to be causes of others in government; as a master, who not only imparts knowledge to his pupils, but gives also the faculty of teaching others." *Ibid.*, I, q. 103, a. 6.

cling to its own being, imitating the divine permanence, and a tendency to communicate its being to others, imitating the divine causality.[71]

The powerful need in man to exercise efficient causality by giving life, creating works of art, putting order into chaos, erecting buildings, cities, and nations, and in an infinite variety of ways seeking to place the stamp of his being on the rest of created reality, is another expression of his desire for maximum being and for the creativity of divine causality. Man's approach to God and godliness involves his growing power and desire to communicate the richness of his being in the exercise of efficient causality.

But such an approach to God and growth in godliness can only take place through the mediation of his positive relation to and identification with the participated divinity of created being. Man, apart from the created order and in a vacuum, is too impoverished in being and goodness to function as an efficient cause. In such a state he has nothing to give, and only hungers to receive. His separation from a positive, enriching, expanding contact with created being, leaves him a hollow shell and sterile. He may surround himself with religious gimmicks and

---

[71] "Divine goodness has this characteristic, that it communicates a likeness of itself to creatures. The perfection of divine goodness entails the double truth that God is good in Himself, and that he leads other beings to goodness. He communicates goodness to creatures under both aspects: they are good in themselves and they lead others to goodness In this way God brings some creatures to goodness through others. The latter must be higher creatures; for what receives a likeness of both form and action from some agent is more perfect than what receives a likeness of form but not of action. Thus the moon which not only glows with light but also illumines other bodies, receives light from the sun more perfectly than do opaque bodies which are merely illuminated but do not illuminate. Accordingly God governs lower creatures by higher creatures. communicates a likeness of itself to creatures. The perfection of divine goodness entails the double truth that God is good in Himself, and that he leads other beings to goodness. He communicates goodness to creatures under both aspects: they are good in themselves, and they lead others to goodness. In this way God brings some creatures to goodness through others. The latter must be higher creatures: for what receives a likeness of both form and action from some agent is more perfect than what receives a likeness of form but not of action." *Compendium*, c. 124

religious rationalizations to justify and support his withdrawal from reality, but in the poverty, paralysis, and impotence of the experience of his inner emptiness, he will find not the experience of the richness and fertile creativity of divinity, but only himself alone.

It is only as man opens himself wide to the embrace of the truth, good, life, beatitude, and power of participated divinity in created being that his own being expands, intensifies, and takes on the richness of the being of God. And as his being and goodness grow through identification with all of created being, his capacity and desire to share his possession of godliness increases. In his activity of giving, ordering, perfecting, sustaining; and creating, he evolves in his experience of the causal creativity of God, and he enters into closer union with the divine act of creation which brings all being into existence, and sustains it.

Justice

The justice (distributive) of a ruler disposes him to give to each of his subjects that which is due to them. Such justice is proper to God who "gives to all existing things what is proper to the condition of each; and preserves the nature of each one in the order and with the powers that properly belong to it."[72] Divine Justice is operative in the act of creating and regulating the universe where we find both in the effects of nature and in the effects of will every creature *ut in pluribus* receiving that which is due to it.[73]

The tendency in humans to see that every being receive what is proper to it, is a created participation in Divine Justice and evidences the drive in human nature for God under the aspect of Justice. The growth in godliness involves man's increasing participation in Divine Justice. Such growth, again, takes place only through the medium of conformity with the expression of Divine Justice found in the created order.

While every aspect of created being is stamped with the impress of Divine Justice, the totality of created being contains and expresses

---

[72] *Ibid.*, I, q. 21, a. 1c.
[73] *Ibid.*, I, q. 21, a. 4.

more fully the Justice of God than any segment or part of creation. The more a man approaches the whole of created being, open to the workings and manifestations of Justice present in each part and in the whole, seeking to discern those workings and endeavoring to conform to their demands by treating every creature as sacred and giving to each that which is due to it, the more he grows in, and approaches union with, the Justice of God.

To be oblivious or indifferent to, ignore or reject, the presence and manifestations of Justice in any part of created being, is to withdraw and shut one's self off from union with Divine Justice. To consider any part of created being insignificant, not worthy of one's time and consideration, and useless for one's spiritual development, is to deny the presence and workings of Divine Justice in that part of the created order and to sever in that area one's point of contact with God.

To draw once more from our model of the artist's presence in his art, the just man approaches the whole of created being as the admirer of a great composer approaches a work of his music. The disciple, by reason of his confidence in the genius of the composer, knows that the stamp of that genius is present not only in every movement and passage of the work, but in every chord and individual note. He knows that each note was chosen by the composer with a definite function in mind and with a specific contribution to make to the perfection of the composition as a whole. And so he does not write off any passage or note as useless, insignificant, unworthy of his attention. He listens intently to each note, relating part to part, and parts to the whole, searching for the experience and revelation of the composer in every facet of the composition.

Likewise, the just man who has confidence in the presence and operation of Divine Justice throughout the work of creation, approaches every aspect of created being as sacred, seeking to discover its nature and function in relation to the whole, and striving to grant to every facet of created being the respect and attention due to it in reflection of, and participation in the care with which Divine Justice treats even the crumbs and particles of created being.

This approach was beautifully expressed in Christ's admonition to the Apostles following the multiplication of loaves and fishes "to gather up all the remains lest one particle be wasted."[74] As the just man gives to each particle of created being and to the whole of the created order, the respect and response due to it, he moves closer to the ordering, directing, controlling workings of Divine Justice out of which the balance and order of created being proceeds.

Mercy

Mercy in its effect seeks to dispel the defects of others. In the broad sense this may be understood of any defect of any being. In the more special sense of defect as misery, this pertains only to rational beings since misery is opposed to happiness which is possible only for intelligent beings.[75] Mercy, which proceeds from the abundance of goodness and expresses itself in a gratuitous act of love, is especially attributable to God.[76] It is an act of divine mercy which lies at the source of all divine activity.

> So in every work of God, viewed at its source, there appears mercy. In all that follows, the power of mercy remains, and works indeed with even greater force; as the influence of the first cause is more intense than that of second causes. For this reason does God out of the abundance of His goodness bestow upon creatures what is due to them more bountifully than is proportionate to their desserts.[77]

Since mercy belongs especially to God, man's participation and growth in Divine Mercy is that which, together with charity, most properly constitutes godliness in Him. Mercy brings man to the most profound and intimate union with God in His work of creation. This growth in godliness through mercy cannot take place apart from the

---

[74] *Jn.* 6.12.

[75] *Summa*, I; q. 22, a. 3.

[76] "In itself mercy takes precedence of other virtues, for it belongs to mercy to be bountiful to others, and what is more, to succor others in their wants, which pertains chiefly to one who stands above. Hence mercy is accounted as being proper to God : and therein His omnipotence is declared to be chiefly manifested." *Ibid.*, II-II, q. 30, a. 4.

[77] *Ibid.* I, q. 27, a. 4.

development of man's relation to the whole of created being's participation in divinity. Man, in the poverty and radical deficiency of his being apart from the rest of the created order, is more the object of mercy than the source of it.

It is only as a man feeds on the presence of participated divinity in the being, truth, love, life, beatitude, power, creativity and justice of created being that he expands and is enriched in that abundance of godly goodness and love. From which alone mercy flows as the highest, finest, and ultimate product in the practical order.

It is only as love grows in a man for the whole of created being, binding him to and identifying him with creation, that the deficiencies of created being become his deficiencies, and especially the miseries of rational beings become his personal miseries.[78] It is then that the godly impulse of mercy stirs in him.

The godly man, therefore, is the merciful man. And the merciful man is the one who is bound in love to created being, identifying with all its aspects, but particularly identifying with its deficiencies that cry out to be dispelled; its poverty of being that seeks to be enriched; its God-hunger that longs to be sated so that it may achieve its full participation in divinity. By the man of mercy's espousal of created being, his destiny and that of the universe become inseparable. It is certainly this binding love and espousal of creation and mankind that lies at the source of Christ's relation to created being.[79] The gratuitous act of love with which on Calvary Christ assumed the deficiencies of created being as his own and gave up his life to alleviate them, was the perfect expression in the human context of the Divine Mercy at the source of all being.[80]

---

[78] "For since he who loves another looks upon his friend as another self, he counts his friend's hurt as his own, so that he grieved for his friend's hurt as though he were hurt himself. Hence the Philosopher reckons 'grieving with one's friend' being one of the signs of friendship, and the Apostle says: 'Rejoice with them that rejoice, weep with them that weep.' (Rom.12.15)." *Ibid.*, II-II, q. 30, a. 2c.

[79] *Ibid.*, II-II q. 30, a. 4.

[80] *Ibid.*, I, q. 27, a. 4.

WHAT GOD AND GODLINESS ARE

Given the poverty of man's being (man's godlessness), no exercise of goodliness in the practical order is more difficult for him or exacts a greater price for him, than mercy. And yet, no perfection more reveals in a practical way the mystery of God and brings man into a more intimate contact with that mystery. Those who strive to be revealing instruments of the presence of God, must seek above all else to be instruments of His mercy, with all that is implied in this most difficult role. Those who look for the experience of God in others must seek this encounter less in the wisdom, joy, power, life, and creativity of men than in the stirring of genuine mercy, and they should not be surprised at the rarity with which they find it—not at the unlikely circumstances under which it appears. This is the thought of Aquinas and of the tradition that he represents.

IV. POSITIVE GODLINESS AND ECUMENISM

It is now possible to flesh out my description of godliness in man in light of this Catholic tradition. The godly man is one who seriously labors to achieve the full realization of his potential for Being, Truth, Love, Life, Omnipotence, Beatitude, Causality, Justice and Mercy, by the expansion and evolution of his capacity for divinity through the possession of the fullness of participated divinity present in created being. His union with God is effected not by an abstract contemplation of divinity otherwise removed from him, but by the concrete evolution of divinity in his own being through which he is rendered disposed for the experience of God. It is by having become god in a sense that he is able to experience God.

As he evolved in the fullness of created being, truth, love, and live, he came to experience the fullness of Being, Truth, Love and Life which was always substantially present to him[81] as to all created being, but which was previously not perceptible by him. His movement toward God was not a movement in place and time, from *here-and-now* where God was not to another *there-and-then* where God was, since God is omnipresent and eternal. His movement rather was one of awakening consciousness, coming alive, evolving love, and growing

---

[81] *Ibid.*, I; q. 8, aa. 1, 2, 3.

capacity for the experience of consuming happiness. It was the expansion of his being, power, and creativity which permits him to experience existentially the divinity always present to him and to all being.

The more profoundly and intensely he loves, lives, exists, and rejoices, the more he experiences Love, Life, Being, and Beatitude. The more generously, creatively, and fruitfully he gives of his being, the more he experiences Mercy, Power and Divine Causality. The wiser he becomes, the more he is one with Wisdom. And, the point I wish to stress, the godly man's growth in being, truth, love, life, and happiness has taken place not in a vacuum but by his intimate, qualitative contact and identity with, and possession of the fullness of participated divinity present in created reality.

If the godly man lives within the Catholic tradition, he will believe further that divinity is not only present in created being by participation, but that God has chosen to elevate created entities as instruments through which He acts in an extraordinary way on humanity by endowing these created instruments with the physical properties and qualities of His Uncreated Being or, better, by grafting onto created being in the moment of instrumental use an extraordinary participation in the properties of Divine Action.

Thus Truth acts on man through truth, endowing truth as an instrument with the perfection and power of Truth, so that man experiences in truth so elevated, an immediate encounter with Truth. So also Love acts through love, Life through life, Beatitude through happiness. Omnipotence through finite power, and Divine Causality through created causality. And in one's encounter with love, life, happiness, power and causality, so elevated and used, one achieves an immediate experience of Love, Life, Beatitude, Omnipotence and Divine Causality.

Since the more actual a being is, the more determined is its nature and, therefore, the more intelligible, identifiable, and specific is its reality,[82] it follows that the godly man, as more realized, will present

---

[82] "Everything is knowable so far as it is in act, and not, so far as it is in potentiality; for a thing is a being, and is true, and therefore knowable, according as it is actual. This is quite clear as regards sensible things, for the

definite, identifiable, specific traits by which he may be recognized. It would be desirable to indicate some of these traits so as to see more clearly the link between godliness and ecumenism.

The godly man will be conscious of the divine presence in the entirety of the created order, and he will perceive that presence as it is differently expressed in all creatures, at all times, in all places, and under all forms. Since he is aware of the limited capacity of truth to express Truth, and knows that all truth is inadequate to exhaust the revelation of Truth, he will be open to the complementary, perfecting, expanding insights into Truth which will be found in the infinite expressions of truth, searching to fill out his possession of the fullness of Truth in the fullness of truth.

The godly man will be profoundly alive not with life in a vacuum or self-constructed test tube, but alive to whatever there is of being, truth, love, life, happiness, power and need in created being, and alive to the presence of Truth and Love in truth and love. He will love the good wherever he encounters it, that is to say everywhere. The universal awareness and love of the infinite expressions of the goodness of created being is an essential element of his godliness.

Conscious of the inadequacy of created good to represent the totality of the Good, he will search always for new manifestations of the Perfect Good in the created good, open to the unique revelation of Divine Goodness which he knows is to be found in every creature and in every situation.[83] He will find his point of contact with Divine Beatitude in the participated beatitude present in every creature and he will endeavor to savor the fullness of joy present in creation as a preparation for, and foretaste of the ultimate encounter with God who is Beatitude.

---

eye does not see what is potentially, but what is actually colored. In like manner it is clear that the intellect so far as it knows material things, does not know save what is in act...." *Ibid.*, I, q. 87, a. 1.

[83] "Every being, as being, is good. For all being, as being, has actuality and is in some way perfect; since every act implies some sort of perfection; and perfection implies desirability and goodness, as is clear from a.1 Hence it follows that every being is good." *Ibid.*, I, q. 5, a. 1c.

He will manifest a reverence for the whole of creation and for each of its parts, seeking to treat every creature with the respect owed to its participation in divinity. The godly man will be expansive, spiritually and psychologically large, in that his being will relate positively to, and identify with every being and all being, and Being. He will unite and not divide; elevate and not lower; inspire and not discourage; radiate love and not fear; be positive and not negative; optimistic and not cynical; expanding and not contracting; transcending limitations and not reinforcing them; opening windows and not closing doors.

Most important of all, according to this tradition, the godly man will be the man of mercy. He will love freely, when there is no necessity or apparent reason to love. He will go beyond the requirements of justice, and give when it is not only not obligatory to give, but when others consider it foolish and madness to give. The merciful person will know great sorrow, since mercy originates in love and love binds to the ones loved.[84] He will, therefore, be bound even more to suffering humanity than he is bound to prospering mankind, so that everyone's cross will be his cross, and everyman's sorrow will be his sorrow. But his sorrow, having its origin in the same source from whence comes his joy, will not obliterate that joy.[85] Rather it will exist alongside his happiness, and add its own special quality which in the end will serve to enhance that happiness.

His experience of mercy in others will be his most profound encounter with God's presence in human nature in the practical order next to the experience of the stirrings of mercy within himself. The former experience will be more pleasant, the latter, more lasting, elevating, revealing, and, in the end, providing the greater joy. The godly man will be the one who by God's grace in some measure realizes in himself the perfections of Christ.

---

[84] *Ibid.*, II-II, q. 30 a. 2.

[85] "The other is the joy of charity whereby we rejoice in the Divine good as participated by us. This participation can be hindered by anything contrary to it, wherefore in this respect, the joy of charity is compatible with an admixture of sorrow, in so far as a man grieves for that which hinders the participation of the Divine good, either in us or in our neighbor, whom we love as ourselves." *Ibid.*, II-II, q.28, a 2c.

WHAT GOD AND GODLINESS ARE

To this description of the positive aspects of godliness I will add one more. The godly man necessarily will be the ecumenical man. The relation between this traditional concept of godliness and ecumenism is clear. Ecumenism, in this context, is simply a label placed on the essential thrust of the godly man to discover, experience, and savor the fullness of God as revealed in the fullness of the perfections of created being. Ecumenism strives to reconstruct and duplicate the inner reality of God where multiple expressions of created being, truth, love, life, power, beatitude, justice and mercy exist in a perfect unity and purity which is the origin of their emergence into the created order. These perfections proceed from God into the created order in a brilliant variety and diversity, each reflecting a different, complementary aspect of its source, and all collectively expressing with a fullness the source present to them somewhat after the manner in which the rays of light coming from a spectrum relate to each other and to the pure light source from which they are derived.

The ecumenical person opens himself to the full variety and diversity of perfections expressed in created being, searching always for the underlying, unifying presence of the source in each, and re-uniting these complementary expressions within himself in the unity, order, and purity which they objectively possess as coming from their source. As he expands through knowledge and love in this possession of, and identification with the full range of created being, becoming that *microcosm* of which Aquinas speaks, he synthesizes within his unified self the richness and diversity of created order and thereby moves into union with that Unified Source from whence the diversity of created beings proceeds.

The more a person grows in godliness, the more ecumenically oriented he becomes. Unlike the finite appetites of man that are surfeited by the attainment of their objects so that the more they have the less they desire, the infinite appetite of man for being, truth, love, life and happiness is stimulated to a new capacity and desire by the partial attainment of its object. The more he succeeds in achieving the objects of these appetites, the more he desires. Thus the rich experience of Truth which is partially expressed in one segment of created being, not only will fail to sate the hunger to know, but it will stimulate a new capacity and more intense desire for further knowledge.

THE THEOLOGY OF ECUMENISM

The more I know, the more I want to know. The more I know about the accidents, the more I crave to understand the substance. The more I know about the effects, the more I yearn to understand the cause.[86] Since my only access to God is through knowledge of His effects, the more I experience the truth of God as revealed in part of His effects, the more I want to know all His effects as my way of gaining more perfect knowledge of Him as Cause. And so also it is with my love of the good and with my desire for life and for happiness.

The partial realization of these appetites intensifies both the capacity and the desire for more.[87] (The person in power who hopes to buy control over his subjects by giving them a little more truth, good, life, and happiness, which he thinks will satisfy their appetites and render them more docile to his tyranny, does not understand human nature.) Thus as godliness grows in man, the hunger to experience more profoundly and fully God's revealing presence in created being is intensified, and the openness and thrust toward further encounters with the expressions of divinity in created reality is heightened.[88]

Just as the approach of Pattern III to the created order is essentially the approach of ecumenism, so the attitudes expressed in Patterns I and II toward created being are opposed to ecumenism. Pattern I, in its atheistic expression, simply denies the existence of the Transcendent either in or apart from created being and thereby removes the basis for ecumenism as a dialogue based on the shared experience of the Transcendent in the created order.

Where Pattern I acknowledges the existence of God and thereby admits the possibility of dialogue based on the experience of His presence in created being, in practice by tending to endow created

---

[86] *Ibid.*, I-II, q. 3, a. 8.

[87] "The capacity of the rational creature is increased by charity, because the heart is enlarged thereby, according to 2 Cor. 6.11: 'Our heart is enlarged;' so that it still remains capable of receiving a further increase." *Ibid.*, II-II, q. 24, a. 9.

[88] "For every natural movement is more intense in the end, when a thing approaches the term that is suitable to its nature, than at the beginning, when it leaves the term that is unsuitable to its nature: as though nature were more eager in tending to what is suitable to it, than in shunning what is unsuitable." *Ibid.*, I-II, q. 35, a. 6.

WHAT GOD AND GODLINESS ARE

being with the qualities of Uncreated Being it results in an arresting in A with a failure to move beyond to B. It further tends to limit the breadth and depth of contact with A, deifying one part of A to the downgrading of other parts. (Aquinas points out that virtue demands unity, whereas vice, the deification of created being, gives rise to divisions and opposition).[89] Finally, this Pattern tends to restrict the experience of A to its surface aspects, and fails to go to the depths of A where the encounter with B takes place, but only at the revelation of the limitations of A.

Pattern II which acknowledges the Transcendent either so separates God from the created order as to deny the possibility of communion with B in A or it so reduces the points of contact with B in A to isolated expressions of A that it is opposed to the full experience of participated divinity in the whole of created being. And to that extent it is negative toward ecumenism.

Pattern III proposes that B is present by participation and in substance throughout the whole of A and in each part of A so that A both in its parts and, better, in its totality, is the point of contact with B. In Catholic tradition and doctrine B is held to act through A as an instrument, offering in A not only a stepping stone to B, but the immediate experience of B acting in and through A. When properly understood this presents the highest expression of ecumenism in that it offers man the possibility of finding in created being not only participated divinity, but the immediate, direct experience of God Himself acting on human nature through the instrumentality of created being.

---

[89] "For sin does not consist in passing from the many to the one, as is the case with virtues, which are connected, but rather in forsaking the one for the many." *Ibid.*, I-II, q. 73, a. 1c

"The love of God is unitive, in as much as it draws man's affections from the many to the one; so that the virtues, which flow from the love of God are connected together. But self-love disunites man's affections among different things, in so far as man loves himself, by desiring for himself temporal goods, which are various and of many kinds: hence vices and sins, which arise from self-love, are not connected together." *Ibid.*, ad. 3.

CHAPTER FIVE

FUNDAMENTAL GOD AND RADICAL GODLINESS

I. FUNDAMENTAL GOD

While affirming the diversity of perfections existing in the unity of the divine essence Catholic theologians question whether one can single out an aspect of the divine reality which is primary and fundamental to, and presupposed by every other aspect of divinity. The more common outcome of this inquiry asserts that in God the identity of essence and existence constitutes the primary, fundamental reality of His divinity that is presupposed in the order of nature, though not of time, by every other aspect.

According to this doctrine, that which fundamentally makes God to be God is the fact that He contains within Himself the total, adequate, and unique explanation of His own existence. God is beholden to no extrinsic reality for any part of His actuality. It is His nature to exist. He is absolutely autonomous in being—self-sufficient, self-contained, pure act. Therefore, to be God means fundamentally to so exist in and of oneself as to find solely and uniquely in one's inner reality the total source of one's actuality—to be Being.[1]

In line with this doctrine all other perfections of God, both negative and positive, are seen to flow from, and presuppose this fundamental aspect of divinity. God, therefore, is not primarily God because He is infinite, perfect, eternal, unique, and immutable. Rather He is infinite, perfect, eternal, unique, and immutable because He is His own existence; which fact excludes the possibility of finiteness, imperfection, temporality, multiplicity, and changeableness, or any other form of

---

[1] *Cf*. R. Garrigou-Lagrange, *God: His Existence and His Nature* (St. Louis: B. Herder Co., 1934), Vol. II, pp. 2-141. And by the same author, *De Deo Uno* (Paris: Desclees, 1937), pp. 126-131. N. Del Prado, *De Veritate Fundamentali Philosophiae Christianae* (Friburg: Ex typis Cons. S. Pauli, 1911), pp. 217-254. E. Hugon, *De Deo Uno*, Ed. Lethielleux (Paris: 1927), pp. 67-73. J. D. Taylor, "Essence and Existence," *NCE*, Vol. 5, pp. 548-552.

limitation. Also, God is not fundamentally God because He is Truth, Love, Life and Omnipotence. Since in the order of nature truth, goodness, life, power, causality, and all other perfections follow upon and presuppose being; God is Truth, Love, Life and Omnipotent, because He is fundamentally Being.

Throughout Aquinas' theological analysis of the negative and positive perfections of God, he always harkens back to the identity of essence and existence in God as the basis from which he builds the logical necessity for every other aspect of divinity.[2] His point of departure in his analysis of the mystery of creation rests on this basis. God is the Creator, the First and Universal Cause, the unique source of all being, because God Himself is uniquely Being.[3] He is the Creator, not primarily because He is Infinite Goodness and Love, although both aspects of divinity are essential to the work of creation, but because He is Being *per essentiam*. The basic distinction between God and all other reality lies in the uniqueness of God's essential identity with being as opposed to the participated character of being common to the whole of creation. Uncreated Being is being *per essentiam*. Created being is being *per participationem*.[4]

II. RADICAL GODLINESS IN CREATED BEING.

That which constitutes the primary, fundamental aspect of divinity should also constitute the most radical aspect of a creature's participation in divinity, that is of its radical godliness. If to contain within

---

[2] For example: "Since everything is knowable according as it is actual, God, Who is pure act without any admixture of potentiality, is in Himself supremely knowable." *Summa*, I, q. 12, a. 1c.

"A thing is prior logically in so far as it is prior to the intellect. Now the intellect apprehends primarily being itself, secondly, it apprehends that it understands being; and thirdly, it apprehends that it desires being. Hence the idea of being is first, that of truth second, and the idea of good third, though good is in things." *Ibid.*, I, q. 16, a. 4.

"Existence is the most perfect of all things, for it is compared to all things as that by which they are made actual. " *Ibid.*, I, q. 4, a. 1 ad 3 - *Cf.* DEL PRADO, *op.cit.*, pp. 217-254.

[3] *Summa*, I, q. 44, a. 1 q. 45, a. 5. See also Del Prado, *op. cit.* pp. 255-283.

[4] *Ibid.*, pp. 284 - 289.

one's self the total source of one's own being (that is, being self-sufficient, self-contained, autonomous in one's existence) is the fundamental reality of the divine essence, then in its own way an analogous "self-sufficiency" would appear to constitute in creatures the most radical possible duplication of divinity in the created order.

Therefore, creatures are similar to God not primarily by reason of their degree of participation in His divine perfections, but radically in so far as they contain in their inner principles the adequate, autonomous source of their own being and perfection. That is to say a creature is radically godlike not primarily by reason of its participation in divine truth, goodness, life, and power, but in so far as it possesses within itself the source and explanation of the truth, goodness, life and power that go to make up its being. God, in turn, will have succeeded in His intention to bestow a radical likeness of His fundamental being upon the created order to the extent that He makes created being autonomous, self-contained, self-sufficient, self-creative, and self-evolving.

This concept of radical godliness in creatures, however, appears to involve an inherent contradiction which places the communication of this aspect of participated fundamental divinity beyond the power even of God to effect. That a creature (being *per participationem*) should so exist as to have within itself the total, adequate explanation and source of its own being (*per essentiam*) is in fact a contradiction. God cannot create a being that exists in such a way as to have not been created in the first place. God cannot create other gods.

Granted the contradiction in such an understanding of radical godliness, another possibility presents itself. God can create beings in a state of potential perfection and endow them individually and collectively with the inner principles (active and passive) by which they can as secondary causes evolve to the state of actualized, realized perfection. In this case created entities would in this qualified sense contain within themselves the proximate, adequate, secondary source of their own being and perfection, and possess the power of self-realization or, in a loose sense, of self-creation. It is this concept of radical godliness in created being which Catholic tradition proposes as essential to the understanding of creation. This is the interplay it sees between Divine

Providence and the created order as created being evolves toward its maximum participation in divinity.

III. RADICAL GODLINESS AND THE DOCTRINE OF AQUINAS

The possibility and fact of the *self-creation* of radical godliness in created being is the constant theme in Aquinas' writing on the relation between God and created entities. He sees this relation as Primary and secondary causes in the evolution of creation toward maturity and self-realization. Aquinas differentiates the levels of perfection in created being by the degree in which creatures contain within themselves the principles of their own activity and development.[5]

The more completely self-contained creatures are, the higher they are placed on the scale of perfection because the more they participate in the self-sufficiency of God. Living beings, therefore, are more perfect than non-living ones because living entities possess more completely within themselves the principles of their activity and self-development. For this reason among living beings sensate beings are more perfect than vegetative ones, and intellectual beings stand above sensate beings.[6]

Where individual creatures are too restricted in nature to contain within themselves the adequate, proximate, secondary principles of

---

[5] "Life is the highest degree properly in God. In proof of which it must be considered that since a thing is said to live in so far as it operates of itself and not as moved by another, the more perfectly this power is found in anything, the more perfect is the life of that thing." *Ibid.*, I, q. 18, a. 3c.

[6] This understanding of perfection is present throughout the teaching of Aquinas. In his analysis of processions as found in creatures and in the divine essence he argues that the more self-contained a procession is, the higher on the level of perfection it belongs. Cf. *Summa*, I, a. 27, aa. 1, 2.

This understanding appears in his analysis of beatitude, *Ibid.*, I, q. 26, a. 1; in the perfection of voluntary acts as being self-contained, *Ibid.*, I-II, q. 6, a. 1; in the necessity of charity being a habit if man is to possess ideally by permanent inner principle the power of such operation. *Ibid.*, II-II, q. 23, a. 2; in the value of virtue in general as equipping man with the means of acting connaturally, from inner principles, *Ibid.*, I-II q. 55 a. 1, 2.; In the notion of merit, I-II, q. 5, a. 7 and q. 21, aa. 3, 4, 5.

their full realization in participated divinity, other created entities will possess the higher participation in divine perfection and causality necessary to elevate these former to their ideal existence. Thus what is lacking to individual creatures in the way of inner principles of self-realization, is found in the inner resources of the collectivity of created being.

The totality of created being, therefore, possesses the inner principles for evolution to actual participation in divinity which are not to be found in isolated individuals and parts of created reality. In this relation of creatures to each other as parts to the whole, with the lower subordinate to the higher as the perfectible to the perfecting, there is present by power and actual exercise in the totality of created being a participation in divine power and causality which otherwise would not be possible.[7] From this point of view also, one finds that the whole of creation shares more fully in divinity than any segment or part.

The totality of created being alone is fully autonomous and self-sufficient in the order of secondary causes, and possesses the full expression of radical godliness by which created being duplicates this primary, fundamental aspect of divinity. To the extent that an individual entity is separated from the totality of created being, it is withdrawn from the proximate, secondary principles of its own full self-realization. When an intellectual being, for example, seeks to achieve autonomy and self-sufficiency in independence of the rest of created being, he withdraws himself from the very source that makes his relative autonomy and self-sufficiency possible.

A second major theme in Aquinas's reflections on the interplay of God as First Cause and creatures as secondary causes, is his constant affirmation of the respect which divine providence always exercises toward the radical godliness that He has instilled in created being. Repeatedly one reads in Aquinas that "God respects the order of causes;[8] divine providence orders all things gently;[9] God provides for

---

[7] *Ibid.*, I, q. 103, a6; *Compendium*, cc. 73, 124.

[8] *Summa*, I, q. 105, a. 5c.

[9] *Ibid.*, I, q. 23 , a 2c.

all things according to the nature of each thing;[10] grace perfects nature."[11]

In all activity of the First Cause in the created order, the full potential of secondary causes to function actively and passively under the influence of the Primary Cause is provided for.[12] The movement of the First Cause in the exercise of providence over created being is never a violent intrusion which ignores, bypasses, or suppresses the active and passive powers of created reality to collaborate in its movement toward full godliness. Thus, under the Providence of God created being becomes in the maximum degree the proximate, secondary source of its own being and perfection.

The full utilization by Providence of secondary causes as intermediaries is to be explained not by a defect in divine power, but by God's desire to impart to created being a share in His causality:

>...there are certain intermediaries of God's providence; for He governs things inferior by superior, not on account of any defect in His power, but by reason of the abundance of His goodness; so that the dignity of causality is imparted even to creatures.[13]

But since things which are governed should be brought to perfection by government, this government will be so much the better in the degree the things governed are brought to perfection. Now it is a greater perfection for a thing to be good in itself and also the cause of goodness in others, than only to be good in itself. Therefore God so governs things that He makes some of them to be causes of others in government; as a master, who not only imparts knowledge to his pupils, but gives also the faculty of teaching others.... If God governed alone, things would be deprived of the

---

[10] *Ibid.*, I, q. 43, a. 7c.

[11] *Ibid.*, I, q. 62, a. 5.

[12] *Summa*, I, q. 105, a. 5.

[13] *Ibid.*, I, q. 23, a. 3c.

perfection of causality. Wherefore all that is effected by many would not be accomplished by one.[14]

In this exercise of their proper causality, secondary causes operate in complete dependency on God as the First Cause:

> Since God wills effects to proceed from definite causes, for the preservation of order in the universe, it is not unreasonable to seek for causes secondary to the divine will. It would, however, be unreasonable to do so, if such were considered as primary, and not as dependent on the will of God. In this sense Augustine says (*De Trin.* iii. 2), "Philosophers in their vanity have thought fit to attribute contingent effects to other causes, being utterly unable to perceive the cause that is shown above all others, the will of God."[15]

This dependency of secondary causes on the First Cause not only does not militate against created being's exercise of its proper causality, but it is the condition for such exercise. The first Cause so moves created causes that they achieve their proper operation:

> Some have understood God to work in every agent in such a way that no created power has any effect in things, but that God alone is the immediate cause of everything wrought; for instance, that it is not fire, that gives heat, but God in the fire, and so forth. But this is impossible. First, because the order of cause and effect would be taken away from created things: and this would imply lack of power in the Creator: for it is due to the power of the cause, that it bestows active power on its effect. Secondly, because the active powers which are seen to exist in things, would be bestowed on things to no purpose, if these wrought nothing through them. Indeed, all things created would seem in a way, to be purposeless, if they lacked an operation proper to them; since the purpose of everything is its operation. For the less perfect is always for the sake of the more perfect; and consequently as the matter

---

[14] *Ibid.*, I, q. 103, a. 7c.
[15] *Ibid.*, I, q. 19, a. 6.

is for the sake of the form, so the form which is the first act, is for the sake of its operation, which is the second act; and thus operation is the end of the creature. We must therefore understand that God works in things in such a manner that they have their proper operation.[16]

In so moving created causes God provides for the modality proper to their operation so that necessary causes produce necessary effects, and contingent causes are moved to act in such a way that they produce contingent effects:

> Since then the divine will is perfectly efficacious, it follows out not only that things are done, which God wills to be done, but also that they are done in the way that He wills. Now God wills some things to be done necessarily, some contingently to the right ordering of things for the building up of the universe. Therefore to some effects He has attached necessary causes, that cannot fail: but to others defectible and contingent causes, from which arise contingent effects. Hence it is not because the proximate causes are contingent that the effects willed by God happen contingently, but because God has prepared contingent causes for them, it being His will that they should happen contingently.[17]

This respect of Providence for the order of nature, and God's maximum utilization of secondary causes in moving created reality toward ideal perfection so as to endow created being with radical self-sufficiency or godliness, is in part the expression of Divine Justice which gives to every creature and to all creatures collectively their due.[18]

Divine Mercy builds upon and surpasses the workings of Justice by assuring that when the ideal perfection of created being requires more than the inner resources of the created order as secondary causes can provide, not only will this perfection be forthcoming from the action of Providence, but it will proceed proximately from created being elevated

---

[16] *Ibid.*, I, q. 106, a. 5c.

[17] *Ibid.*, I, q. 19, a. 8c.

[18] *Ibid.*, I, q. 21, a. 4.

as the instrument of the First Cause.[19] Thus created being is the proximate source of its evolution to full godliness either as a principal secondary cause or an instrumental secondary cause.

The work of creation as seen in Diagram 5-1 by this tradition proceeds in two stages:

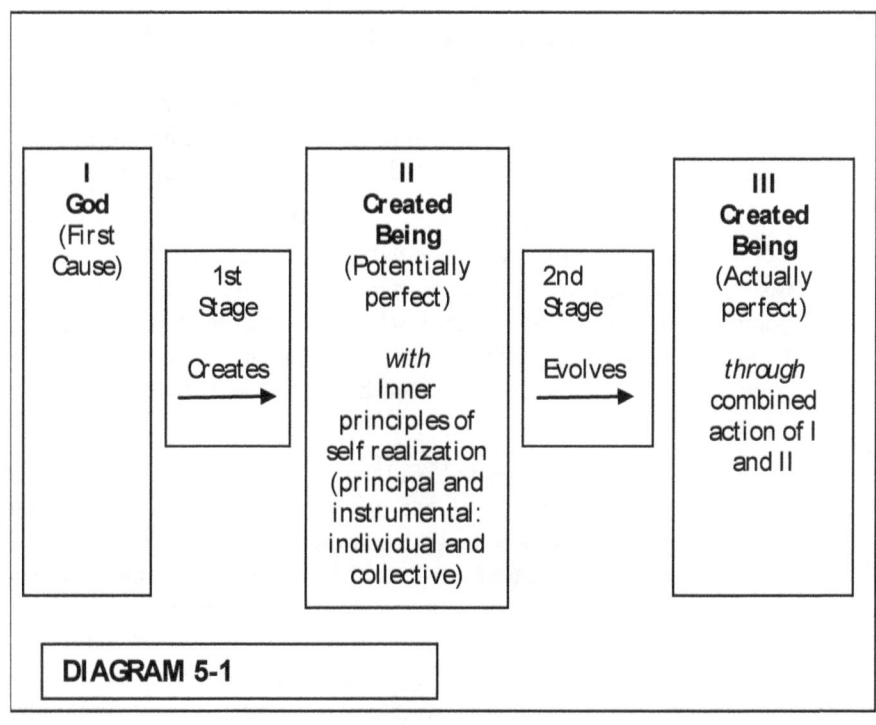

DIAGRAM 5-1

The first stage in which created being comes into existence more in the state of potential than actual perfection, is an instantaneous one proceeding uniquely from the creative act of God since no instrumental

---

[19] *Ibid.*, I, q. 21, a. 4.

intermediary is possible in the act of creation.[20] Created being in this initial stage is endowed individually and collectively as secondary causes with inner principles (active and passive) of self-actualization and self-realization.

The second stage of creation is an ongoing one in which created being evolves from its potential participation in divinity to the actualized, fully realized achievement of godliness. In this stage God as first Cause activates the potential of created being for perfection, acting on created being mediately through secondary causes in the fullest degree possible, moving higher created entities to perfect lower ones, and immediately when the instrumental use of created being is not possible.[21] Thus through the combined subordinated action of the first Case and secondary causes, created being evolves to full perfection.

This movement of the second stage to III proceeds totally from God as First Cause, and totally from created being as secondary cause.[22] It is this latter element in the evolutionary process which expresses created being's radical godliness that I wish in particular to stress. No perfection is found in the term of the second stage (III) which does not in some manner proceed from created being (II) as activated by the First Cause.

In this evolution of created being from the potential perfection of II to the actual perfection of III, we are witnessing the work of creation being brought to completion. To expect to find the full perfection of III in the transitional stage from II to III, is to fail to understand that creation as we know it is not the finished product but an ongoing process.[23] Many of the problems that are encountered in the endeavor to reconcile the imperfections of the present condition of created being with Divine Providence stem from the faulty premise that created being as we now experience it is in its competed, finalized state. If one grants this premise, it is impossible to provide a satisfactory answer to these objections.

---

[20] *Ibid.*, I, q. 45, a. 5.
[21] *Ibid..*, I, q.105, a. 6.
[22] *Ibid.*, I, q. 105, a. 5.
[23] *Ibid.*, I, q. 58, a. 3; q. 62, a. 5; q. 85, aa4, 5.

FUNDAMENTAL GOD AND RADICAL GODLINESS

Just as one could not answer the criticism of persons surveying the efforts of a superb architect who has partially completed a masterpiece of a building, when they attack the quality of his work on the assumption that the incomplete, and therefore necessarily imperfect, structure is already in its finished state. One can only point out that granted the deficiencies in the structure in its state of partial completion, its evolving perfections offer ample evidence of the genius of the builder, and warrant one's suspending final judgment until the building has been completed.

What makes this form of criticism of Divine Providence particularly poignant is the fact that the principal reason for the imperfect, potential state of parts of created being is that human nature may actively share with God the ongoing work of creation. It is in order that man may participate in the providence and causality of God that created being awaits his perfecting presence to be brought to completion.[24] Like an architect who deliberately leaves his work partially unfinished so as to allow the workers to share the privilege and glory of cooperating with him in completing his masterpiece, and then suffers the barbs of criticism from these same workers for the deficiencies which they find in his work, God must suffer criticism from men for the unfinished character of creation which invites man to share with God the glory of completing it.

IV. RADICAL GODLINESS AND THE NATURAL MAN

Man is the most perfect among visible creatures because he more than others contains in his inner reality the source of his activity and development to perfection—thereby sharing more fully, and coming more closely to the "self-sufficiency" of God. While his inner faculties of will equip him with the potential for a consciousness, love, fullness of life, happiness, power and causality, which provides him with his unique participation in divinity beyond that of other visible entities, it is not these perfections that constitute his radical participation in divinity. It is the way in which these perfections evolve in him from his inner resources that constitutes his radical godliness. While mercy in man is

---

[24] *Compendium*, cc. 73, 124; *Summa*, I, q. 19, a. 5 ad 3; q. 19, a. 8, q. 22, a. 3.

the highest expression of his participated divinity in the practical order, its evolution in him from inner principles provides his point of similarity to fundamental divinity.[25]

In terms of human perfection, man's initial stage is more that of a potential existence rather than an actual human existence. He begins life literally as a seed in which the mature adult potentially exists. Although endowed early in life with intellect and will as well as sensitive and vegetative powers, he is initially that *tabula rasa* in whose inner vitality there is no intellectual consciousness nor affective movement—no stirring of happiness, power, and creativity; no just and

---

[25] For Aquinas the primary meaning of freedom is found in the power it gives to human nature to determine for itself its development in being when acting under God as a secondary cause. "The intellect can be a cause of its own judgment whereby it desires a good and performs an action for the sake of an end. But what is a cause unto itself is precisely what is called free." See *Compendium*, c. 76. By reason of his freedom, then, man causes as a secondary agent under God his evolution in perfection. This is the meaning of his power to merit whereby he causes an intrinsic goodness in his actions which justly demands compensation. This is also the basis for his being subject to reward and punishment, praise and blame. It is in the implications of the fact of man's freedom that he most approximates the self-sufficiency of God. Aquinas says:

"Free-will is the cause of its own movement, because by free-will man moves himself to act." *Summa*, I, q. 83, a.1, ad. 3.

"The will is mistress of its own act and to it belongs to will and not to will. But this would not be so, had it not the power to move itself to will. Therefore it moves itself." *Ibid.*, I-II, q.9 a. 3c.

"Now man differs from irrational animals in this, that he is master of his actions. Whereby those actions alone are properly called human, of which man is master." *Ibid.*, I-II, q. 1, a. 1c.

"But those things which have a knowledge of the end are said to move themselves because there is in them a principle by which they not only act but also act for an end. And consequently, since both are from an intrinsic principle, to wit, that they act for an end, the movements of such things are said to be voluntary." *Ibid.*, I-II, q. 2, a.1.

"Now an action is imputed to an agent, when it is in his power, so that he has dominion over it; and this is the case in all voluntary acts: because it is through his will that man has dominion over his actions." *Ibid.*, I-II, q. 21, a. 2c.

merciful impulse toward created being.[26] Slowly, gradually, through the interplay play of the created order and his inner vitality, the awakening takes place and his evolution toward maturity in the realization of his potential for godliness advances.

In this evolution of man toward perfection his freedom is not, as some seem to believe, a vague luxury and unspecified power that permits him to choose indiscriminately from and savor the multiplicity of created delights to no lasting effect. Rather, it is a godly power which permits a man, in harmony with the basic thrust of his nature, to relate to the whole of created being. To relate in such a manner as to feed generously on the participated presence of divinity there and evolve toward that state of fully realized godliness for which he was created. It is primarily through his exercise of choice that a man becomes to himself the proximate source of his own perfection and duplicates in himself the participation in fundamental divinity which is his radical godliness.[27]

Since the specifics of man's natural thrust toward divinity originated in the ordering, willing act of the mind of God which is the eternal law, and since man's nature is the temporal embodiment and revelation of that law, man's conformity to the true requirements of his nature in the exercise of freedom, is likewise his conformity to the ordering mind of God.[28] Thus man becomes the conscious, active, free instrument of the perfecting action of the divine will, and in cooperation with the First Cause, causes his own beatitude.

Given the limitations of individual man as a fragment of humanity and his inability to possess within himself the full perfection or potential for perfection of human nature, God grants to the totality of humans the inner potential for the realization of the full range of human perfection which is not to be found in any individual or segment of mankind. Different complementary expressions of the potential for human perfection are given to different individuals. Each man is so

---

[26] *Summa*, I, q. 84, a. 6.
[27] *Summa*, I-II, q. 13.
[28] *Ibid.*, I-II, q. 90 a. 2.

ordered to every other human as part to a whole, with the less perfect subordinate to the more perfect, that in the interplay of humans and in the experience of the richness of the totality of human nature, man finds in humanity as a whole the inner potential for full human perfection.[29]

However, man's self-sufficiency and power of self-creativity is not negated by his dependency on the rest of human nature since it still lies within the power of his inner choice to open himself wide to the full experience of divinity in humanity, or to close himself off to that presence.[30] Therefore by reason of his freedom he remains the immediate proximate source of the evolution in godliness which takes place in him through his virtuous free submission to the godliness he finds in the rest of human nature.

If radical godliness constitutes man's special participation in fundamental divinity, then man's natural desire for godliness must include an instinct to search for and desire to find in himself and in human nature the immediate source of his evolution in perfection. Man will not only hunger for the fullness of being, truth, love, life and happiness but instinctively yearn to find in himself and in human nature in general the source and means by which these perfections may be achieved.

What he fails to find by way of positive means of growth in his own hold on human nature, he will, by instinct more than choice, search for in other humans in obedience to this radical aspect of the built-in, necessary thrust of his nature toward godliness. Underlying all the dynamics of man's social instinct whereby he is automatically drawn to other humans for help in his groping toward realization, is this

---

[29] *Ibid.*, I-II, q. 97, a. 4c. *Ethics*, bk. 1, lect. 1, no. 4.

[30] "So therefore, in the parts of the universe also every creature exists for its own proper act and perfection, and the less noble for the nobler, as those creatures that are less noble than man exist for the sake of man, whilst each and every creature exists for the perfection of the entire universe.
Furthermore, the entire universe, with all its parts, is ordained towards God as its end, in as much as it imitates, as it were, and shows forth the divine goodness, to the glory of God. Reasonable creatures, however, have in some special and higher manner God as their end, since they can attain to Him by their own operations, by knowing and loving Him." *Summa*, I, q.65, a. 3c.

expression of the duplication in human nature of the self-sufficiency fundamental to divinity.

This instinct of man to seek in human nature the immediate source of his perfection was instilled in him by God as the expression of His will for man's radical godliness. And since God respects the order of nature which He Himself created, it is to be expected that God would not frustrate this instinct for radical godliness by ignoring, bypassing, suppressing, or frustrating, man's instinctive searching in his own humanity for the proximate source of his evolution to perfection and fully participated divinity. This God-given potential of human nature for radical godliness, invites a just, merciful response from Providence, which incorporates its utilization as a basic component in the plan whereby God moves man to full perfection. Catholic doctrine finds this incorporation at the basis of the Incarnation. Wherein God responds to man's instinct for radical godliness by disposing that he actually find in his humanity the proximate principle and source of his salvation, perfection, redemption and beatitude, in the advent and presence of Christ. As with the rest of created reality, the creation and movement of human nature toward full perfection involves the same two stages as seen in Diagram 5-1.

Man according to traditional Catholic doctrine is a composite of spiritual and material being. His initiation into full reality requires the presence of two principles, the animating principle of rational life and animated material being.[31] The first principle comes into existence instantaneously from the creative act of God without instrumental intermediaries.[32] The material principle, however, is rendered from pre-existing reality for its incorporation into human reality by the vital instrumentality of human agents—his parents.[33] Already, therefore, in this first stage of man's existence we find the expression of his radical godliness because human nature possesses within its inner resources the capacity to contribute directly and vitally to its own continued and expanded existence in providing the material principle of human life.

---

[31] *Ibid.*, I, qq. 91, 92.
[32] *Ibid.*, I, q. 91 , a. 3.
[33] *Ibid.*, I, q. 99 , aa. 1, 2.

Thus the new expression of living humanity comes into existence through the combined action of God and subordinated human nature— through God's just and merciful utilization of the maximum potential of human nature as a vital secondary cause in this work of special creation. Through this interplay of divine and human forces we can in a loose sense say that human nature has the power to create itself, to cause human life. Man creates man.[34]

The whole Catholic interpretation of the work of the Incarnation and Redemption is based on the assumption of an analogous interplay between divine and human causality. God utilizes the potential of human nature for radical godliness by the elevation and incorporation of man's power as a vital secondary agent in causing not merely new human life, but causing Divine Life to exist in a new, extraordinary created presence in human nature through grace. The effect of the Incarnation, therefore is, that man as a vital instrument causes God to come alive in human nature through created grace. In a very loose sense it is as though God have given to man the power to create God.[35]

The fullest expression of godliness in human nature is found in the term (III) of the second stage of man's existence. However, the expression of man's radical godliness is not to be sought in III, but in the evolution of III out of II. It is to the extent that the perfections of III originate proximately in the inner resources of II that man achieves the

---

[34] As I have already noted (*Cf.* Chapter 5, Section III.) Catholic tradition holds that creation in the strict sense of the production of something from nothing, transcends the power of any created agent to effect and remains possible uniquely to God. This tradition opposes those views proposed by certain existentialists and others which attribute to human freedom an autonomous power of self-realization and self-determination which approaches the power of strict creation and thereby identifies divine and human action. While unequivocally rejecting such understanding of human freedom Catholic tradition holds that the plan of providence intends that man share in the fullest possible degree both as a secondary cause in the realization of his natural capacity for perfection, and as an instrumental cause in his development in participated divine Life through grace. In this understanding Christianity goes substantially beyond humanism in attributing to human nature not only the proximate principles of man's evolution in the supernatural life of grace.

[35] *Summa*, III, q. 62, a. 1.

self-sufficiency which is his participation in fundamental divinity.[36] Since God wills this perfection for man, He not only creates and sustains II, but also He acts in and through II. In the maximum degree the perfection of III are made to evolve proximately from II. God does not in the exercise of His causality leapfrog the potential of II as a secondary cause, to effect perfections in III independently of II.[37] In effecting as first cause this transition from II to III, God acts both immediately in an individual by activating his powers, and mediately on the individual through the instrumentality of other humans, so that the movement from II to III proceeds from the secondary causality of the whole of human nature.

This interplay between the actions of God as the First Cause and the radical godliness of man as a free agent prompted to action by God, raises a knotty question about the reconciliation of man's freedom with God's universal causality. And in the Christian sphere the question concerns the reconciliation of grace with free will. Controversy over this question has plagued Catholicism from the first centuries down to the present time. Interpretations have been proposed, condemnations have been uttered, schools have been formed. While the question still remains open to discussion it is not my present purpose to expound on this controversy. I would only point out that this debate centers on the fact of man's potential for radical godliness implicit in his possession of freedom.

What comes through with striking clarity from this controversy about man's freedom is that all Catholic parties concerned agree that man in a very real sense contributes actively to his redemption and final

---

[36] This is not to say that human nature in the instrumental role in its growth in grace is superior to human nature in the state of beatitude, since beatitude implies that man has already exercised his power under God of contributing to his growth in grace through his use of sacraments, and through the merit of good work and prayer. "But if he (an angel) had no grace before entering upon beatitude, it would then have to be said that he had beatitude without merit even as we have grace. This however, is quite foreign to the idea of beatitude; which conveys the notion of an end, and is the regard of virtue, as even the Philosopher says." *Ibid.*, I, q. 62, a. 4c.

[37] *Summa*, I, q. 105, a. 5.

perfection. No party to this controversy denies this aspect of man's radical godliness. The whole point at issue is the reconciliation of this universally accepted aspect of man's participation in fundamental divinity with the prerogatives of God as the First and Universal Cause.

At first one may be surprised, and even dismayed, to encounter the wide diversity of opinion among Catholic theologians on this question. But when one stands back and observes the controversy from a distance, the underlying unity present in the midst of diversity comes through with equal force. One is awakened to the universality of conviction in the Catholic tradition from the outset that man is in some way to a significant degree the secondary source of his own redemption and ultimate beatitude. The presence and continuity of this conviction in the community of Catholic believers on the significant role of man's radical godliness in his spiritual development, is further highlighted by the total rejection of this concept by Conservative Protestantism, and in some cases by Liberal Protestantism as well.

The point of unity amidst the wide diversity of opinion among the early Protestant reformers was that salvation came to man wholly from outside of him. That he is in no way the source of his redemption. It is this Catholic understanding of the role of man's radical godliness in his redemption which constitutes the fundamental point of difference between Catholic and Conservative Protestant thought and provides a basic obstacle to ecumenical activity.[38]

V. RADICAL GODLINESS AND THE ORDER OF GRACE

In his initial state of existence (II), man had a true potential for perfection (III) that lies within the limits of his natural power to achieve as shown in Diagram 5-1. The actualization of this potential in the transition from II to III constitutes a development or evolution which is natural in him. The state of perfection of III, which is the realized potential of II, can be called the natural godliness of man.[39] The active role that man exercises under God in his evolution from II to III expresses a participation in the fundamental aspect of divinity which can likewise be termed man's *natural radical godliness*. His

---

[38] L. Bouyer, *op. cit.*, pp. 148-158.

[39] *Summa*, I-II, q. 109, a. 3.

development from II to III may be described in terms of man's perfections as an evolution in him from potential being, truth, love, life, happiness, power, causality, justice, and mercy, to the full, ideal, actual possession of these perfections in the way that constitutes his natural participation in the Being, Truth, Love, Life, Happiness, Omnipotence, Causality, Justice and Mercy, which is God.

The traditional Catholic understanding of the message of Christ is that God intends for man the full realization of his natural potential for participated divinity attained in the transition from II to III. Not only that, but He further wills in His Mercy to build on this natural development of godliness by grafting onto human nature an extraordinary participation in His Divine Life that essentially transcends the natural potential for life present in II. Further, Catholic doctrine teaches that in elevating human life to its extraordinary participation in Divine Life God does not abandon the accommodation of Divine Justice to the natural radical godliness of man. In a gratuitous expression of love He builds upon and surpasses His Justice by implanting higher principles of spiritual development in man that permit him to exercise an active and vitally passive role in the evolution of his new possession of Divine Life.

Therefore, God does not suddenly infuse into man a full participation in Eternal Life so as to effect his instant redemption and beatitude. As in the natural order, God initially implants the seed of Eternal Life, the basic potentiality in man, to evolve to a full participation in Being, Truth, Love, and Divine Life. Thus Christ teaches that the kingdom of heaven comes initially in the form of a seed that possesses the inner vital potentiality for the fullness of Divine Life.[40]

---

[40] "For we see that all things which, in the process of time, being created by the work of Divine Providence, were produced by the operation of God, were created in the first fashioning of things according to the seed like forms, as Augustine says, such as trees, animals, and the rest. Now it is evident that sanctifying grace bears the same relation to beatitude as the seed like form in nature does to the natural effect; hence (Jn.3.9) grace is called the *seed* of God. As, then, in Augustine's opinion it is contended that the seed like forms of all natural effects were implanted in the creature when

Having implanted this divine seed (called in the Catholic tradition sanctifying grace, that is the physical, entitative participation in the Being and Life of God) with its potential for development, God infuses together with this new life the necessary active and passive powers (that is, the infused virtues and gifts of the Holy Spirit) as permanent inner principles in man. These permit him under God to express and develop this new life in such a manner that he becomes the proximate, secondary instrumental cause of its evolution to maturity.[41]

In this vital role that man exercises in his sanctification we find the elevation of his natural radical godliness to a higher level of operation. Humanity becomes the proximate source of God's birth in man by way of created grace and the evolution of grace to maturity. The evolution of this new life in human nature can be described as a transition in man from potential Being (sanctifying grace) and potential Truth, Love, Life, Beatitude, Power, Causality, Justice, and Mercy (the infused virtues and gifts of the Holy Spirit) to the actual, ideal, fully participated Being, Truth, Love, Life and other perfections of the divine essence, through which he is brought into immediate union with, and possession of Uncreated Being, Truth, Love and Life.

Aquinas argues for the presence in man of the infused virtues and gifts as *permanent* principles of supernatural growth—not as mere transitory movements of the Holy Spirit in him. He appeals to the fact of radical godliness in lower creatures whereby they are internally equipped with the full range of powers necessary to allow them to express their being and develop from within to full natural perfection. He argues that God would not do less for those whom He loves more than He has done for the lesser creatures:

> Secondly, man is helped by God's gratuitous will, inasmuch as a habitual gift is infused by God into the soul; and for this reason, that it is not fitting that God should provide less for those He loves, that they may acquire

---

corporeally created, so, straightway from the beginning the angels were created in grace." *Ibid.*, I, q. 62 a. 3.

[41] "Ordinarily, the increase of grace is produced in two ways: *ex opere operato* by the sacraments, and *ex opere operantis* by supernatural meritorious acts and by the impetratory efficacy of prayer." A. Royo, *op. cit.* p. 105.

supernatural good. Now He so provides for natural creatures, that not merely does He move them to their natural acts, but He bestows upon them certain forms and powers, which are the principles of acts, in order that they may of themselves be inclined to these movements, and thus the movements whereby they are moved by God become natural and easy to creatures according to *Wis.* viii.1: "she...ordereth all things sweetly." Much more therefore does He infuse into such as He moves towards the acquisition of supernatural good, certain forms or supernatural qualities, whereby they may be moved by Him sweetly and promptly to acquire eternal good; and thus the gift of grace is a quality.[42]

That God should infuse into man an extraordinary physical participation in His Eternal Life with its unlimited potential for development and expression and then fail to endow him with the powers necessary to exercise, express, and develop that life, would, in the mind of Aquinas, be equivalent to creating a monster. It would, for example, be similar to generating human life that is lacking in the faculties of sight, speech, touch, smell, hearing, and self movement, by which alone this life can be developed and expressed.

An interesting light on the emphasis that Aquinas places upon the importance of radical godliness in man, is found in his doctrine on charity as a created quality in the soul. He directs his attention to the position of those who argue that the movement of charity comes not from a permanent principle in the soul, but from a special action of the Holy Spirit upon the soul. Since charity is the highest expression of godliness in man, his participation in Divine Love, one's concept of its mode of presence and operation in human nature is particularly expressive of one's essential understanding concerning the place of human activity in the work of man's sanctification. I will quote this doctrine at length because it expresses so well the concept of elevated radical godliness which I have been expounding. Also it throws special light on the difference between traditional Catholic understanding of the work of redemption by intrinsic grace with man's vital cooperation

---

[42] *Summa*, I-II, q. 110, a. 2.

and Conservative Protestant doctrine which affirms that salvation comes to man completely *ab extrinseco.*

The Master looks thoroughly into this question in Q. 17 of the First Book, and concludes that charity is not something created in the soul, but is the Holy Ghost Himself dwelling in the mind. Nor does he mean to say that this movement of love whereby we love God is the Holy Ghost Himself, but that this movement is from the Holy Ghost without any intermediary habit, whereas other virtuous acts are from the Holy Ghost by means of the habits of other virtues, for instance the habit of faith or hope or of some other virtue: and this he said on account of the excellence of charity.

But if we consider the matter aright, this would be, on the contrary, detrimental to charity. For when the Holy Ghost moves the human mind the movement of charity does not proceed from this motion in such a way that the human mind be merely moved without being the principle of this movement, as when a body is moved by some extrinsic motive power. For this is contrary to nature of a voluntary act, whose principle needs to be in itself, as stated above. (I-II, Q. 6, A. 1): so that it would follow that to love is not a voluntary act, which involves a contradiction, since love of its very nature, implies an act of the will.

Likewise, neither can it be said that the Holy Ghost moves the will in such a way to the act of loving, as though the will were the instrument, for an instrument, though it be a principles of action, nevertheless has not the power to act or not to act, for then again the act would cease to be voluntary and meritorious, whereas it has been stated above (I-II, Q.114, A.4) that the love of charity is the root of merit: and, given that the will is moved by the Holy Ghost to the act of love, it is necessary that the will also should be the efficient cause of that act.

Now no act is perfectly produced by an active power, unless it be connatural to that power by reason of some form which is the principle of that action. Wherefore God, Who moves all things to their due ends, bestowed on each thing the form whereby it is inclined to the end appointed to it by Him: and in this way He "ordereth all things sweetly (Wis.viii.1)." But it is evident that the act of charity surpasses the nature of the power of the will, so that, therefore, unless some form by superadded to the natural power, inclining it to the act of love, this same act would be less perfect than the natural acts and the acts of the other powers; nor would it be easy and pleasurable to perform. And this is evidently untrue, since no virtue has such a strong inclination to its act as charity has, nor does any virtue perform its act with so great pleasure. Therefore it is most necessary that, for us to perform the act of charity, there should be in us some habitual form superadded to the natural power, inclining that power to the act of charity, and causing it to act with ease and pleasure.[43]

The limits to this concept of man's active role in his growth in grace would appear to be reached in the realm of mystical experience. The common opinion of all schools of mysticism in the Catholic tradition is that the soul is ordinarily passive during the experience of the movements of the Holy Spirit in the mystical state.[44] These promptings of the Spirit occur independently of the recipient's power, and he lacks the inner resources either to initiate or sustain this activity coming from without. Therefore, it would appear that in the higher stages of spiritual growth and activity, man ceases to be the proximate cause of his development and experience of the divine. The more he advances in the spiritual life, the less he possesses within himself the proximate principles of his spiritual activity—the less he is moving and the more he is moved. A significant diminution of the radical godliness aspect of his participated divinity appear to accompany his approach to divinity

---

[43] *Summa*, II-II, q. 23, a. 2.

[44] "The mystic has a clear awareness of the fact that what he is experiencing is not produced by himself. He is restricted to receive an impression produced by an agent completely distinct from himself. He is under the passive influence of an experience which he did not cause and which he cannot retain for a second longer than is desired by the one who produces it." A. Royo, *op. cit.*, p. 167.

in the sense that the closer he comes to God the less active he is in contributing to his spiritual development.

On the contrary, even in this realm of mysticism, one might say especially in this realm, Aquinas teaches that man's radical godliness is sustained in that the gifts of the Holy Spirit which render him docile to the promptings of the Spirit, are permanent, active-passive, inner principles of vital response in his soul. True, the human modality of operation by which his radical godliness is normally in his active initiation and direction of his activities, is not operative in the mystical experience. But the inner disposition of soul by which he is disposed to respond to the Spirit's promptings, are permanent qualities and perfections of his being, and function as the proximate source and explanation of his dynamic, vital response to these inspirations:

> But it must be noted that in man there is a twofold principle of movement; one within him, namely the reason, and the other extrinsic to him, namely God.... Now it is evident that whatever is moved must be proportionate to its mover; and the perfection of the mobile as such consists in a disposition whereby it is disposed to be well moved by its mover. Hence the more exalted the mover, the more perfect must be the disposition whereby the mobile is made proportionate to its mover. Thus we see that a disciple needs; a more perfect disposition in order to receive a higher teaching from his master. Now it is evident that human virtues perfect man, according as it is natural for him to be moved by his reason in his interior and exterior actions. Consequently, man needs yet higher perfections whereby; he can be disposed to be moved by God. These perfections are called "gifts," not only because they are infused by God, but also because by them man is disposed to become amenable to the divine inspiration, according to Is. 50:5: "The Lord God hath opened my ear, and I do not resist; I have not gone back" Even the Philosopher says, ...that for those who are moved by divine instinct there is no need to take counsel according to human reason, but only to follow their inner promptings, since they are moved by a principle higher than human

reason. This, then, is what some say, namely, that the gifts perfect man for acts which are higher than acts of virtue.[45]

Now man is not completely passive when so inspired by the Holy Spirit.[46] While he cannot initiate these movements that proceed entirely from the Spirit, he is the conscious, free recipient of their activity. He can second and concur in what is taking place in him by removing obstacles to the movement of the Spirit prior to His action, and by checking any tendencies or responses which would interfere with, or restrict, the inspirations of the Spirit while they are taking place.[47]

In this sense man is not only moved in the mystical experience, but he also moves with his movement and works along with what is being worked in him. By his free, conscious, concurrence in this movement which is initiated entirely by the Spirit independently of him, he is able even to gain merit.[48] To the objection that man as moved by the Spirit is somewhat of an instrument and therefore does not require a special habit for such a role since it benefits only principal causes to be perfected by habits, Aquinas replies:

> This argument holds in the case of an instrument which has no faculty of action, but only of being acted upon. But man is not an instrument of that kind for he is so acted upon by the Holy Ghost, that he also acts himself, in so far as he has a free will. Therefore he needs a habit.[49]

The workings of the Holy Spirit in man complement and complete the normal development of his spiritual life that proceeds from his active exercise of the virtues infused into him. The operation of the gifts then is not a substitute for or alternative to man's expression of radical godliness in the active working out of his salvation through

---

[45] *Summa*, I-II, q. 68, a. 2.

[46] *Ibid.*, I-II, q. 68, a. 3 ad 2

[47] A. Royo, *op. cit.* p. 87.

[48] "The mover that is moved moves through being moved. Hence the human mind, from the very fact that it is directed by the Holy Spirit, is enabled to direct itself and others." *Summa*, II-II, q.52, a. 2, ad.3.

[49] *Ibid.*, I-II, q. 68, a. 3 ad 2.

meritorious acts, prayer, the reception of the sacraments, and general active exercise of all the virtues. It is that person who has been the most intense, effective, successful, active secondary cause of his own spiritual development (who has exercised *active*, instrumental, radical godliness in the fullest degree), that normally becomes the habitual recipient of the movements of the Holy Spirit that constitute the mystical state.[50]

---

[50] This follows from the teaching of Aquinas concerning the nature and relation of the infused virtues and gifts of the Holy Spirit. According to Aquinas the infused virtues normally operate under the active direction of reason enlightened by faith after the manner in which reason in the natural order controls and directs human activity. The gifts are not intended to be substitutes for, or supplant, the virtues. Their function, as Aquinas understands them, is to supplement the operation of the gifts where reason elevated by faith is inadequate to the task. As grace intensifies in the soul, the ability of man actively to express and direct the inner life of grace becomes less adequate, and the operation of the gifts becomes more necessary and frequent. Since this increase of grace normally follows from the active exercise of the infused virtues, it follows that it is ordinarily those persons who have developed most in the life of grace by the intense, qualitative exercise of virtues in this human modality, who become the habitual recipients of the movements of the Holy Spirit which constitute the mystical state.

"But in matters directed to the supernatural end, to which man's reason moves him, according as it is, in a manner, and imperfectly, informed by the theological virtues, the motion of reason does not suffice, unless it receive in addition the promoting or motion of the Holy Ghost, according to Rom. 8.14,17: 'Whosoever are led by the spirit of God, they are the sons of God...and if sons, heirs also' and Ps. 142.10: 'Thy good Spirit shall lead me into the right land,' because, to wit, none can receive the inheritance of that land of the Blessed, except he be moved and led thither by the Holy Spirit. Therefore, in order to accomplish this end, it is necessary for man to have the gift of the Holy Spirit." *Summa*, I-II, q. 68, a. 2c.

Cf. John of Saint Thomas, *The Gifts of the Holy Ghost*, tr. by Dominic Hughes, O.P. (New York: Sheed and Ward, 1951), pp. 17 and 41-72.; R. Garrigou-Lagrange, *Three Ages of the Interior Life*, tr. by Sr. M. Timothea Doyle, O.P. (St. Louis: B. Herder Book Co., 1954), pp.78-82.; And by the same author, *Christian Perfection and Contemplation*, tr. by Sr. M. Timothea Doyle, O.P. (St. Louis: B. Herder Book Co., 1949), pp. 272-277, 324 ff. A. Royo, *op. cit.*, pp. 79-88.

FUNDAMENTAL GOD AND RADICAL GODLINESS

I have already referred to a pattern of behavior of some persons who endeavor to leapfrog, or bypass their own humanity and the role of active human effort in their endeavor to achieve union with God directly and independently of the created order.[51] Their appeal to the fact of direct dependency on the workings of the Holy Spirit in them, as opposed to the recourse others have to human effort (with its implied inferiority as an approach to God), is the more common defense of, and justification for this form of Quietism.[52] Just as "charity covers a multitude of sins" so the workings of the Holy Spirit are hopefully made to cover vast, empty spaces where the blood and sweat of human effort should be found.

Mysticism that does not rest upon, and complement an intense development of man's potential for active radical godliness, is like the house built on sand which collapses under the first pressure of the elements. In such mysticism the Holy Spirit in the end invariably turns out to be a rather "holy and *unwholesome* spirit" of flawed groping of human nature instinctively trying to create a substitute dream world replete with the divine presence by reason of its inability to experience that presence in the only place in which it is to be truly found—reality.

To the two stages of man's creation and evolution to natural godliness, Catholic tradition adds a third which is initiated in man's second stage, and develops in an ongoing process which intermingles with, and elevates into its higher level of vitality, that second stage. These stages of man's creation and evolution in natural and supernatural godliness may be expressed in Diagram 5-2

---

[51] *Cf.* Chapter Three, Section III.
[52] T. K. Connolly, "Quietism," *NCE*, Vol. 12, pp. 26-28. R. Garrigou-Lagrange, *Three Ages of the Interior Life, op. cit.*, pp. 289-292.

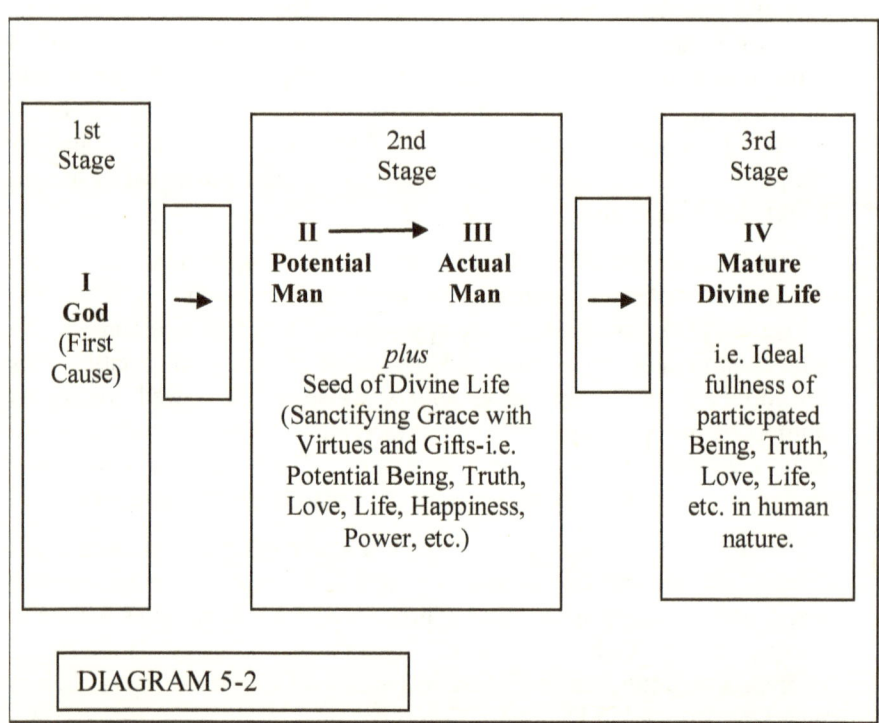

DIAGRAM 5-2

Using this outline of traditional Catholic doctrine as my reference point, I now will locate within its framework the major, differing views about man's evolution towards perfection which I have already briefly touched upon in my analysis of the three general patterns according to which persons in practice and theory work out their movement toward godliness.[53]

---

[53] *Cf.* Chapter Three, Section III.

VI. RADICAL GODLINESS AND THEORIES OF HUMAN PERFECTIBILITY

In my analysis of the three patterns which I suggested as a valid division of the principal ways in which men tend in practice and in theory to work out their perfection, I proposed that:

Pattern I is characterized by the tendency of persons to identify Uncreated Being with created being. This tendency is most frequently found in an implicit form in the practical order. Although it does proceed at times from a conscious explicit theoretical basis.

Pattern II is expressed in the tendency of those who not only strongly assert the distinction between Uncreated Being and created being, but also either place them in strict opposition to each other or so minimize their degree of similarity and positive relation as to make created being relatively useless, or an obstacle, as a point of contact with Uncreated Being.

Pattern III represents the position of those who both stress the distinction between Uncreated Being and created being and, at the same time, affirm the similarity and positive relation between them in so far as created being proceeds from Uncreated Being as effect from its cause. Therefore created being is similar to, present in, sustained by, and the point of contact with Uncreated Being.

This division was offered as a most general one, uniting a wide variety of divergent views in terms of their broadest common features. Therefore it allows positions which otherwise are fundamentally different, to be grouped under the same category. If these patterns were to be described specifically in terms of their attitude toward man's radical godliness and were to be symbolically expressed after the manner of my scheme in Diagram 5-2 (First Stage, Second Stage, Third Stage) setting forth the traditional Catholic understanding of man's existence and evolution toward natural and supernatural perfection, the results would be as follows:

Pattern I places maximum importance on man's natural radical godliness exercised in the second stage of his development in the transition from II to III. At the same time this pattern tends to diminish or eliminate entirely the significance of the first and third stages either by the outright denial of the existence of I (God) and, therefore, of IV (Supernatural Godliness), or by their absorption in a practical way into the second stage, that is the absorption of I into II, and IV into III. This pattern's optimistic appraisal of the positive potential of II (created being and man) for perfection likewise results in the tendency to absorb Grace into II (nature). Therefore, in terms of my diagram *Pattern I* would assume a form in which the first and third stages, as well as Grace are either negated or absorbed into the second stage, reducing the whole reality to this stage.

Pattern II stresses the existence and transcendence of God and emphasizes His activity as the unique source of man's perfection to the total exclusion or severe diminution of man's active role (radical godliness) as the proximate cause of his perfection. The potential for perfection initially in human nature (II) is downgraded, and the capacity of man's second stage of being (II→III) to be receptive of Divine Life (Grace) is likewise diminished or excluded.

This pessimistic view of man's potential (II) for perfection (III), which is characteristic of Pattern II, tends to put human nature beyond the possibility of a positive, intrinsic rehabilitation and elevation to divine life so that Grace as an intrinsic alteration and perfection of human life is radically reduced or excluded, and salvation comes uniquely from outside of man (that is from I—God) without internal change in the person redeemed. Man's attainment of union with God (IV) comes from the action of I on II, bypassing the second and third stages of human development and reducing Grace to this extrinsic action of I (God) on II.[54]

Pattern III emphasizes the importance of all three stages in the dynamic order in which they proceed from each other, in man's evolution to final perfection. This pattern moves between the opposites of Pattern I with its maximum stress on man's radical godliness to the rejection or diminution of God's primary causality and man's dependence on Grace, and Pattern II with its outright rejection or severe restriction of man's active role as the proximate cause of his evolution to perfection. It affirms that man's development to natural

---

[54] Bouyer, *op. cit.*, pp. 139-159. P. De Letter, "Justification in Protestant Theology," *NCE*, Vol. 8, pp. 88-92.

perfection (that is his second stage of being (II→III) provides the ideal environment (the good soil) receptive of, and responsive to, the vivifying, animating, perfecting presence of Grace (the seed of Divine Life), and that from the human organism so perfected, proceeds proximately under the primary causality of God, the evolution to Supernatural Godliness (IV) as illustrated in Diagram 5-2.

Having located the three patterns in broad outline on my scheme expressing the Catholic doctrine on man's evolution to perfection, it would now be desirable to relate to this Catholic tradition the specific, divergent positions categorized under these patterns.

Pattern I
Among the principal positions on the evolution of human perfection that I have placed in this first pattern are Humanism, Atheism, Deism, Liberal Protestantism, Existentialism, Positivism, Pantheism and a general classification representing all those who in their exercise of freedom tend in a practical way to deify created being.

Humanism in general places strong emphasis on human nature's capacity to evolve to ideal perfection. It thereby represents an optimistic view of man's radical godliness in the positive potential of II to evolve to the ideal perfection of III. Together with this optimistic evaluation of man's natural potential for self-evolution goes a tendency to diminish or reject the concept of grace and man's third stage of evolution to supernatural godliness (IV), since his nature (II) already possesses the potential that Grace is supposed to provide, and the second stage of his development effects the perfection that others attribute to the third stage.

Atheistic Humanism denies the reality of God (I) and thereby denies the existence of the first and third stages of man's being as expounded in Catholic doctrine. Atheism reduces all reality to the second stage (II→III). In so doing it tends to absorb qualities of I (God) into II, and similarly identify IV (Supernatural Godliness) with III (natural perfection). As long as the atheist retains his optimism in the positive potential of man (II) to evolve to full perfection—an optimism based on his 'faith' in the godly component, or radical godliness—he ascribes to human nature (II) by way of a human equivalence to divine self-sufficiency in its autonomous, intrinsic power to effect its own ideal realization. In this way he continues in the humanist school. However, if he should lose his optimism in this autonomous potential of man for self-realization—that is, lose faith in man's divine self-sufficiency—he would remove himself from the camp of humanism and see life pessimistically as a II which came from nowhere, is going nowhere, and therefore is nothing.

Deism[55] acknowledges the existence of God (I) and the first stage of man and created being (I→II). Since God (I), according to Deism, so created the universe as to have endowed it with powers of independent existence, activity, and self-development, apart from His presence, He is able, so to speak, to withdraw from created reality after having completed the work of creation (first stage). Then the second stage, wherein created being and human nature evolve from potential to actual perfection, takes place independently of the First Cause: I creates→II, II evolves→III (independently of I).

Since the full potential for perfection is present in II, and God (I) no longer intervenes in the process of man's self-development, the third stage of man's evolution is absorbed into the second stage. In the substantial expansion of man's radical godliness (II) to the state of divine self-sufficiency in which it functions as the first cause to itself of its evolution to perfection, we find the withdrawn God re-emerging in unidentified form in the divine power attributed to II.

One expression of *Christian Humanism* may be found in the form of a modified Deism. In this Christ serves to reveal to man his potential for perfection, that is the radical godliness of II achieves III of its own power. God continues to be withdrawn from the process of man's self-realization and exercises no efficient causality in motivating this development. It is Christ by the example of his life who reveals the ideal perfection of human nature and makes known to men that they too possess within themselves a similar capacity for such perfection. Here we find God's re-emergence in the self-sufficiency of II taking place through II's identification with the divine self-sufficiency revealed in the person of Christ. Just as God exercises no efficient causality in man's evolution to the perfection of Christ, so also Christ himself

---

[55] R. Z. Lauer, "Deism," *NCE*, Vol. 4, pp. 721-724.

provides no efficient motivation in this development, acting only as a final and exemplary cause in man's movement toward perfection.

Christian Atheism like atheism in general, denies the existence of God (I) and, therefore, the first and third stages of man's evolution, reducing the entire reality of man's being to the second stage of his existence. Christ exercises an essential role in this development by awakening in mankind through his preaching and example a consciousness of its autonomous, divine self-sufficiency, and motivates it to the activating of this divine power in an act of self-creation. One could say that according to this view Christ not only succeeds in helping men become *like* God, but he succeeds further in convincing them that they *are* God.

Some branches of *Liberal Protestantism* tend to follow a pattern similar to Christian Deism in placing significant emphasis on the self-contained power of human nature (II) to evolve to perfection (III) without depending on the efficient causality of God (I).[56] In its optimistic appraisal of human nature's potential for self-realization, and its emphasis on the active power of man to exercise aggressively the good works preached in the gospel, Liberal Protestantism stands in striking contrast to Conservative Protestantism with its rejection of man's radical godliness and his active power to cooperate in the work of his sanctification.[57] Liberal Protestantism ascribes to man's godliness an autonomy of power that takes it completely outside of and beyond, the traditional Catholic understanding of this aspect of man's godliness.

Existentialism belongs to Pattern I, especially by reason of the stress it places on the absolute power of man's freedom to determine for himself what human nature is to be. In its atheistic form Existentialism equates the participated radical godliness of man whereby he contributes to his evolution to perfection, with the ultimate self-determination and self-sufficiency of God Himself. Existentialism emphasizes the indeterminate character of initial human nature (II) so that its evolution to III depends entirely on man's exercise of free choice. The transition from II to III, therefore, takes on more the character of a creation than an evolution. Man does not so much evolve from potential to actual perfection in this act of choice as he brings himself into existence as a determined reality, becoming that kind of being which he chooses to be.[58]

Whereas Catholic tradition understands that initial human nature (II) as the effect of creation (I), possesses a definite, objective form with a specific, predetermined thrust toward an established, definite final state of perfection (III), so that man's freedom enjoys a relative and mediating role assisting in the actualization of this fixed potentiality, and not an absolute role of autonomously determining what this very potentiality (II) is to be.[59] Existentialism in its affirmation of man's absolute power of self-determination absorbs the causality of I (God) into II, and conceives II to be creating itself. In Atheistic Existentialism where I (God) is denied independent existence, this identification of I with II is complete. In Deistic Existentialism the tendency is toward a partial identification of I with II by the expansion of the self-determining power of II beyond the more restricted view of man's freedom (radical godliness) which Catholic tradition attributes to it.

Positivism was touched upon when I mentioned the influence of the empirical mentality on western culture disposing persons to accept as reality only that which can be immediately verified by sense data.[60] As a consequence of this empirical approach, Positivists concentrate totally on the second stage of man's existence as that which alone can be accepted as reality since it alone offers the basis for scientific verification.[61] The first and third stages, along with I and IV, cannot be acknowledged as part of reality since there is no basis on which their existence can be verified. Even man's second stage of existence (II→III) can be accepted only under those aspects that permit verification. Thus the concept of II as 'nature', and III as 'final cause' cannot be acknowledged. In this focusing upon the purely empirical aspects of II and its evolution to III to the exclusion of all else,

---

[58] J. Collins, *op. cit.*, pp. 77-87.
[59] *Summa*, I-II, q. 10, a. 1; q. 93, a. 3.
[60] *Cf.* Chapter Three, Section III.
[61] R. L. Cunningham, Article: "Positivism," *NCE*, Vol. II, pp. 621-3.

Positivism implicitly tends to absorb all aspects of the total process of man's creation and evolution into the surface aspects of this second stage so that, once again, man's radical godliness is not only accepted but it is implicitly assumed to possess the ultimate self-sufficiency and self-determinacy of divinity.

Pantheism[62] follows Pattern I in its explicit identification of I (God) with II (created being) whereby created being and human nature become not only endowed with the self-sufficiency of God, but become identified with God Himself. According to Pantheism created being's first and second stages of existence (I--creates→ II--evolves→ III) are telescoped into a single stage so that the movement of II to III is a process in which God, created being, and human nature together, in a radical unity and identity, advance in a creative evolutionary process to full being. With this divination of man's radical godliness (II) by his identification with divinity (I), the third stage of man's existence is negated since there can be found no divinity outside of the universe and human nature to implant in man a new potential (Grace) through which a vital development beyond the natural one takes place in him. The pantheistic view, therefore, reduces the various stages and elements of man's growth to perfection as understood in Catholic tradition, to the second stage.

This understanding of the radical godliness in created being and human nature as identical with divine causality is an essential component in process theology, and is congenial to the empirical mentality when it seeks ultimate answers in the restricted realm of the sensibly verifiable that it equates with the whole of reality. As an expression of a psychological, affective experience of the dynamic, creative unity of reality, it is also congenial to that pantheism that comes from an artistic-mystical approach to the universe. When this psychological experience of the dynamic unity of being is made the uncritical basis of a metaphysical definition of reality, a dynamic pantheism emerges in its explicit form as a philosophy.

Finally, under Pattern I there is that block of heterogeneous persons who in theory may accept the existence of I as the sources of II,

---

[62] E. R. Naughton, "Pantheism," *NCE*, Vol. 10, pp. 947-950.

acknowledging the first stage of man's being and often accept also the third stage of Catholic tradition, but in practice by reason of their psychological, affective absorption in finding complete fulfillment in the immediacy of the second stage of their existence, project into that stage of self-development qualities of efficient and final causality that belong rather to the first and third stages. The consequence of this choice is their practical attribution to man's radical godliness the independent power to effect ultimate beatitude and perfection from the finite materials of created being, giving both to their active powers of self-development and to the finite objects of their choice qualities of creativity and goodness which belong uniquely to God.

This is the dynamic at work in the sinful act, as I have already proposed[63] wherein the sinner attributes to his exercise of choice (radical godliness) a divine efficaciousness in achieving perfection and to the finite object of choice the infinite goodness of divinity. In the sinful act, therefore, the first and third stages are negated or absorbed into the second stage as II becomes the equivalent in causality to I (First Cause) and III to the Final Cause. In this sense sin may be described as a practical form of atheism, a practical extermination from one's act of the living presence of the God whose existence is acknowledged in theory.

If one were to locate Pattern I on the age scale of human existence, it would appear that this pattern is most congenial to and embraced by youth. Youth tends to have a confident, optimistic appraisal of its own good intentions and creative powers while experiencing uncritically in itself the instinctive thrust toward the fullness of life, love, truth, and power, which is man's natural, necessary, hunger for godliness. Not having had this thrust exposed to the chastening, purifying pressures and blows of prolonged experience in which it has been battered, frustrated, stomped upon, and especially betrayed by its own vacillation; youth instinctively asserts an exaggerated confidence in its own powers of self-development (radical godliness).

Now granted the wide divergences of these positions that I have placed in Pattern I, they do share the common characteristic of giving priority to the second stage of human development (II→III), and

---

[63] *Cf* Chapter Three, Section III.

FUNDAMENTAL GOD AND RADICAL GODLINESS

emphasizing the primacy of man's radical godliness in working out his search for perfection. At the same time they share the tendency to reduce or eliminate entirely the role of the First Cause in man's development by absorbing divine efficient causality into human efficient causality.

Pattern II

Pattern II moves in the opposite direction away from Pattern I by affirming above all else the transcendence of God and the predominance of divine causality in the evolution of created being and human nature to perfection. By reason of the Dualism which characterizes Pattern II, whereby it severely reduces or rejects entirely any positive relation between Uncreated Being and created being the role of man's radical godliness in working out his perfection is similarly diminished or completely negated.

Theoretical Dualism which explicitly affirms the fundamental opposition of created being and Uncreated Being, denies entirely any active, contributory role to man in his attainment of perfection. Given this position, since man's second stage of development (II→III) involves his growing identification with created being, this stage not only fails to contribute to his union with God, but it takes him away from such union. It is by suppressing or transcending this second stage of his development that man springs free from the hold which material, multiple, finite changeable being has on him, and can thereby gain union with the spiritual, unique, infinite, immutable reality of God. Theoretical Dualism frequently leads to an extreme Quietism in which the total suppression of man's radical godliness in his active response to created being, becomes the ideal, necessary condition for his union with divinity.

Practical Dualism[64] As I have already mentioned Theoretical Dualism is incompatible with Catholic doctrine which asserts that

---

[64] I have already noted in Chapter Three the distinction between those systems of thought which affirm in explicit manner that created being or parts of created being, for example visible reality, are derived from an ultimate principle distinct from God, and stand in positive opposition to God. I have pointed out that while Catholics may not affirm such a theoretical dualistic

created being comes from the creative act of Divine Love and, having been fashioned in His likeness, exists in, is sustained by, and provides the point of contact with God. Notwithstanding this theoretical affirmation of the divine likeness of created being and the positive contact with divinity which it provides, a modified form of implicit, practical dualism has continually emerged in the Catholic community under the guise of such movements as Jansenism, Puritanism, modified quietism, and subtle forms of Manichaeism. These movements express a recurring tendency among many Catholics to downgrade the natural evolution of man to perfection (II→III) and his exercise of radical godliness implicit in this development, as possible instruments for the growth to Supernatural Godliness.

Underlying these movements is a negative evaluation of the perfectibility of human nature itself (II) which is usually justified by a pessimistic interpretation of the consequences of original sin in tainting man's nature. From this attitude toward the corruption of human nature there proceeds a diminution of the possibility of intrinsic rehabilitation and elevation of man through grace, and a consequent movement in the direction of seeing man's salvation as coming totally from outside of his nature. Since Catholic doctrine affirms that man's sanctification takes place through the action of God's grace intrinsically altering and perfecting human nature, it is not possible to reject in theory this concept of grace and remain within the community of Catholic believers. I allude here, therefore, to a practical tendency among Catholics rather than to an explicit theoretical position though the practice has always tended to articulate itself in theory, and has given rise to periodic tensions and controversy in the Catholic community over the centuries.

According to practical dualism, man's evolution in natural godliness and the radical godliness at the proximate source of this evolution, do not represent a good soil receptive to the new life of Grace implanted therein. Human nature's development from potential to actual truth, for example, contributes little, and is often an obstacle to his growth in

---

world view, in the light of Church doctrine, many, along with other Christians, tend in practice to adopt some of the attitudes and implications of such an interpretation of created reality. Their position is somewhat parallel to those who are theists in theory but atheist in practice. For want of a better label of identification I am terming this position *practical dualism*.

Truth (IV). His transition from potential to actual love for the goodness of created being, is also more an obstacle than an aid to the infusion of Love in his soul. Likewise, man's movement from potential life, happiness, power, and creativity, are negative influences or indifferent contributors to his elevation to Divine Life, Beatitude, Power, and Creativity. The less intense is man's second stage of development, his evolution to natural perfection, the more ideal are the conditions for the implantation and development of Grace. Other practical expressions of this tendency may be found in the concept of religious life as a place of relative suspension of the second stage of man's development by the diminution of the vigorous, independent exercise of freedom (radical godliness) as the ideal environment for the development of the life of Grace.

All forms of spiritual counseling which fail to stress the importance of evolution in natural godliness (that full development of the natural man equals III) as the necessary condition (good soil) for the development of the life of grace, reflect this modified dualism. The indifference in some Catholic circles to the Church's involvement in the temporal, economic, and social spheres of human life, is another expression of the downgrading of the role of man's evolution in natural perfection and radical godliness in the plan of his sanctification.

In areas where Catholic doctrine demands the explicit use of human nature and created beings as active, instrumental principles of man's growth in Grace (that is in the sacraments, and also the priesthood, teaching and preaching activities of the Church, and meritorious works) this modified dualism expresses itself in a particular manner. It sees these instrumental uses of created being as rare, extraordinary, isolated instances of God's utilization of secondary causes, rather than the revelation of the potential in the radical godliness of created being and human activity to be continuously, universally functioning as instruments of God's sanctifying activity in human nature. For persons of this position the sacraments serve to reinforce their conviction about the absence of radical godliness in created being rather than reflect its presence.

For example, the presence of the priest in society does not serve to remind men everywhere that God intends to use all men in varying ways as the sanctifying instruments of human nature. Rather it dramatizes the basic deficiencies of human nature which require very special persons with very special power to do for men what they can in no way do for themselves, even under God. And so the priest is not a symbol of the radical godliness of human nature, but a reminder of the fundamental godlessness of man.

According to this tendency the Church's mission is not, as some hold, to awaken men to the radical godliness present throughout created being that God intends to activate through their use as instruments. Rather the Church should preach the absence of godliness in the created order. It should inculcate a pessimism in men towards divinity's presence in created being and in humanity so as to motivate them to turn away from the universe and their own humanity, and seek salvation purely and solely in God.

This practical dualism which is a recurring phenomenon in Catholic history, comes very close in some instances to the attitudes and concepts that control Conservative Protestant thought. In both positions we encounter the same downgrading of the radical godliness of created being as human instruments of man's sanctification. As a consequence, this orientation looks for salvation to come totally from outside the created order, has the same sense of the radical corruption of human nature as a result of original sin, and the same evaluation of the futility of man's second stage of existence as a contributory factor to effective union with God.[65] A principal difference between these two positions lies in the fact that among Conservative Protestants these attitudes and concepts are articulated clearly as the explicit, theoretical expression of essential doctrine. Whereas among Catholics the various versions of this modified dualism represent practical tendencies and convictions that constantly give rise to tension whenever the effort is made to provide them with an explicit theoretical basis in Catholic doctrine.

Conservative Protestantism affirms above all else the transcendence of God and His unique absolute position as the Beginning and the End of created reality.[66] Together with this affirmation goes the rejection of

---

[65] L. Bouyer, *op. cit.* pp. 139-159. de Letter, *op. cit.*, pp. 88-92. Dillenberger-Welch, *op. cit.*, pp. 26-42.

[66] L. Bouyer, *op. cit.*, pp. 68-96.

the power of human nature (radical godliness) to function under God as the proximate source of its own sanctification. It is this rejection of man's radical godliness which underlies Conservative Protestantism's denial of validity to sacraments, the priesthood, meritorious good works, and to the Church as an active, efficient, physical instrument through which God teaches and sanctifies mankind.

Implicit in this rejection of created being as the proximate cause of Uncreated Being's new presence in human nature, is also the denial that being, truth, love, life, happiness, power, and causality, can be the physical instruments whereby God brings into existence in human nature a new, extraordinary participation in Being, Truth, Love, Life, Beatitude, Omnipotence, and Divine Causality. According to Conservative Protestantism, reality is so far transcended by the Divine Being that it would be a blasphemous degradation of Divinity to the created level if one were to affirm a positive content in created reality that possesses true similarity to Uncreated Being and which permits created causes to communicate to other beings a share in their participated divinity.

Aquinas on the contrary asserts the similarity (analogous) of created being to Uncreated Being. But he also affirms that it would be a lessening and degradation of Divine Omnipotence and Causality to deny to God the power of imparting to created entities both an imperfect participation in His Being and a participation in His Causality whereby created causes possess by virtue of their natural forms the active power to communicate to others a share in their participated divinity.[67] It would be a further lessening of Omnipotence to deny to God's power the capacity to elevate the natural causality of creatures (radical godliness) to a level of instrumental performance under His Causality. Thus where Conservative Protestantism considers it blasphemous to attribute to created being a true similarity to the Being and Causality of Divinity, Aquinas reflecting the Catholic tradition holds that it is blasphemous to lower the power of God to a finite, restricted level by denying to that power the capacity to effect just such a similarity in created being.

---

[67] *Summa*, I, q. 105, a. 5.

Because of the essential inferiority of human nature to Divine Being, and the further flawing of human nature as a result of original sin, Conservative Protestantism holds that man is incapable of being intrinsically altered and perfected by Grace, and thus salvation comes to him wholly from without through the mercy of God's extrinsic altering of man's relation to Him. The redemption of human nature, therefore, is not effected by the infusion of Divine Life into the soul—rejection of the third stage of man's existence with its principle (Grace) and term (IV)—but by God's gratuitous, extrinsic act of mercy whereby man is brought back under the special providence of the Creator without being intrinsically perfected in the process.

There is one other grouping that I propose to place in Pattern II, although its inclusion in this division is a subtle one and open to discussion. According to Catholic doctrine the natural evolution of man to godliness involves an expansion in human perfection which comes from man's healthy, full relation to divinity's presence in the entire created order, but particularly to divinity's special participated presence in human nature. Man evolves in his potential for actual, full, being, truth, love, life, happiness, and power by his encounter with the participated being, truth, love, life, happiness and power, of the created order in general, but primarily and principally by his encounter with the participated being, truth, love, life, beatitude, and power of God which is to be found in its riches, highest, and most intense expression human nature itself. Now there are those who celebrate God's presence in nature and created being as a whole, without granting to human nature that primacy of divine presence and revelation which Catholic doctrine attributes to it. In their affirmation of contact with God through created being, they identify with Pattern III, and stand opposed to Pattern II. However, to the extent that they ignore the substantial primacy of human nature as the principal revelation and point of contact with divinity, they slip by default into Pattern II.

I have in mind the tendency reflected at times in the writings of persons who celebrate God's presence in nature and, certainly also, in man, but man as filtered through the somewhat depersonalized vision of the scientist. I propose this classification because I believe that with the technological, scientific emphasis of the future and its concomitant mechanization, depersonalization, and dehumanization of life there will develop a tendency in men to move further and further away from the profound experience of their humanity, and their religious encounter with God's presence in reality will tend to take place more in the bottom of a test tube than in the depths of the human spirit, more in the marvels of increasingly rarer contacts with sunsets and natural phenomena than in the miracle of the stirrings of love in the heart of one who has only reason to hate, and the surging of hope where one expects to find only despair.[68]

As for Pattern II's location on the age scale of human life, I would identify her with experienced adulthood. If, as I have proposed,[69] one aspect of man's radical godliness is his instinct to search in his own humanity for the proximate source of fulfillment of all human needs, then optimism about the inner capacity of human nature to effect its own evolution to ideal perfection would be the initial, instinctive attitude of man toward his humanity. The pessimistic evaluation of human nature as wanting in the radical godliness necessary to bring about from its own resources the perfection it necessarily hungers after, could only come about as a consequence of intense, prolonged, experience of the deficiencies not just of one human or a group of men, but of mankind in general. Since it is such an evaluation of human nature which dominates Pattern II, this pattern should be recognized as the expression not of an initial, innocent, inexperienced attitude toward human life, but of a judgment which proceeds from multiple, painful experience of human inadequacy.

Pattern III

Pattern III represents the traditional Catholic understanding of created being (and human nature) as proceeding from God and bearing a likeness to its Source by its participated divinity. Initially, created being possesses more the potential for godliness than actual godliness. Its evolution to full, actual participated divinity proceeds proximately from its own inner principles whereby it participates in the self-sufficiency of fundamental divinity by being the proximate source of its actualized

---

[68] Rahner, Theological Investigations, No. VI, op. cit., pp. 5-11.
[69] *Cf.* Chapter Five, Section IV.

godliness. God then adds to this natural godliness a new, vital potential for an extraordinary participation in the Divine Life.

This new life is initiated in human nature in such a way that it also evolves to full perfection from active and passive principles infused together with Grace so that man becomes the proximate source of his evolution to Supernatural Godliness. According to this Catholic understanding, then, there are three stages to man's existence and evolution to full participated divinity, with each new stage proceeding in dependency from the preceding one as shown in Diagram 5-2:

1. First Stage. Created being and human nature (II) proceed from God (I) in the likeness of I with a fixed, determined nature, and specific thrust toward ideal realization (III), and possesses the inner principles (radical godliness) to be the proximate source of their evolution to III.

2. Second Stage. The actual evolution of II to full natural godliness (III) proceeds under the dual causality of God as First Cause and man in his radical godliness as the secondary principal cause. What is lacking in man's individual existence by way of active principles of perfection, is present in other humans so that the fullness of radical godliness is found in the collectivity of human nature. In the movement toward full godliness man is activated by the participated divinity of all created being, but primarily and principally by divinity's participated presence in the totality of human nature.

3. Third Stage. God implants an extraordinary participation in His Divine Life (Grace) as a new vivifying principle in human nature so that Grace relates to the whole human organism as an organizing, animating principle in the way that the soul relates to the body as the substantial principle of life in the body.[70] The natural godliness of man

---

[70] Grace is said to make pleasing, not efficently, but formally, that is because thereby a man is justified, and is made worthy to be called pleasing to God...."*Summa*, I-II, q. 111, a. 1 ad. 1

"Grace, as a quality, is said to act upon the soul, not after the manner of an efficient cause, but after the manner of a formal cause, as whitness makes a thing white, and justice, just." *Ibid.* II - II, 110, a. 2, ad. 1.

"Now in the manifestation of faith, God is the active cause, having perfect knowledge from all eternity; while man is likened to matter in receiving the influx of God's action." *Ibid..*, II - II, q. 1, a. 7, ad.3

is the good soil, that is the material principle receptive to the vivifying presence of Grace) so that the evolution of man to IV builds upon the continued development of man in his natural godliness.[71]

The tension in man between the old and new life (Grace) of which Saint Paul speaks,[72] comes not primarily from the godliness of man's natural perfection, but from the absence of such godliness (that is godlessness equals sin) in his second stage of existence. It is to the extent that man fails in his natural evolution to full, participated godliness that an opposition of contradiction exists between the defective condition of his natural state and the life present through Grace (for example between hatred in him and the presence of Love). This is not to say that man's natural perfection (godliness) provides the basis of a quick, easy transition to the higher levels of supernatural life. Since the divine life initiated in man by Grace substantially transcends the limitations of his natural life, this new life will severely stretch and strain the dynamics of his natural vitality.[73]

---

[71] "So long as nature endures, its operation remains. But beatitude does not destroy nature, since it is its perfection. Therefore it does not take away natural knowledge and love. Natural knowledge and love remain in the angels. For as principles of operations are mutually related, so are the operations themselfes. Now it is manifest that nature is to beatitude as first to second; because beatitude is superadded to nature. But the first must ever preserved in the second. Consequently nature must be preserved in beatitude: and in like manner the act of nature must be preserved in the act of beatitude….The advent of a perfection removes the opposite imperfection. Now the imperfection of nature is not opposed to the perfection of beatitude, but underlies the perfection of the form, and the power is not taken away by the form, but the privation which is opposed to the form…All things which make up beatitude are sufficient of themselves. But in order for them to exist, they presuppose the natural gifts; because no beatitude is self-subsisting, except the uncreated beatitude." *Ibid*. I, q. 62, a. 7.

[72] I. Cor. 15.45 ff.

[73] "Now, since charity surpasses the proportion of human nature, as stated above (A.2) it depends, not on any natural virtue, but on the sole grace of the Holy Spirit Who infuses charity. Wherefore the quantity of

The tension, however, will not be one of contradiction but one of degree between the *less* of man's natural participation in Divine Life and the substantial, essential *more* of his extraordinary share in Divine Life through Grace—between the love proper to his natural perfection and Love. The evolution of the new organism (since Grace is not merely something new added to man, but man himself divinized) to the fullness of participated Divine Life (IV) proceeds primarily from God as First Cause, and secondarily from supernaturalized human nature as proximate, instrumental cause.

This traditional Catholic understanding of man's evolution to perfection agrees in part both with Pattern I's affirmation of the immanence of God in created being, and with Pattern II's affirmation of the transcendence of God and His radical, essential distinction from created being. According to Catholic doctrine there is no contradiction between affirming the essential distinction between God and created reality, and at the same time espousing an analogous similarity of created being to its Source and asserting the intimate presence of that Source to the whole of the created order. Therefore Pattern III rejects Pattern I's tendency to identify God and created being, while rejecting also the absoluteness of separation between the two as proposed in Pattern II. Pattern III also agrees both with Pattern I's positive appraisal of the radical godliness of human nature whereby man has the principles of self-growth within himself, and with Pattern II's evaluation of the inadequacy of human nature to effect its ideal self-realization and with its emphasis on the causality of God as the essential condition of man's salvation. At the same time Pattern III rejects what it considers to be Pattern I's naïve exaggeration of the kind and degree of autonomous self-sufficiency of human nature's radical godliness in her supposed capacity to attain perfection independently of the efficient and final causality of God, and Pattern II's withdrawal from this same radical

---

charity depends neither on the condition of nature nor on the capacity of natural virtue, but only on the will of the Holy Spirit Who 'divides His gifts according as He will.' Hence the Apostle says (Eph 4.7): 'To every one of us is given grace according to the measure of the giving of Christ.' " *Summa*, I-II, q. 24, a. 3

godliness of human nature any power whatsoever to participate actively as a proximate cause in the work of its redemption.

In terms of the human age scale, I would classify Pattern III as "enlightened middle age." Essential to Pattern III's understanding of the workings whereby he actively contributes to his own development in perfection, and the recognition of the limitations and deficiencies of this radical godliness which demands that he seek in God's grace what he fails to find in his own powers while newly conscious of the fact that even his natural perfections are totally the product of Divine Mercy.

Patterns as stages of human development

It would appear that these three patterns represent not radically distinct attitudes of life, but three successive stages in human development. The first stage is that of Pattern I with its instinctive confidence in the power of human nature to accomplish man's full realization. The second stage of Pattern II emerges from the first by way of a crisis-conversion which involves man's loss of confidence in human nature's self-realizing powers as the result of a bitter experience of human inadequacy (crisis) with a turning away entirely from human nature to seek salvation outside the created order and uniquely in God (conversion). The third stage of Pattern III reflects a re-conversion of man back to his humanity when acting as the instrument of Divinity, as the proximate source under God where he finds salvation and perfection.

This re-conversion of man back to human nature comes from his experience of what God's mercy can accomplish in him and others using humanity as the instrument of His Divinity. This experience of the sanctifying power in human nature as an instrument of God, reveals to man that God cannot only act in and through his humanity in spite of his deficiencies, but that He will incorporate these very deficiencies into His action so that, for example, strength comes to him from his humanity not merely in spite of his weakness, but out of these weaknesses when properly embraced. So also wisdom comes to him out of foolishness; love out of hatred; life out of death; and fruitfulness out of impotence.

Pattern III accepts and incorporates the positive insights of Patterns I and II, and unites them in an understanding which discloses a complete, balanced, unified picture of the relation of Uncreated Being and created being. One can find an exemplification of these three stages in the development of the Apostles. Pattern I holds sway in the confused, uncritical optimism in their powers of self-development which they manifested prior to the events of Calvary. This first pattern gave way to Pattern II in their shocked confrontation with their own human frailty and the deficiencies of human nature in general which was revealed in Christ's death (crisis). This frightening, dismaying encounter with the godlessness of human nature drove them to an anguished search outside and beyond their human nature for whatever salvation they might hope to achieve (conversion).

With the coming of the Holy Spirit at Pentecost, they underwent a totally new experience of the Spirit within their humanity (re-conversion back to the radical godliness of human nature as an instrument of the Holy Spirit) and they issued forth from behind the locked doors with an unshakable confidence in the power of their fragile human nature, when operating as an instrument of the Spirit, to breathe Divine Life into the anemic, flagging natural vitality of human beings.

VII. RADICAL GODLINESS AND ECUMENISM

Proceeding on the basis that the dialogue of ecumenism builds on the shared experience of Divinity's presence in created being and human nature, I will now draw some conclusions about the implications for ecumenism present in the various positions that I have examined concerning the relation of Uncreated Being to created being, and the role of radical godliness in man's movement toward perfection. I have already argued in a general way that both Patterns I and II are not congenial to ecumenism, while Pattern III presents the approach to Uncreated Being through created being which is most open to ecumenism.[74] I now propose to pursue this evaluation in more detail, and then elaborate on the specific implications for ecumenism of Pattern III.

Pattern I

Three basic positions are found under this pattern:

---

[74] *Cf.* Chapter Three, Section III.

FUNDAMENTAL GOD AND RADICAL GODLINESS

1. The position of those who deny the reality and existence of God, implicitly absorbing into created being the characteristics of Uncreated Being. For example, note the various atheistic forms of humanism, existentialism, and positivism.

2. The position of those who acknowledge God's existence but separate Him from created being in such a way that created entities are held to evolve to perfection independently of God's efficient and final causality. Hence they have attributed to themselves qualities of divine efficient and final causality. For example note Deism, deistic forms of humanism, and some branches of Liberal Protestantism.

3. The position of those who acknowledge God's existence and identify Him with created being, either by explicit theory or in the practical order by deifying created being through their endeavors to find perfect happiness in finite good. For example note pantheism.

In atheism's denial of the existence of God the theoretical basis of ecumenism is effectively eliminated since ecumenism as a very minimum presupposes God's existence. The atheist in theory cannot be open to dialogue based on the shared experience of a God who does not exist. He can only take part in a dialogue in which he offers his reasons and insights in support of his convictions while listening with openness of mind to the evidence offered by those who affirm the reality of God.

However, the atheist is still able in practice, not withstanding his theory, to possess a genuine sense of God's presence in created being which he will refuse to identify in traditional terminology, and thereby find himself open to dialogue about his sense of the ultimate without conferring on that experience the label of "experience of God." I have been struck by my personal encounters with individuals who call themselves atheists or agnostics while evidencing to me a remarkable openness to the mystery and miracle of life, and a sense of the sacredness and goodness of created being together with a respect and wonder for all the best in the created order. This has led me to conclude that they are genuine mystics and, in one case at least, I would say a Christian mystic. I have found in these cases that their so called atheism stems in part from a profound religious sense which has made them draw back from, and refuse to identify with conventional forms of religion precisely because of their experience of abuses and hypocrisies which scandalized their refined religious instincts. I do not wish to say, therefore, that the atheist cannot possibly be an ecumenist in practice, but only that this theoretical position logically rules out such a development.

My evaluation of the other positions is also offered by way of the logical consequences of their theoretical positions. This does not exclude the possibility of an intense, admirable ecumenical spirit in their position in the practical order.

Among those who acknowledge the existence of God but separate Him entirely from the created order (for example the various forms of Deism) ecumenism cannot take the form of a dialogue based on the experience of God's immediate presence to created being. The ecumenical dialogue of the Deist would have to be built around the shared experience of created reality's revelation of the distant, separated God who is revealed to us by the participated divinity of the created order. It is one thing to experience divinity present in created being; it is something else to experience created being as the symbol and revelation of divinity which is far removed from it. Deism offers the theoretical basis only for the latter kind of ecumenical dialogue.

Among those who in theory or practice identify God with created being, the experience of God which created reality offers is not that of divinity's presence and revelation in created being, but the experience of created being itself as divine. In pantheism, which substitutes the symbol for the reality, the participation for the essence, ecumenism would be based on the experience of the higher, nobler, more mysterious and unified aspects of created being as though this were the experience of God Himself. When the object of this experience of created being as divinity is human nature in its more divine aspects, pantheistic ecumenism fulfills Durkheim's definition of religion as man's worship of himself in community. In the place of the golden calf such pantheism substitutes the mystique of divine humanity on the high altar of worship. For those who pursue in practice a more concrete deification of tangible created being and prefer to reserve the altar for the golden calf, a kind of ecumenism may be found, for example, in a group of tired business men describing to each other the form of perfect happiness that they will purchase when they get their hands on that elusive first million dollars. Such ecumenical encounters take place more comfortably in a cocktail lounge with martini in hand after a long, hard day in the office than in the gothic atmosphere of a chapel.

Pattern II
Dualism which asserts the basic opposition of created being and Uncreated Being, eliminates even more effectively than atheism the possibility of an ecumenical dialogue based on the shared experience of God's presence in the created order. While atheism in theory denies the existence of God, the atheist in practice is not explicitly compelled to shut off his attention from those aspects of created being that place him in an unarticulated encounter with divinity. The Dualist, while acknowledging the existence of God, is forced to focus only upon those aspects of created being that reinforce his views on the radical opposition between Uncreated Being and created being. Ecumenical dialogue for the adherents of Dualism will logically take the form of the shared experience of the godlessness and opposition to Uncreated Being of created being rather than the experience of created being's godliness and similarity to Uncreated Being.

The practical dualism present in some Catholic schools of the spiritual life and in Conservative Protestantism leads to somewhat the same position. In their stress on the transcendence of God and the inability of created being to reflect Divine Being by similarity, still less to be the active secondary cause of God's extraordinary presence in transformed human nature by Grace, they substantially alter and lessen the theoretical basis for ecumenism found in traditional Catholic doctrine. According to these views men are able to share not in the positive experience of God's presence in created reality, but only in the absence of God from the created order. Ecumenical dialogue serves to reinforce their convictions about this absence or the basic godlessness of human nature. I have already dwelt upon the similarities between Conservative Protestantism and these Catholic schools which represent a modified dualism.

The similarity of the two positions provides me with the occasion for making an important comment on ecumenism which applies to every form of ecumenical dialogue between various groups. I am certain that such likeness of outlook between Conservative Protestantism and this strain of thinking in some Catholics provides the basis for a congenial, mutually supportive relation between them, and that ecumenical dialogue in such circumstances comes easily and is painless. Now, if the shared convictions which would be at the basis of this friendly ecumenical rapport are true reflections of God's actual relation to created being and human nature, then the dialogue that ensues from these shared views constitutes an expression of true ecumenism. However, if their shared attitudes are flawed, defective understandings of the presence of divinity in created being, and represent a kind of godlessness (absence of truth), then the dialogue that proceeds on this basis and serves to reinforce these convictions, proceeds from and reinforces an expression of godlessness under the guise of godliness, and represents a distorted, defective ecumenism.

The purpose of ecumenism is not that of merely allowing men to exchange views and experiences of a religious nature in a friendly environment, but of serving as a means toward achieving a fuller experience of God's presence in the created order. If the dialogue serves to distort that presence or to reinforce convictions which impede the valid experience of that divine presence, then ecumenism fails in its primary purpose irrespective of the fraternity and goodwill which accompanies the dialogue.

Pattern III
From my analysis of the three patterns of approach to God's presence in created being, it is clear that Pattern III represents the approach which, in theory at least, is most congenial to ecumenism. This pattern asserts that in the natural order whatever being, truth, goodness, life, or other positive perfection is present, is totally derived from the reality of God, is revealing of that reality, and is a point of contact with divinity. This theoretical position, therefore, demands of its adherents that they approach all created being and, especially, that they approach any and every aspect of human nature, with the explicit consciousness of the divine presence and open to the experience of that presence.

Further it asserts that in the present economy the experience of God may be attained only through such openness to the divine presence in created being. In addition to this possible encounter with God present in the natural order, Pattern III affirms also an extraordinary divine presence taking place through the workings of Grace in the supernatural order. This elevation of natural human life to the level of a special participation in Divine Life provides the basis for an essentially higher, more perfect experience of God and, therefore, an essentially higher and more perfect form of ecumenism.

Prescinding from the question of the objective validity and truth of Pattern III's approach to created being, it should be clear that from the theoretical point of view alone, it provides the basis for the highest and most inclusive form of ecumenism by reason of its teaching on both the ordinary and the extraordinary presence of divinity in humanity. Since Pattern III is simply the experience of traditional Catholic doctrine, it is equally clear that ecumenism not only can be reconciled with traditional Catholicism, but it must be accepted as inseparable from that Catholicism when it is properly understood. When Catholics, who by their faith are adherents to this pattern of approach to God through created being and human nature, fail to evidence in practice this openness to the divine presence in the full range of created reality, with primacy given to this presence in human nature, it will be found that they have abandoned their theoretical position and have in the practical order slipped over into the approaches of Patterns I and II.

Keeping in mind that ecumenism is the openness to the experience of God's presence in created being in general and in human nature in particular, some of the implications for ecumenism of Pattern III's understanding of man's radical godliness are as follows:

1. Since God makes His reality and presence known through visible entities and since in the maximum degree He acts in and through secondary causes in imparting a share in His being to the created order, my search for God will not lead to an encounter with him in a state of disembodied, independent existence, floating about in space, but it will find His reality and presence revealed primarily in the depths of human existence and at the source of whatever perfection is present in every human act. Therefore, the more profoundly and fully I experience the miracle of man, individual and collective, and the closer I come to the depths of the mystery of human life and the ultimate source of human consciousness, love, joy, creativity, strength, and mercy, the more I will experience and the closer I will come to the reality of God. The most direct, immediate, perfect, and ideal way to God is through human nature. In fact it is ultimately the only way. In my loving penetration

into the depths of human nature, I will penetrate into the Love from which that nature proceeds.

2. The presence of God that I am searching for in human nature is not the full, mature, perfect, triumphant presence of God who exists apart from created being, but the partial, immature, imperfect, infant presence of Grace which is struggling to be born, to come alive and remain alive in the relatively hostile environment of human life. If I find God at all, I will find Him creating Himself in the human context, bringing Himself into existence as a visible, tangible, palpable, audible, living presence in the conscious, affective world of human life, and utilizing man's active and vital-passive cooperation as a kind of combination parent and midwife in assisting at this birth of participated divinity.

In the beginning God created man. Now man finds the God who created Him in the success of his own efforts to re-create God. The experience of God that men fundamentally share in the ecumenical dialogue of man's present state of existence, therefore, is not the soul-filling, joy-bringing experience of the perfect God of the beatific vision, but the experience of sharing in the birth pangs by which men collectively give rise to the elusive, obscure vulnerable quickening of participated Divine Life in the human spirit. "A woman in childbirth suffers because her time has come."[75]

It is one thing to hold hands and share in the joyful experience of God's radiant presence in the sunsets and awesome beauties of nature. This is an ecumenism analogous to that which is found in the communion of saints. It is quite something else to attempt to soothe and relax pain-writhing hands of a mother who struggles for a new vision to come alive and transform the horror of the present one and make acceptable the mind-stunning, heart-shattering sight of her young son dying on a hospital bed.

She had searched in reality for a glimpse of God's face, and finds staring back at her from that reality the lifeless features of her son. She refuses to succumb to an instinct that tempts her to turn away entirely from reality and in a dream world, wipe from her mind and memory the meaningless horror of the lifeless face looking up at her. And so she

---

[75] Jn. 16.21

remains and stares long, hard, and deep through a filter of pain into the death mask that was her son. At length the scales drop from her eyes, and she thinks thoughts that she had never thought, and sees meanings and values that she had never seen, and experiences affective movements in her that she had never before felt. A new wisdom and love quickens within which leaves her permanently and ineradicably transformed.

The sorrow is not lessened but heightened as she now freely embraces it and holds the reality of that lifeless face constantly before her mind. But in that womb which is her sorrow, a new life is implanted, takes root, quickens, and grows. And the true ecumenism instinctively seeks to live as closely as possible to that sorrow so that by sharing in it, he may share also in her experience of Wisdom and Love being conceived and growing in her through the Life-giving and Life-nourishing power of the lifelessness of her son.

3. Since God comes alive through the radical godliness of human nature, I must search for His imperfect emergence primarily in the struggles that men make under God to transcend their personal defects and natural limitations in order to achieve true godliness. Therefore I should not look in human nature for the experience of Love in its maturity and purity. Rather I should look for the man who is filled with bitterness, distrust, and even hatred of one much abused by life, and yet who prays and struggles that his hatred may be purged, his negative responses to others curbed, and the narrow confines of his natural affection transcended by the power to forgive and love which he finds in Christ. As his painful memories and resentments persist, and his instinct for vengeance and distrust continue to gnaw at him, his struggles and prayers also continue so that gradually, in spite of many lapses, the power to love intensifies and finally achieves a fragile primacy over the negative forces in him. As I experience his struggle with knowledge of his background necessary to appreciate the enormity of the obstacles which he must overcome in order to succeed, and marvel at the gradual emergence of Love to its place of effective primacy in his life, I am experiencing the coming alive of God in him.

So also my encounter with God as Truth in human nature will not be the clear, illuminating experience of consummate wisdom in a man who understands all the problems and knows all the answers. It will more likely take the form of my wonder at the habitual, intense hunger for, and groping after ultimate answers that goes on in one whose vision of reality is dimmed and flawed by ignorance, error, and limited insight. As I watch the emergence of new understanding and consciousness slowly, painfully coming out of the darkness of his mind, as he tenaciously and prayer-fully persists in daily searching, meditating, turning over every aspect of life in his mind, I am seeing Truth being generated in the human mind. "The Light coming into the darkness"[76]

And so it is with my experience of the other aspects of Divinity. I find Life, Joy, Power, Creativity, Justice and Mercy in human nature, if I find them at all, never in a state of mature perfection, but always as emerging in a process of continuous birth out of individual and collective human struggle.

4. Since the God who is being born and is evolving out of human effort and toil is infinite, no one form of human activity can be the adequate instrumental cause of the total expression of Divine Life. God uses different forms of human activity to generate different facets of His being. He comes alive and reveals Himself in one way through the innocence and simplicity of the child and in another way through the more sophisticated behavior of the adult. Thus, I must live close to all varieties of human activity and struggle so that I may experience more fully the emergence and revelation of God.

To experience God's acting in and through the spectrum of human life effecting His living presence in human nature I must approach all with openness and sympathy. The unique presence and emergence of divinity is to be found differently in the artist, intellectual, working man, contemplative, activist, parent, offspring, young, old, very old, sick, lonely, learned, simple, disappointed, happy, primitive, sophisticate, and in every other form of human existence. And the more different the life states and life experiences of others are from my own, the more important it is that I am open to God's presence therein in order to fill out my experience of divinity.

5. Since my initial and continuously primary encounter with reality is in the encounter with myself, so it is that all other experiences filter

---

[76] *Jn.* 1.5.

through this essential one.[77] I must in particular experience the birth and evolution of God in my own being and come to know the manner in which God uses my activity as the proximate instrument of His emergence and growth, if I am to experience His coming alive in the struggles of others. Most important, I must experience how God can use my natural limitations and personal deficiencies as instrumentalities of His birth and evolution in me—how His Joy, Love, Wisdom, Power, Causality and Mercy can come alive in me not only in spite of my sorrow, lovelessness, foolishness, weakness, sterility, and deficiencies, but in, through, and out of these limitations when they are embraced by me with confidence in His creative power to bring being out of my nothingness. The man who has never experienced God transforming godlessness into godliness in his own person, has no basis for an ecumenical dialogue that will allow him to experience God's creative emergence in and through the deficiencies of others.

6. The ecumenical thrust in me that impels me to search more broadly and deeply in others to fill out my experience of God is itself the fruit of godliness evolving in me. Since this evolution in godliness conflicts with many of my natural tendencies it encounters intense resistance and only grows out of my struggles and prayers. I should be prepared to encounter in my ecumenicity the same pitfalls, ups and downs, lagging interest and will, and all the other phenomena which exercise a curbing and negative influence on my spiritual development.

7. I should be prepared to discover three basic, successive patterns at work in my approach to human nature, my own and others, as the point of my experience of divinity. In the first stage there will be the inevitable, often unconscious, exaggerated confidence in the radical godliness of human nature as contributing to the experience of divinity. The second stage will involve the equally inevitable disillusionment with human nature, my own and others, as an active source of contact with God. The third stage will entail a reconversion to human nature with renewed confidence in its power to provide the primary, principal contact with God when it is approached with the explicit, purified awareness of the essential role of God as first and universal cause in the

---

[77] *Cf.* Chapter Three, Section III.

being and activity of man. It is as this third stage of reconversion to human nature as the active, proximate source of the experience of God's emerging out of the creative efforts of man's radical godliness operating as the instrument of divine action, that mature ecumenism commences.

8. Since God is present more fully in the whole of humanity than in any of its parts, and since His presence is interwoven throughout, and emerges from the deficiencies and inadequacies of human life as much as it proceeds from man's positive perfection, and since each part is related to the whole in such a way that it cannot be fully understood apart from the whole, I must embrace the entire of human nature in my ecumenism if I am to experience the fullness of God's presence in the whole and in each of its parts. I cannot approach human nature piecemeal, picking and choosing those aspects which I feel will offer contact with divinity, while eschewing other aspects which appear negative to me for the experiences of God, separating the cockle from the grain without throwing away the best with what seems to be only the worse.

If I am to espouse God's presence in reality and human nature, then like the young man in love who wishes to take his beloved to be his bride, I must take unto myself the totality of humanity for better or for worse, in sickness and in health until death.

If the young man in making his vows intends only to relate to those aspects of his bride that promise to be pleasant and satisfying to him while from the outset eliminating from their relationship any aspect of her that may cause tension and prove demanding or frustrating to him, it means that he does not love her as a person (that is in her totality), on the basis of equality. He wants her only as a means to serve his ends. And since her perfections and limitations are intimately interwoven so that one cannot be experienced apart from the other, in refusing to bring into his life her limitations, the young man effectively shuts out the experience of her true goodness and loveableness. Which is to say, he effectively shuts out her. His so called love for her turns out to be simply another expression of his egotistical love of himself.

Likewise, the ecumenist who approaches other men with his defenses up, filled with misgivings and built-in distrust, and unconsciously determined to relate to them on his own terms and in a way amenable to himself, is not searching for God's presence in other humans. He is only looking gingerly and inanely for himself.

Ecumenism, like ice water, must be plunged into at once and all the way. The person who dips his toe into ecumenism in order to determine whether the temperature is comfortable enough to allow him a painless entrance further, will be more repelled by it than attracted to it. Just as trial marriages rarely succeed because of the radical flaw in the whole of a conditional human relationship, so trial ecumenism is doomed to a similar fate since conditional ecumenism is not ecumenism at all.

9. In the demand of ecumenism that one relate in depth to the totality of human nature, we encounter the inevitability of the cross. Calvary was the predictable end effect of Christ's encounter with human nature as a whole. On Calvary Christ confronted the godlessness of human nature which he himself had flushed to the surface by threatening its existence with his appeal to the godliness of man.

Godliness and godlessness are so intimately inter-related in man that a person cannot address himself to one without confronting the other. If I am to experience God's presence in human nature, both my own and others, I must first experience His absence from human nature. And since God comes into existence through the radical godliness of man in a creating, evolving process, so that my experience of Him is found in my experience of man creating Him. The human nature I must draw close to for the experience of divinity, is the flawed, partially godless, evolving humanity out of which Divinity is emerging.

If I refuse the pain of this experience of man's radical godlessness, I withdraw from the experience of divinity in man's radical godliness. If I am to reach the third stage of development where I find mature ecumenism in the discovery of God's use of my humanity as an instrument effecting His presence, I must previously pass through the second stage by experiencing what my human nature can accomplish of its natural power without the special assistance of God. This experience in turn serves to purge me of the illusions of the first stage in which I have exaggerated the presence of divinity in my natural being.

The Apostle Peter became the conscious instrument of Divinity's presence in him only after he had gone through the hell of experiencing himself apart from that special presence. In Peter's encounter with the nothingness of Peter without God, He found the moment of conversion whereby he became everything with God. The cross for Peter was not some terrible sorrow inflicted upon him by forces from without. It was the agony and personal hell of confronting his own true humanity in its depth and naked nothingness without illusion or pretence of being something apart from God. The cross, therefore, was the violence done to Peter's illusions about the divinity of Peter in his discovery of the full implications of his creatureliness apart from God. Only by the agony of finding and accepting himself fully as a creature that is nothing apart from God was Peter able to find, and accept, and experience God as God.

The experience of God in human nature is inseparable from and follows upon the experience of human nature as godless apart from God. It is the acceptance of the violence present in this emerging, evolving vision of one's nothingness apart from God, that is the cross, which distinguishes incipient ecumenism from mature ecumenism—separating the child from the adult.

As I have already proposed, it can be seen that all men are by nature ecumenically inclined in the sense that initially all instinctively seek to find in their individual and collective humanity the fullness of godliness (See Chapter Five Section IV). There is no merit in this since the impulse comes more from nature than from choice. It is only after they have discovered the struggle that must be undergone and the price that must be paid in order to earn the experience of God's evolving in the evolution of their own humanity that a few men continue along this path by conscious choice.

Again, all men naturally enjoy the easy, unearned experience of God's radiant presence in the sunsets of life. Few, however, are willing to make the sacrifice necessary to create His presence out of the poverty of their being and to share with others the pain of giving birth to God. The cup that Christ held out to the Apostles to be drained by them as the price they had to pay for the vision of God and which he himself consumed to the final drop on the Calvary, contained the bitter dregs of man's godlessness which must be experienced in depth before the experience of God's coming alive in human nature is to be earned and caused. The reason why we do not clearly see God in our humanity is that we are not willing, or too frightened to first truly see ourselves.

CHAPTER SIX

IMAGE OF GOD BY NATURE

I. IMAGE AND LIKENESS

Catholic doctrine affirms that created being is made in the imperfect likeness of its unique source—God the Father. Man. who represents the highest expression of participated divinity among visible entities by reason of his intellectual nature, boasts a special likeness to divinity. In order to differentiate this special likeness of human nature to God from the more imperfect likeness of created being in general, man is said in the biblical sense to have been made in the *image* of God. This doctrine of the imperfect likeness of created being in general to God and man's special likeness as image to the divine, expresses the traditional Catholic understanding of the divine presence in the created order.

Since in Catholic understanding it is the shared experience of divinity's presence in created being and human nature which provides the basis for ecumenical dialogue, this doctrine is particularly illuminative of the Catholic approach to ecumenism. It therefore merits special consideration in my efforts to develop a concept of ecumenism that is in harmony with traditional Catholic doctrine.

In his treatise on Man in the *Summa*, Aquinas devotes an entire question to man's special likeness to divinity as the image of God.[1] Since his treatment of this material presents the essential component of Aquinas' ecumenism, I will set forth his doctrine in detail and in his own words.

In the first article of this question Aquinas asks in a general way whether the image of God is in man. In his response he differentiates between image and likeness, and then excludes equality from belonging to the essence of image. In the context of this differentiation and clarification he responds that man is imperfectly the image of God:

> As Augustine says (QQ.83; qu. 74): "Where an image exists, there forthwith is likeness; but where there is likeness,

---

[1] Part I, Question 93, the End or Term of the Production of Man

there is not necessarily an image." Hence it is clear that likeness is essential to an image; and that an image adds something to likeness—namely, that it is copied from something else. For an image is so called because it is produced as an imitation of something else; wherefore, for instance, an egg, however much like and equal to another egg, is not called an image of the other egg because it is not copied from it.

But equality does not belong to the essence of an image; for as Augustine says (*ibid.*): "Where there is an image there is not necessarily equality," as we see in a person's image reflected in a glass. Yet this is of the essence of a perfect image; for in a perfect image nothing is wanting that is to be found in that of which it is a copy. Now it is manifest that in man there is some likeness to God, copied from God as from an exemplary. Yet this likeness is not one of equality, for such an exemplar infinitely excels its copy. Therefore, there is in man a likeness to God; not indeed a perfect likeness, but imperfect. And Scripture implies the same when it says that man was made *to* God's likeness; for the preposition *to* signifies a certain approach, as of something at a distance.[2]

Next, in article 2, Aquinas inquires whether the image of God is to be found in irrational creatures. After expounding further on the difference between image and likeness he concludes that it belongs only to intellectual creatures properly speaking to be the image of God:

Not every likeness, not even what is copied from something else, is sufficient to make an image; for if the likeness be only generic, or existing by virtue of some common accident, this does not suffice for one thing to be the image of another. For instance, a worm, though from man it may originate, cannot be called man's image, merely because of the generic likeness. Nor, if anything is made white like something else, can we say that it is the image of that thing, for whiteness is an accident belonging to many species. But the nature of an image requires likeness in species; thus the image of the king exists in his son: or at least, in some

---

[2] *Summa*, I, q. 93, a. 1c.

specific accident and chiefly in the shape; thus, we speak of man's image in copper. Whence Hilary says pointedly that "an image is of the same species."

Now it is manifest that specific likeness follows the ultimate difference. But some things are like to God first and most commonly because they exist; secondly, because they live; and thirdly because they know or understand; and these last, as Augustine says "approach so near to God in likeness that among all creatures nothing comes nearer to Him." It is clear, therefore, that intellectual creatures alone, properly speaking, are made to God's image.[3]

After concluding in article 3 that, absolutely speaking, angels are more in the image of God than man, while granting that in some respects human nature is more like to God than the angelic nature, for example, man's ability to beget man, Aquinas questions in article 4 whether the image of God is found in every man.

Since man is said to be to the image of God by reason of his intellectual nature, he is the most perfectly like God, according to that in which he can best imitate God in his intellectual nature. Now the intellectual nature imitates God chiefly in this, that God understands and loves Himself. Wherefore we see that the image of God is in man in three ways. First, inasmuch as man possesses a natural aptitude for understanding and loving God; and this aptitude consists in the very nature of the mind, which is common to all men. Secondly, inasmuch as man actually or habitually knows and loves God, though imperfectly; and this image consists in the conformity of grace. Thirdly, inasmuch as man knows and loves God perfectly; and this image consists in the likeness of glory. Wherefore on the words, "The light of Thy countenance, O Lord, is signed upon is" (*Ps.* iv. 7), the gloss distinguishes a threefold image, of *creation*, of *re-creation*, and

---

[3] *Summa,* I, q. 93, a/ 2c.

of *likeness*. The first is found in all men, the second only in the just, the third only in the blessed.[4]

In distinguishing the three ways in which man is the image of God, Aquinas makes no mention in this text of man's status as the image of God by reason of his actual knowledge and love of God achieved through purely natural resources. This way stands between the first by which man has conformity to divinity through his natural aptitude for knowledge and love of God and the second in which man has such conformity through grace. In other texts, however, where he treats of man's realization of his natural aptitude for such knowledge and love of divinity, Aquinas affirms that man possesses the likeness to God of image, though he finds this to be a *disfigured* and *clouded* image.

> The meritorious knowledge and love of God can be in us only by grace. Yet there is a certain natural knowledge and love as seen above (Q.12,a.12;Q.56,A.3;Q.60,A.5). This too is natural that the mind, in order to understand God, can make use of reason, in which sense we have already said that the image of God abides ever in the soul; "whether this image of God be so obsolete" as it were clouded, "as almost to amount to nothing, as in those who have not the use of reason;" "or obscured and disfigured," as in sinners; or "clear and beautiful," as in the just; as Augustine said (*De Trin.* xiv.6).[5]

It is this status of man as the image of God in the natural order by reason of his realized natural godliness that is the object of my present concern since it provides the theoretical basis in Aquinas of an ecumenical dialogue in the natural order. In Chapter Seven I will examine the ecumenical implications of Aquinas' doctrine on man's likeness to God as image by reason of grace.

Having set forth the general basis on which human nature is considered to be the image of God, in article 6 Aquinas probes to determine under what specific aspect of his humanity man is constituted the image of God. He concludes that it is man's mind alone which is properly the subject of this conformity of image, whereas the other aspects

---

[4] *Ibid.*, I, q.93, a. 4c.
[5] *Ibid.*, I. q.93, a. 8, ad 3.

of human nature possess only the more imperfect likeness to God which is found in created being in general.

> While in all creatures there is some kind of likeness to God, in the rational creature alone we find a likeness of *image* as we have explained above (AA.1,2); whereas in other creatures we find a likeness by way of a *trace*.
>
> Now the intellect or mind is that whereby the rational creature excels other creatures; wherefore this image of God is not found even in the rational creature except in the mind; while in the other parts, which the rational creature may happen to possess, we find the likeness of a *trace*, as in other creatures to, which in reference to such parts, the rational creature can be likened. We may easily understand the reason of this if we consider the way in which a *trace*, and the way in which an *image*, represents anything. An *image* represents something by likeness in species, as we have said; while a *trace* represents something by way of an effect, which represents the cause in such a way as both to attain to the likeness of species. For imprints which are left by the movements of animals, are called *traces*: so also ashes are a trace of fire, and desolation of the land a trace of a hostile army.[6]

Finally, Aquinas argues in article 7 that it is not simply the mind, which is the subject of conformity to God as image, but it is the mind in operation with the very act by which man knows and loves God that first and foremost constitutes him the image of God:

> As above explained (a. 2), a certain representation of the species belongs to the nature of an image. Hence, if the image of the Divine Trinity is to be found in the soul, we must look for it where the soul approaches the nearest to a representation of the species of the Divine Persons are distinct from each other by reason of the procession of the Word from the Speaker, and the procession of Love connecting both. But in our soul word "cannot exist without actual thought," as

---

[6] *Ibid.*, I, q. 93, a. 6c.

Augustine says (*De Trin.* xiv.7). Therefore, first and chiefly, the image of the Trinity is to be found in the acts of the soul, that is, inasmuch as from the knowledge which we possess, by actual thought we form an internal word; and thence break forth into love. But, since the principles of acts are the habits and powers, and everything exists virtually in its principle, therefore, secondarily and consequently, the image of the Trinity may be considered as existing in the powers, and still more in the habits, forasmuch as the acts virtually exist therein.[7]

From this doctrine of Aquinas the following conclusions may be drawn:

1. All created being is made in the imperfect likeness of God and therefore provides an imperfect revelation of, and point of contact with divinity. Wherever in the created order we encounter participated being, truth, goodness, love, life, beatitude, power and causality, we find there an imperfect likeness of, and point of possible union with essential Being, Truth, Love, Life, Beatitude, Omnipotence, and First Causality.

2. By reason of his intellectual nature man possesses the special likeness of image to God and provides an essentially higher revelation of divinity and, therefore, a more ideal point of contact with divinity.

3. Man is most properly constituted the image of god and, therefore, best reveals and provides access to God when he is in the very act of loving contemplation of God.

4. The quality and perfection of this act of loving contemplation, and the intimacy and depth of our encounter with it, will determine the quality and perfection of our encounter with divinity in the created order.

5. Since the act of loving contemplation of God is the highest expression and revelation of man's aptitude for godliness and being, it is in this act in which man comes closest to God that he comes closest to himself and realizes his own true identity.

---

[7] *Ibid.*, I, q. 93, a. 7c.

IMAGE OF GOD BY NATURE

6. One cannot separate the encounter with the highest expression of divine life in the created order from the encounter with the fullest realization of human life in the same order. The closer one comes to the complete, ideal realization of human existence in breadth and in depth, the closer one is to the fullest presence of participated divinity in created being.

The doctrine of Aquinas can be expressed in terms of my analysis concerning the relationship between the positive perfections of created and Uncreated Being as understood in Catholic tradition. According to this tradition God is defined as essential, eternal, infinite, perfect, immutable, personal Being, Truth, Love, Life, Beatitude, Omnipotence and First Cause. By nature God is wrapped in the eternal loving contemplation of Himself. This loving conscious self-possession constitutes His Life and Beatitude. Within this eternal consciousness is present the ordering and controlling divine act from which all other being comes into existence and is sustained in existence as the expression of Himself.

Whatever perfections of being, truth, love, life, beatitude, power, and causality are present in created entities come from and imperfectly reflect the Being, Truth, Love, Life, Beatitude, Omnipotence, and Causality of God. Man as part of the created order shares in his irrational parts in the general likeness of created being to God. That is to say apart from his mind, man's nature manifests the same *traces* of divinity, which are found in all irrational aspects of created being. There is the same non-conscious intelligibility, goodness, natural appetite, expressions of divine life, beatitude, power, and causality, which created being in general manifest.

However, by reason of his intellectual nature, there is also present in man a conscious dimension of reality, existing in and operating along with his irrational aspects. This endows him with a unique participation in divine consciousness and life, and constitutes his special likeness to God as image. By reason of this conscious dimension man is not only intelligible, but he is also capable of actually knowing himself, created being, and God; man has not only natural goodness and appetite, but he can consciously love the good, both created and uncreated; human nature is not only the expression of divine life and beatitude, but it boasts a consciousness and self-possession, which is analogous to divine life and beatitude; human nature not only participates in divine power and causality in the manner in which irrational being shares in this power and causality, but it is capable of a conscious mastery by which man can order himself and created entities to the ends determined by God, and consciously under God impart a share in his special participated divinity to other beings.

Therefore, in man's aptitude for loving consciousness of God with all that this implies in terms of hold on life, beatitude, power, and causality, he transcends the general likeness to God of his irrational aspects and of created being in general, and achieves the unique status of image of God. As long as this aptitude for knowing and loving God remains unrealized, man is only potentially the image of God. To the extent that he exercises this aptitude in the actual attainment of such knowledge and love, man becomes in actuality the image of God. And to the extent that he is actually the image of God—he is fully human, realizes his true identity, and becomes both the highest natural expression of divinity in the visible created order and the ideal point of contact with God.

II. THE EVOLUTION OF MAN AS IMAGE OF GOD

Man's natural perfection as the actual image of God is not something that comes together with the gift of existence itself. It is not a state that is instantaneously realized in him. Man begins existence on the rational level with nothing more than a specific potentiality for knowing and loving; possessing the potentiality of mastering, to a degree, reality both created and uncreated.[8]

His movement from potential to actual perfection as image of God, which is to say from potential to actual true self, is a gradual, difficult, lifelong, partially merited transition in which the full utilization of his inner principles of development (that is this radical godliness) exercises an essential role under the movement of God. In his transition from

---

[8] "Now the intellect is only a potentiality in the genus of intelligible beings, just as primary matter is a potentiality as regards sensible beings; and hence it is called *possible*. Therefore in its essence the human mind is potentially understanding. Hence it has in itself the power to understand, but not to be understood, except as it is made actual." *Ibid.*, I,q.87, a.1c .

potential to actual godliness (image of God) man reverses the pattern of movement by which created being proceeds into existence from the actual perfection of God. In order to understand this transition better and to grasp the reversal of the work of creation involved in it, it would be desirable to reflect once again on the stages of creation and on the relation of God to created being as the opposite of man's relation to it in his evolution to godliness.

The Beginning
In the beginning God alone exists, personal, essential Being who is eternal, immutable, perfect, self-sufficient, self-contained. The act of creation originates in the autonomous existence of God's eternal, loving, conscious possession of Self wherein we find the essential, actual Being, Truth, Love, and Life which is the divine essence. This Being, Truth, Love, Life, Beatitude, Omnipotence, Causality, Justice, and Mercy, which is God, in no way depends upon the being, truth, goodness, life, beatitude and other perfections of created being, and therefore is not altered, expanded or contracted, enriched or impoverished, by the existence or non-existence of created being.

God does not grow in His truth by knowing the truth of created being, but the truth of created being is derived from and imperfectly reflects the eternal, immutable Truth of God. God does not love creatures because they are good, but they are good because He creatively loves them, imparting to them a share in His infinite goodness.

God does not come alive to the perfections of created being but these perfections come into existence out of the self-contained Life of God. God does not find fulfillment and beatitude in created goodness, but from His essential, infinite Beatitude He endows creatures with their limited power to fulfill.

God does not achieve inner unity and power by ordering created entities to a unified goal as parts of a whole, but created beings proceed into, and are sustained in existence in an ordered, unified, responsive way out of the inner power and unity of God.

God does not become just by giving to creatures their due, and merciful by giving them more than their due, but because God is Just and Merciful creatures come into existence possessing all that is due to them and more.

The First Stage
Out of God's perfect, unalterable, self-contained, eternal, infinite, loving, conscious possession of Self proceeds created being made in the image (in its rational parts) and likeness (in its irrational parts) of its source; containing individually and, more fully, collectively (as parts ordered to a whole) the perfections of its source. Man comes into existence as an integral part of the visible universe. In his irrational parts he shares in the likeness (*traces*) of divinity common to created being in general. By reason of his mind with its aptitude for knowing and loving God he possesses the special likeness to god of image. However, whereas in God His loving self possession is actual, eternal, immutable, essential, and perfect; in man the capacity for God-consciousness is radically potential, temporal, changeable, accidental, imperfect.

Man begins his existence as far removed from the actuality of God's conscious self-possession as an intellectual being can exist and still be intellectual.[9] The next step down in the scale of being from man's purely potential aptitude for divine consciousness takes one out of the intellectual order entirely. A being that is neither actually or potentially conscious, is one that is simply not intellectual. Thus man starts his existence on the periphery of intellectual existents. As he moves from this periphery of purely potential knowledge and love toward the center of actual divine consciousness by the actualization of his aptitude for knowing and loving God, man becomes more fully the actual image of God and his own true human reality.

The Second Stage
In this initial stage of existence in which man possesses the capacity for knowing and loving God while in fact being bereft of any actual consciousness whatsoever, he finds himself surrounded by the visible universe which, in both its rational and irrational parts, possesses in varying degrees actual participated divinity; that is actual being, truth, goodness, love, life, power, and causality. Man comes into existence as an integral part of this visible universe, oriented by nature to achieve

---

[9] *Ibid.*, I, q. 58, a. 3; q. 79, a.8; q. 93, a. 3.

IMAGE OF GOD BY NATURE

his realization and special expression of godliness through his identification with the fullness of God's presence in created being.

Initially man is that *tabula rasa*[10] in whom no movement of conscious love, life, happiness, power, and creativity is to be found, but who is vitally disposed to respond to the actual being, truth, goodness, love, life, beatitude, power and causality of the created order. In whatever direction he turns, man encounters the participated divinity of created being. His first contact with reality takes place through his senses whereby on the visible, tangible, audible level he confronts the actual godliness of created being.[11]

In a word, it is the actual godliness of the visible universe that causes the transition in man from potential godliness to actual godliness; from his potential self to his actual self; from being the potential image of God to the state of actual image of God.[12] It is the actual image of God in rational creatures and the actual likeness to God in irrational creatures that proximately causes the actual image of God to evolve in the individual—who is by nature the potential image of the divine.

In this initial development we find the reversal of the pattern of creation whereby created being is related to God. In that pattern the

---

[10] Blank Slate—The mind in its hypothetical blank or empty state before receiving outside information.

[11] *Summa*, I, q. 84, a. 6; q. 85, a. 1.

[12] "What is contained in the intellect as an interior word is by common usage said to be a conception of the intellect. A being is said to be conceived in a corporeal way if it is formed in the womb of a living animal by a life giving energy in virtue of the active function of the male and the passive function of the female, in whom the conception takes place. The being thus conceived shares in the nature of both parents and resembles them in species. In a similar manner what the intellect comprehends is formed in the intellect, the intelligible object being as it were, the active principle, and the intellect the passive principle. Thus what is comprehended by the intellect, existing as it does within the intellect, is conformed both to the moving intelligible object of which it is a certain likeness, and to the quasi-passive intellect, which confers on it the intelligible existence. Hence what is comprehended by the intellect is fittingly called the concept of the intellect." *Compendium*, c.38.

actuality of God causes the potential and actual godliness of created being. The Being, Truth, Love, and Life of God causes the being, truth, goodness, love and life of created entities. In man's initial relation to created being, this order is reversed. It is not the truth and love in man that causes the truth and goodness of created being, but the truth and goodness of created being cause truth, love, and life in man. It is the actual godliness in created being that proximately stirs to actuality the potential god in man.

III. THE UNIVERSE AS THE WOMB OF GOD

Given our understanding of man's evolution in perfection, the universe may be conceived of, in a manner of speaking, as the womb of God. In it a man finds himself in the first stage of his existence in an ideal habitat of enveloping godliness. It sustains and nourishes through every aspect of its being the potential godliness (image of God) proper to him. The more broadly and profoundly he unites his being with the godliness of this environment and the more fully he feeds upon divinity's presence in the universe, the more he will mature in his own godliness and advance toward the realization of his true identity as the actual image of God.

While man can nourish his aptitude as image of the divine by feeding on God's presence in the participated divinity of both irrational and rational aspects of created being, it is not an either/or choice which confronts him. Man is not free to feed the hunger for special likeness to God with the godliness of irrational creatures to the exclusion of human nature, or purely with the godliness of human nature to the exclusion of irrational beings. The godliness of irrational and rational creatures is so interwoven as mutually perfecting parts of a unified whole, that one cannot exist fully without the other.

Human nature begins to be actualized on the level of mind by its encounter with the actual truth and goodness of irrational creatures. It is only as man becomes actually knowing and loving as a result of this encounter that he in turn can feed the hunger for knowledge and love in other humans and also impart new perfection to the potential, perfectible aspects of irrational beings.

Apart from this initial encounter with the actual truth and goodness of irrational beings, human nature on the level of mind remains purely an *aptitude* for knowledge and love. Since the potential is not intelligible of itself, human nature in this state of non-conscious existence is neither known or loved by itself, and presents nothing knowable and loveable on the level of mind to other men.[13] Nor does it exercise a perfecting activity on irrational creatures. It is therefore through the possession of the truth and goodness of the visible universe that man as mind becomes knowing and loving—and thereby perfecting of both rational and irrational creatures. When he possesses this truth and goodness of created being in such fullness and depth as to be able to lovingly contemplate the revelation of truth and the Perfect Good in the truth and goodness of the universe, then man becomes the actual image of God. He becomes capable both of elevating other men to a similar level of perfection, and of bringing the potential godliness of irrational creatures to ideal realization by using them to sustain in humans their loving encounter with divinity.

Consider the example of a man who is rapt in the contemplation of the awesome beauty and mystery of a sunset. In his loving contemplation of this godly phenomenon, we can distinguish three distinct encounters implicitly, if not explicitly, taking place in him. First, there is his encounter with the godliness and participated divinity of the sunset. Secondly, since man's potential as one who can wonder at the beautiful and mysterious is actualized by the power of the sunset, evoking conscious, affective responses from him, there is also an encounter with his own reality as a contemplator of sunsets. Third, implicit in these first two encounters is an encounter with God as revealed to the man both in the awesome spectacle of the sunset, and, more perfectly and mysteriously still, in his own conscious response to that phenomenon.

If the first encounter remains a relatively superficial one, so that the man's consciousness rests in his wonder at the sensible beauty without encompassing the full dimensions of his experience, he will fail to

---

[13]"Now the human intellect is only a potentiality in the genus of intelligible beings, just as primary matter is a potentiality as regards sensible beings; and hence it is called *possible*. Therefore in its essence the human mind is potentially understanding. Hence it has in itself the power to understand, but not to be understood, except as it is made actual.... Therefore the intellect knows itself not by its essence, but by its act." *Summa*, I, q. 87, a. 1.

advert to the even more wonderful revelation of the mystery of human life that vainly awaits him in the unrealized second encounter with himself as a contemplator of the miracles and beauties of nature. However, if his first encounter goes to the next level of awareness he will find himself marveling both at the miracle of the sunset and at the created miracle of his own reality as a contemplator of sunsets.[14]

Should he go to the final depths of the mystery of his experience he will find himself contemplating in awe the Source both of the miracle of the godliness of the sunset (*trace*) and the miracle of the godliness of his own existence as a loving contemplator of a God (*image*) who reveals Himself in and through both sunsets and man's contemplating sunsets.[15] In this encounter with himself (human nature) not merely as one who knows and loves God's revealing presence in sunsets (that is in the *traces* of God), but as one who knows and loves God in his substantially more revealing presence in himself as one who knows and loves God (that is an *image* of God), he is in the presence of the highest natural revelation of divinity in the created visible order. He touches upon that point in reality that on the natural level provides the most ideal contact with God.

Among those who hold that created being imperfectly reveals divinity and serves as the point of man's contact with God, some tend

---

[14] "Therefore the intellect knows itself not by its essence, but by its act. This happens in two ways: In the first place, singularly, as when Socrates or Plato perceives that he has an intellectual soul because he perceives that he understands. In the second place, universally, as when we consider the nature of the human mind from knowledge of the intellectual act. It is true, however, that the judgment and force of this knowledge, whereby we know the nature of the soul, comes to us according to the derivation of our intellectual light from the Divine Truth which contains the types of all things as above stated. There is however, a difference between these two kinds of knowledge, and it consists in this, that the mere presence of the mind suffices for the first; the mind itself being the principle of action whereby it perceives itself, and hence it is said to know itself by its own presence. But as regards the second kind of knowledge, the mere presence of the mind does not suffice, and there is further required a careful and subtle inquiry. Hence many are ignorant of the soul's nature, and many have erred about it." *Summa*, I, q. 87, a. 1c.

[15] Ibid., I, q. 93, a. 7.

IMAGE OF GOD BY NATURE

to emphasize man's encounter with God in nature (in our example the sunsets) as offering a more ideal basis for the experience of the divine than that which is provided by human nature itself. Traditional Catholic doctrine rejects this position in which the likeness to God of irrational beings is given a greater capacity to reflect and reveal divinity than man himself created in the image of God.[16] It is man (human nature) contemplating the sunset who effects the conscious link between nature and God. The sunset has no consciousness of itself—to say nothing of an awareness of its source. Man by reason of his intelligence is capable not only of conscious awareness of the sunset, but of the whole of irrational being as well. Human nature thereby qualitatively transcends the accumulative perfection of irrational creatures.

The visible universe itself is not fully intelligible without the presence of man. For example, the existence of sunsets achieves final, full meaning, only with the presence of the contemplator savoring their magnificence.[17] The diversity of creatures proceeds from the divine unity, and all creatures are ordered to each other as parts of a unified whole—the lower being ordained to the higher. For this reason any effort to find ultimate meaning in a particular being when it is isolated from the rest of creation, and especially when isolated from the higher levels of created being which it is intended to serve, is doomed to failure.

---

[16] Ibid., I, q. 93, a. 2.

[17] "Now if we wish to assign as end to any whole, and to the parts of that whole, we shall find, first that each and every part exists for the sake of its proper act, as the eye for the act of seeing; secondly, that the less honorable parts exist for the more honorable, as the senses for the intellect, the lungs for the heart; and thirdly, that all parts are for the perfection of the whole, as the matter for the form, since the parts are, as it were, the matter of the whole. Furthermore, the whole man is on account of an extrinsic end, that end being the fruition of God. So, therefore, in the parts of the universe also every creature exists for its own proper act and perfection, and the less noble for the nobler, as those creatures that are less noble than man exist for the sake of man, whilst each and every creature exists for the perfection of the entire universe." *Summa*, I, q. 65, a. 2c.

THE THEOLOGY OF ECUMENISM

The experience of god in created being entails, among other things, the experience of the underlying unity from which the diversity of creatures proceeds. Any fragmentation or isolation of a part of created being separates it from the whole. It separates us also from the full experience of God's presence in that part which can be attained only when it is related to the whole.

Others stress contact with God through human nature to the relative exclusion of irrational being as exercising a significant role in the experience of the divine in created being. Urbanization and the technological age, which surround man with human artifacts and separate him from any significant contact with nature, tend to force this condition on him.[18] Irrational beings are seen more as providing material for man's use and manipulation than as providing objects for contemplation. Catholic tradition while affirming the priority of human nature as the primary, principal point of contact with God in the created order, emphasizes also the significant, substantial role that irrational creatures exercise in contributing to man's experience of the divine in the totality of created being.

Among others considerations this tradition asserts that man exists as an essential part of the visible universe and that he cannot achieve his full development of self and experience of God's presence in his own humanity without existing in a mutually perfecting relation with the rest of the universe. This contribution of the visible universe to man's experience of God's presence in the entirety of created being is admirable highlighted in the sanctifying role of irrational creatures in the liturgy and sacramental practices of the Catholic Church. And yet, while *affirming* this role of the visible universe in man's encounter with himself and God, the Church teaches always that man's primary and principal contact with God takes place in and through human nature as the image of God. It is man's experience of his humanity in the act of loving contemplation of God that brings him closest to himself and to God. And it is the sharing of this conscious loving experience of God by men that is the essence of ecumenical dialogue.

---

[18] H. Cox, *op.cit.* pp. 21-24; K. Rahner, *Theological Investigations*, No. VI, pp. 5-11.

IMAGE OF GOD BY NATURE

As the individual evolves to the perfection of actual image of God, his relation to surrounding reality undergoes a significant change. While continuing to feed on the actual godliness of created being to sustain the perfection already achieved and to develop further the remaining potentiality of his being, he begins to impart to the perfectible aspects of his environment a share in that perfection (godliness) that has matured in him. The cosmos still remains a womb for him, but he ceases purely to feed on it and now commences to fecundate its perfectible aspects with his partially realized godliness.[19]

As the child image of God in him becomes in certain respects the adult image of God, he in a godly exercise of power and causality begins to perfect the potential godliness of his surroundings while the child image part of him continues to feed on the actual godliness of those same surroundings. This relation of the individual to the visible universe in which he is first perfected by its actual godliness while continuing to be nourished by it in his own potential parts, creates a continuing cycle of mutually perfecting dialogue between the individual and the universe. This cycle is expressed by the diagram 6-1.

If I were to elaborate a description of this cycle in terms of my analogy to the cosmic womb, I would say that in the first phase of this circulatory movement (A →B →C) the actual godliness of created being (A) as a kind of father principle acts on the potential godliness of the individual (B) as the mother principle, giving birth in him to the actual knowledge and love of God in the image and likeness of God's revealing presence in created being (A) as the Author of Nature.[20] That is to say, the actual being, truth, goodness, love, life, beatitude and power of created being (A), as a participation in, and revelation of, the Being, Truth, Love, Life, Beatitude, and Power of God, acts on man's

---

[19] *Compendium*, c. 24.

[20] "What is conceived in the intellect is a likeness of the thing understood and represents its species; and so it seems to be a sort of offspring of the intellect. Therefore when the intellect understands something other than itself, the thing understood is, so to speak, the father of the word conceived in the intellect, and the intellect resembles rather a mother whose function is such that conception takes place in her." *Compendium*, c. 39.

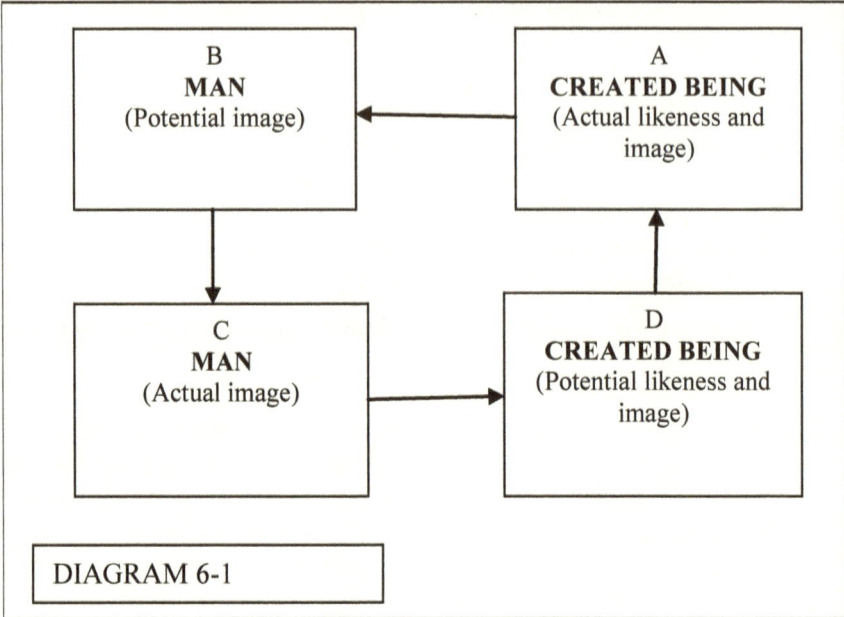

DIAGRAM 6-1

aptitude for conscious being, truth, love, life beat-itude, and power (B) effecting in him the emergence of the actual knowledge and love of God (C) with its concomitant participation in the being, life, beatitude, and power of God after the manner of God's participated presence in created being (A). In the second phase (C ➔D ➔A) the actual knowledge and love of god now present in the individual (C) permits him to impart to the perfectible aspects of cre-ated being (D), his own and others, a share in the actual godliness which has come alive in him through the medium of the actual god-liness of created being (A). That is to say, by virtue of the actual truth, love, goodness, life, beatitude, and power now present in him, he can act on the perfectible aspects of created being (D), both in its irrational and rational parts, and effect in them a development of their potential godliness to actual godliness.

He may act on irrational creatures by consciously ordering them to those uses and purposes which, from his acquired knowledge of God, he knows to be in harmony with the divine will; thus assisting them to achieve their ideal participation in divinity by functioning in the cosmos according to the plan decreed for them by the eternal law. He may perfect rational beings especially by sharing with them the knowledge and love of God which has come alive in him, thus assisting them both to develop from potential images of God to actual images of the divine, and to realize their own true identity.

In this circulatory, mutually perfecting movement between the individual and the universe, in which created being under God develops collectively and in a self-sufficient process to actual godliness, we find a form of ecumenical dialogue in which the individual feeds on the actual godliness of created being and shares his own godliness with it—it is the underlying dynamic of this evolution.

At the center of this cycle, as the heart whose beat sustains the movement toward godliness between the individual and the cosmos, is man's exercise of free will. Through free will he can consciously choose both to open himself to the actual godliness of created being and to impart a share in his acquired godliness back to the perfectible aspects of created being.

IV. FREEDOM AS MIDWIFE

In his evolution from potential to actual image of God, man's exercise of freedom functions somewhat in the role of a midwife. By opening himself to the actual godliness of created being in general—rational and irrational—so as to effect in man actual knowledge and love of God as the Author of nature, freedom nurses man into existence as the actual image of God. Thereupon freedom serves to enhance further man's likeness to God as image by imparting a share of his newly acquired godliness back to the perfectible aspect, that is the potential godliness of created being. In addition freedom functions as a midwife while it assists at bringing into existence the actual likeness and image of god in *other* creatures as they are perfected by the activity of the person in whom freedom resides. In the performance of this function freedom enjoys a limited, relative role since it is consciously realizing a plan already predetermined by eternal law, and not in an absolute manner creating a plan of its own.[21]

---

[21] In like manner neither is natural necessity repugnant to the will. Indeed, more than this, for as the intellect of necessity adheres to the first principles, the will must of necessity adhere to the last end, which is happiness: since

Nature precedes intellect and, therefore, freedom. A man's power of self-determination exists in a nature already determined in its specific potentiality, thrust, and final goal. Man's freedom cannot ignore or alter the basic structure of his nature and the ultimate goal to which it is directed. Also, the created reality that freedom encounters is already determined independently of man in its potential and actual godliness, and in its radical capacity to actualize the potential godliness of human nature. Since man's nature is ordered by God to its final goal and created reality in general is fixed in its capacity to contribute to man's attainment of that goal, freedom, with its power to act or not act, and to choose from among various means by which this goal may be pursued, functions to implement the divine plan.[22]

The perfection of freedom therefore consists in the ability to operate in conscious harmony with the divine will,[23] by the ability to grasp the nature and thrust of man's potential, by understanding the contribution that the godliness of created being is to make man's development, and by consciously relating his potential to the entirety of created being. In this way the divine intention is realized whereby man becomes the actual image of God through the mediation of the created universe.

Since human nature is created to achieve its perfection in the actual knowledge and love of God, man comes into existence as an intellectual being endowed both with the faculties necessary for such knowledge and love, and with an unalterable, necessary thrust toward

---

the end is in practical matters what the principle is in speculative matters. For what benefits a thing naturally and immovably must be the root and principle of all else appertaining thereto, since the nature of a thing is the first in everything, and every movement arises from something immovable..... We are master of our own actions by reason of our being able to choose this or that. But choice regards not the end, but the means to the end....Wherefore the desire of the ultimate end does not regard those actions of which we are masters. *Summa*, I, q. 82, a. 1c.

[22]"Now it is from the eternal law, which is the Divine Reason, that human reason is the rule of the human will, from which the human will derive its goodness.... It is therefore evident that the goodness of the human will depends on the eternal law much more than on human reason; recourse to the Eternal Reason." *Summa*, I-II, q. 19, a. 4 c.

[23]*Ibid.*, I-II, q. 19, a. 9 c.

IMAGE OF GOD BY NATURE

Truth and the Perfect Good. Man thereby is the potential image of God by nature with all that this implies.

Human life in its initial stage of existence not only contains the seed of its evolution to the participated divine life of actual knowledge and love of God, but it is that seed! To the extent that man knows and loves God, he achieves his potential for being in actuality. As part of the visible universe man is oriented by nature toward the whole of created being so as to evolve through the medium of God's participated divinity in the created order to his natural perfection as image of God. This is to say that by nature man is designed to experience the presence of God in the created order, and to seek union with Uncreated Truth, Love, Life, and Being through encounter with His participated presence in the being, truth, goodness, and life of created reality. This is to say, further, that man by nature is ecumenical in the sense that his natural, necessary thrust is to search instinctively for the experience of God in his encounter with created being.

Aquinas offers many examples of this naturally ecumenical thrust of human nature. For one, Aquinas argues that by nature man loves himself as *part* of the *whole* of created being, loving more the whole than himself as part, and loving still more the Source of the whole than the whole itself.[24] Were man by nature to love himself, a part, more than he loved the whole and the Source of the whole, this love, which is essential to him, would be perverse. It is because man is disposed by nature to love God more than created being in general and himself in particular, that charity, the divinely infused, supernatural love of God, does not destroy this aspect of man's nature, but elevates and perfects it.[25]

---

[24] *Ibid.*, I - II, q. 109 , a. 3.

[25] "Consequently, since God is the universal good, and under this good both man and angel and all creatures are composed, because every creature in regard to its entire being naturally belongs to God, it follows that from natural love angel and man alike love God before themselves and with a greater love. Otherwise, if either of them loved self more than God, it would follow that natural love would be perverse, and that it would not be perfected but destroyed by charity." *Ibid.*, I, q. 60, a. 5c.

Thus by nature man looks for the Perfect Good in his encounter with the mutable good of created being. He naturally tends to relate the particular good to the whole of created good, and this whole of created good to the Perfect Good. So also man naturally, necessarily loves Truth, and instinctively seeks the experience of Truth in the truths of the created order. Therefore by nature, and not initially by choice, man is inclined to relate particular truths to the fullness and totality of created truth as the revelation and point of contact with Uncreated Truth. Thus man naturally will not rest until he come to the attainment of Ultimate Truth.[26]

When man knows an effect, by nature he yearns to understand its cause. When he encounters accidents, necessarily he seeks to know the substance. The more he knows, the more he naturally hungers to know. This pattern holds, as I have argued, with regard to man's hunger for Beatitude, Life, and Being itself. The point of all this is that the natural thrust which instinctively, necessarily impels man to seek his encounter with Being, Truth, Love, and Life, in the being, truth, goodness and life of the created order shows that the dynamics underlying the ecumenical impulse come not from a free, conscious, arbitrary choice which man is able to indulge in or reject at will, *but from the necessary inescapable workings of human nature itself.*

The objective order of the visible universe is so structured by God as to respond ideally to the natural, ecumenical thrust of human nature whereby man instinctively seeks the experience of God in the fullness of created being. This is another way of saying that the visible universe is designed by God to function as the womb of participated divine life, sustaining and nurturing in man his natural movement toward actual knowledge and love of God. The variety and multiplicity of created beings so proceed in an orderly fashion from the unity of God, as I have mentioned previously,[27] that each is related to the other, the lower to the higher, the perfectible to the perfecting and the part to the whole.[28] Only in the totality does one find the fullest expression of the participated divinity of created being. By reason of this order of the

---

[26] *Ibid.*, I-II, q. 3, a. 8.
[27] *Cf.* Chapter Three, Section III.
[28] *Ibid.*, I, q.47; *Compendium* cc. 73, 102.

parts of created being to a unified whole, each part opens up to every other part and to the whole, and to the Source of the whole and its parts. For example, the encounter with a particular good in the created order objectively leads to the encounter with other particular goods, which, in turn leads to the encounter with the fullness of created good, and finally to the encounter with the Perfect Good present in and revealed through the fullness of created good.

So also contact with a particular truth of the created order objectively leads to contact with other particular truths. In turn these lead to the encounter with the fullness of truth in created being and to contact with Truth at the source of created being, and finally, to contact with Truth at the source of created truth which is revealed in the truth of the universe.

This same objective pattern holds with regard to the other simple perfections of created being such as being itself, life, beatitude, and power. These in an orderly manner proceed in their diverse and multiple forms of created existence from the unity of God. In this ordering of multiple, diverse created beings in which the encounter with any part objectively opens one to other parts, then to the whole and finally to the source of the whole and its parts, we find the objective ecumenical disposition of created being which perfectly corresponds to the subjective ecumenical character of man's natural thrust toward his ultimate goal of knowing and loving God as experienced in and through created being. This perfect harmony between the subjective movement of man's nature and the objective ordering of created being is considered by Catholic tradition to be one more expression of the divine unity from which the diverse existences of the individual human nature and the cosmos distinct from that individual have proceeded and toward which by nature they are both ordered to return.[29]

In the exercise of his freedom man must be true to his own nature and to this structuring of the visible universe by consciously acting in harmony with the ecumenical character both of his subjective thrust for perfection and the objective ordering of created being. He is con-

---

[29] *Summa*, I, q. 47, a. 4.

sciously true to his nature when he understands that his instinctive, necessary hunger for perfection is specifically a hunger for Perfect Happiness in the attainment of the Perfect Good and Truth which is his ultimate goal and when he acts in a willed conformity with this awareness.

This entails, among other things, his recognition that in its depths his attraction toward created being takes place by reason of its participated divinity. It is the actual godliness of created being as the revelation of and point of encounter with the Creator Himself that naturally and necessarily draws man to his embrace of the visible universe. His conscious implementation of this fact of his being by a controlled, willed approach to created being which seeks always in the finitude, multiplicity, changeableness, and temporality of created being the Infinite, One, Immutable, and Eternal, and in the being, truth, goodness, life, and beatitude of created existence Uncreated Being, Truth, Love, Life and Beatitude, represents the perfection of man's exercise of freedom. Through this ideal use of free will the individual becomes proximately the cause of his own evolution from potential image of God to actual image. Thus, in a manner of speaking creating the god in him by causing the actual godliness and image of the divine in his person.

At the same time man is consciously true to the ecumenical character of the objective structure of created being when he approaches created reality explicitly as *created*—affirming the objective unity of created being whereby part is linked to part, and parts to the whole, and the whole to the Creator. In this way he is consciously open to the objective presence of the Infinite, One, Immutable and Eternal, in the finite, multiple, changeable, and temporal. He finds contact with Being, Truth, Love, Life, and Beatitude in the being, truth goodness, life and beatitude of created being. It is by reason of this objective link between parts, whole and Creator that man, in his encounter with parts of created reality, can consciously recognize, embrace, and achieve affective and effective union with God as his ultimate end in and through the mediation of created being.

Because man can achieve immediate contact with the Creator, the individual, while only part of the created reality, is in a sense able to transcend the whole of creation by reason of this direct link with his ultimate end.[30] However, in thus transcending the created order, it does not follow that man acts independently of, or outgrows the whole of created being since he still must achieve this transcending union with God in and through created reality.

It is also by reason of this objective link between part, whole, and Creator, that man, who as a finite agent cannot perform an act of infinite positive content, can in his encounter with the finite consciously close himself off to its objective link to the Infinite. He can thereby be consciously responsible for the absence of effective union with the Infinite and effect an infinite privation in his act. It is this understanding that explains in part the traditional Catholic doctrine on grave sin and the possibility of immeasurable evil in man's conscious behavior.

Since true love is a conscious attraction to the objective reality and goodness of the beloved object, man's love for the created universe, if it is to be true, must embrace the diversity of created goods in their relation to the unity of the Perfect Good from which they are derived. That is to say, true love for the visible universe requires that man love the parts of the created being (including himself) as *parts*, inseparable from and subordinate to the *whole*, and that he love the created whole as both *whole* and *created*, which is to say inseparable from and subordinate to the Creator. When man in a defective use of his freedom chooses to love the part as though it were the whole—the finite, temporal, imperfect, and multiple as though it were the Infinite, Eternal, Perfect, and One; being truth, goodness, life, and beatitude as though they were Being, Truth, Love, Life and Beatitude—he does violence both to the subjective thrust of his natural appetite and to the objective reality of created being.

This defective use of freedom also involves violence done to his relation to his Creator. In such defective behavior his conscious choice is out of harmony with his power of free choice circumscribed by the fixed demands of his nature concerning his ultimate end, and by the objective limitations of created being to function as a substitute for that

---

[30]Ibid., I, q. 65, a. 2.

end. Such defective exercises of freedom cannot radically alter or eliminate man's necessary thrust toward perfect happiness, or the limited capacity of created being to actualize that thrust. They can only retard it by presenting the particular good as though it were the universal good; created being as though it were Uncreated; and the means to the ultimate end as though they were the ultimate end—an effort at creating false gods for man to worship in the place of the true God to whose worship by nature he is impelled.

Such a defective exercise of freedom consists not so much in a form of non-ecumenical behavior as it does in an expression of false ecumenism in which a creature-god is made the object of shared experience in the place of the true God. The proper, perfect exercise of freedom entails a true ecumenism. In this a man's choice of means to his ultimate end is in conscious harmony with the ecumenical character of his subjective, natural appetite and the objective order of creatures whereby he consciously relates to the participated divinity of created being so as to achieve contact with God in and through the objective relation of the created universe to the Creator. This ecumenical character of man's use of freedom is also in harmony with the eternal law which decrees that man come to the experience of God in and through created being. It is through this ecumenical quality of his exercise of freedom that man causes himself to become the actual image of God.

V. IMAGE IN COMMUNITY

According to Catholic tradition man becomes the actual, natural image of God and the highest expression of and point of contact with divinity in the visible order by the act of knowing and loving God. Now no finite person can encompass in his limited knowledge, love, and power the infinite Truth, Love, and Omnipotence of God even in its restricted expression in the participated character of created being. As we have seen[31] the diversity and multiplicity of created beings are explained primarily by the divine will to share more fully with the collectivity of creatures His infinite goodness which cannot be given in such fullness to any individual creature.[32]

---

[31] *Cf.* Chapter Three, Section III.
[32] *Summa*, I, q. 47, a. 1.

IMAGE OF GOD BY NATURE

The closer creatures approach God by their participation in His divine perfections, the higher on the level of being and perfection they are and, therefore, the greater is the possibility of multiplication and diversification among them.[33] Since man comes closest to God in his act of knowing and loving divinity and in his actions in the practical order that proceed directly from such knowledge and love, it is especially true of human nature as the actual image of God that no one person can possess fully this participated likeness. Hence it is in this state that the possibility of multiplication and diversification of man's possession of such perfection is the greatest.[34]

A great many men reflecting diverse and complementary aspects of the Truth, Love, and Power of God are therefore required in order that human nature may more fully achieve the perfection of actual image of God. In the collectivity of men who are actual images of God, knowing and loving divine Truth and Goodness according to its diverse aspects as experienced on the human level, one finds a fuller expression of divinity in human nature than can be found in an isolated individual.

---

[33] "The possibility of multiplication applies to a thing in its intelligible being. For we grasp with our intellect many things which cannot have being in matter.... Now separate substances have intelligible being by their nature; and consequently a greater multiplicity is possible in them than in material substances, taking into account their respective properties and natures.... Therefore the multiplicity of separate substances surpasses that of material bodies" *Contra Gentiles*, Vol.II, p. 283.

[34] Aquinas argues for the existence of a vast number of angels both because their higher level of being permits of such multiplication and because it serves the purpose of creation for God to multiply the more perfect and noble beings. "Hence it must be said that the angels, even inasmuch as they are immaterial substances, exist in exceeding great number, far beyond all material multitude.... The reason whereof is this because, since it is the perfection of the universe that God chiefly intends in the creation of things, the more perfect some things are, in so much greater an excess are they created by God.... Hence it is reasonable to conclude that the immaterial substances as it were incomparably exceed material substances as to multitude." *Summa*, I, q. 50, a.3. These same arguments may be justly advanced in support of the existence of a multitude of actual images of God among men.

When the individuals of this collectivity enter into a community in which they mutually share their respective knowledge and love of God, and act concertedly in their exercise of the power over created being that proceeds from this knowledge and love, one finds in such a community of images of God the ultimate expression and revelation of divinity in human nature and the visible order. The embrace of, and active participation in, such a community of actual images of God, therefore, provides the most direct and ideal access to the experience of God in and through the visible universe that is available in the natural order.

Now such a community implies more than just a quantitative multiplication of men with their diverse insights into, and experiences of God. The very act of mutually sharing their encounter with God in the visible order not only enlarges the knowledge and love of God in them, but it provides an entirely new revelation and experience of divinity. In order to illustrate this I will draw once again on my example of the man's experience of God in his contemplation of the sunset. Let me add to this individual in his act of contemplation, the presence of a friend who shares with him this experience of God's revealing presence both in the sunset and in their response to His presence. In this instance each of them, as before, is able to experience an encounter with; first, the beauty of the sunset; secondly, the revelation of his reality as a contemplator of sunsets; and third, in depth, the revelation and experience of God as the Creator both of sunsets and men who contemplate sunsets.

To these three encounters which each is able to achieve independently of the presence of the other, several new encounters now take place in them by reason of their shared experience. First, there is the added contact with and experience of each other as persons who are able to contemplate God's revealing presence both in sunsets and in their enjoyment of sunsets. This entails a particularly profound experience of each other's human reality since, as I have noted,[35] a man is closest to himself and most fully himself in the act in which he knows and loves God. To experience a friend in that moment in which he is lovingly contemplating God, therefore, is to know him at the moment in which he is most fully himself.

---

[35] *Cf.* Chapter Six, Section III.

IMAGE OF GOD BY NATURE

Second, by reason of their shared experience each can fill out something of what is wanting in his knowledge and love of God Himself, and the sunset by what is present by way of complementary knowledge and love in the other. Since knowledge and love effect an indwelling of the known and loved in the person knowing and loving, something of what is wanting in knowledge and love in one friend while present in the other, becomes the possession of the former by his experience shared with the latter.[36]

Third, in the very act of sharing their mutual experience of God, they encounter a new revelation of God as one who creates not only sunsets and contemplators of sunsets, but also friendships and communities of images of God that are bound together by their shared experience of God. It is in the actual interplay of the truth and love of God binding men together in such friendships and communities as images of God in which they know and love God as the Creator of such communities of wisdom and love that God provides the ultimate heights of the revelation of Himself in the visible order.[37]

Now let us alter this example somewhat. In place of the two persons who are merely friends let us posit a husband and his wife. And for the sunset which they are contemplating let us substitute an infant, their offspring. These two changes introduce a significant new dimension into their experience of God's revealing presence in their shared relation. Now they not only marvel at the miracle of the child (far more wonderful than the sunset) and God's revelation of Himself as the Creator of children and themselves as contemplators of children, but they especially marvel at the mystery of their own being as proximate creators of the child and at God's revelation of Himself as the one who has endowed them with the divine power of begetting through co-operative effort an offspring made in their image and in the image of God Himself.

---

[36] "In like manner when a man loves another with the love of friendship, he wills good to him, just as he wills good to himself; wherefore he apprehends him as his other self, in so far, to wit, as he wills good to him, as to himself. Hence a friend is called man's other self...." *Summa*, I-II, q. 28, a.lc.

[37] *Ibid.* II-II, q. 23, a. 1.

THE THEOLOGY OF ECUMENISM

Over the years as the child matures they struggle in a complementary effort to grow in their shared knowledge and love of God so that together they may impart their perfection as actual images of God to their child, thereby assisting him to evolve as an actual image of God. Throughout this lifelong process of evolution in godliness, their shared experience of God in each other is not the experience of persons who posses mature, defined, terminal knowledge and love of God, but of persons who are struggling intensely in confusion and obscurity with mutual dependency to develop such knowledge and love in themselves not only for their own sake but in order that they may impart this perfection to their child. Thus their shared experience of God is the experience of one Who reveals Himself to them in their very effort to create His likeness in themselves and to impart this achieved likeness to others.

Since, as we have seen, men begin their existence as only potential images of God and must struggle with the aid of the actual godliness of created being to evolve in the knowledge and love by which they become actual images of God and capable of imparting their acquired perfection to others, a community of images of God assumes more the form of a husband-wife relationship than that of the two friends who share their experience of God in the contemplation of the sunset. In this latter experience, the friends do not create God's presence in the sunset, but finding Him already resplendently present, they can only marvel at the revelation. In the husband-wife relation, however, they themselves create God's presence in their begetting of the son as the actual image of themselves and the potential image of God. Having created the child-image of God in their son, they continue the process of causing God's participated presence by evolving from potential to actual images of God both for their own sakes and in order that they may assist the child to undergo a similar evolution in actual godliness. Thus the image of God that they experience in each other is an evolving image on which human nature is proximately the cause of the evolution. And so it is with men in general.

The image of God that is found in men in the present economy is an evolving image in which men, in a mutually perfecting and sustaining effort, must struggle and grope together in partial confusion and obscurity to acquire further insight into the Truth of God and more intense love for the Goodness of God in so far as His Truth and

Goodness are revealed in created being. Therefore, the person who seeks in the fullest degree possible to experience God's presence in the totality of human nature, must open himself not to a community of perfectly evolved images in whom the knowledge and love of God radiates in a mature, clear, and fully developed, errorless state, but to a community of partially realized images at best who continue to struggle in obscurity and doubt to develop further their imperfect knowledge and flawed love of God, and to impart the godliness already achieved to the rest of created being.

It is as an active member of such a community of imperfect images of God, struggling to evolve further in divine likeness, that man on the natural level encounters the highest expression of participated divinity in the visible universe and his point of ideal contact with God. It is in the manner and degree in which a man enters into dialogue with the knowledge and love of God found in the totality of actual images of God among men whenever and wherever they may be encountered, and collaborates with such images in the effort to impart this godliness to the rest of created being, that he himself evolves as an actual image of God and enters into an intimate union with his Creator. *Why* a man must enter into community with actual images of God in order to evolve from potential to actual image, and *how* in fact he enters into such community, invites more specific reflection since these questions touch on the essential dynamics of ecumenism and the ecumenical dialogue in the natural order.

Image in Community of Truth

Man's natural evolution as the image of God by way of his actual participation in Divine Truth is effected through his union with Uncreated Truth as revealed in and through created truth. Since the totality of created truth contains a fuller participation and revelation of Truth than any part, the more a man possesses the truth of created being in breadth and depth, the more ideal is his point of possible contact with Truth.

Now the attainment of truth in breadth and depth is not possible except in community with minds that already partially possess such truth. Therefore, in order that a man gain maximum access to created truth as a means of ideal access to Truth, he must enter into the broadest and deepest dialogue possible with truth in the minds of men wherever it is to be found.

Truth in Breadth

Created being and, therefore, created truth is so diverse and multiple in form that no one person or group of persons has access to its full range of expression. It requires many minds experiencing in a variety of ways over many years the richness and complexity of the created universe in order for the human mind collectively to begin to have some comprehension of the seemingly inexhaustible intelligibility of being. A constant cry of unhappiness that comes from the world of empirical sciences is that a person simply does not have the time and energy necessary merely to digest all the information being published in research journals, to say nothing of engaging in broad, serious research himself. Yet the truth of created being, which is revealed in empirical investigation, is only one relatively narrow aspect of the intelligibility of the visible universe. There remain to be digested other aspects of truth such as those expressed by the philosopher, artist, historian, and intuitive but unlettered person, as well as by cultures differing radically from our own with their special and valid approaches to being and truth.

In this regard the human intellect manifests something of a seeming infinity in its capacity for truth which responds to the apparent infinitude of created truth itself. Therefore, in order that one may have some measure of access to the fullness of created truth in breadth, one must live in continuous, intimate dialogue with the truth in the minds of all other men since only such a community of minds and truth can begin to provide a relatively complete reflection of the sweep of the truth of created being. Thus the most direct, effective access that men have to truth in breadth is through the minds of other men in a dialogue in which ideas, insights, experiences, doubts and convictions are shared together with the evidence upon which they depend. *Men of great learning are invariably those who evidence a profound respect for the minds of all persons and live in a continuous dialogue with the truth in the minds of men wherever they encounter it.*

IMAGE OF GOD BY NATURE

Truth in Depth

Just as dialogue with other minds is essential for the attainment of created truth in breadth, a similar dialogue is even more necessary in order that a man have access to truth in depth. Men pursue truth in depth when they search for ultimate causes and answers, thereby seeking to trace created truth back to its origin in Truth and to find the revelation of Truth in truth. Such a pursuit of truth in depth is in the Catholic tradition the pursuit of wisdom.[38]

Since truth originates in Truth,[39] the infinite variety and multiplicity of created truth proceeds from the unity and simplicity of Uncreated Truth.[40] As one pursues truth to its source, therefore, the diverse and multiple character of its surface expression and diffusion is replaced by a unity and simplicity which encompasses in a synthesized form what is disparate and, therefore, more easily digestible in its surface manifestations. Such a movement into the depths brings the mind into the realm of the intellectually arduous and obscure. This is not by reason of the poverty of intelligibility it encounters there, but by reason of the richness of the truth and the intensity of the light with which the weakness of the human intellect is unable to cope.[41] And so men move into these depths with great difficulty and no little peril.

This undertaking requires a combination of special gifts and a lifetime of disciplined concentration in order that one may become habituated to his surroundings there. Rarely is this endeavor made without a significant quantity of error being mixed with the truth that is

---

38

[39] *Ibid.*, I, q. 16, a. 7.

[40] *Ibid.*, I, q. 16, a. 9.

[41] "Since everything is knowable according as it is actual, God, Who is pure act without any admixture of potentiality, is in Himself supremely knowable. But what is supremely knowable in itself, may not be knowable to a particular intellect, on account of the excess of the intelligible object above the intellect; as, for example, the sun; which is supremely visible, cannot be seen by the bat by reason of its excess of light." *Ibid.*, I, q.12, a. 1c.

brought forth.[42] And here, least of all, is the solitary human intellect self-sufficient in its quest. In order that one gain some mastery and measure of success in his efforts it is necessary that he avail himself fully of all the light and insight that is to be found in other minds similarly engaged in this undertaking, whether it be the sophisticated speculations of the philosopher and theologian, or the intuitive penetrations of the mystics and sages of both the East and the West. It is especially in this effort, according to Aristotle, that one must act in a community of truth and build his insights upon the truth previously attained by others.

He who pursues truth by embodying in his own vision whatever truth has been discovered by those who have gone before him is, in the mind of Aristotle, in the happy position of the midget who is standing on the shoulders of a giant.[43] Whereas the man who wades into these depths while ignorant of, or indifferent to the truths previously discovered by others so that he moves outside the community of such minds, either drowns or ends up bobbing about on the surface like a cork while foolishly thinking that he is swimming masterfully in the depths.

Man's natural, necessary thrust toward his final end entails an ever operative desire for ultimate truth and, therefore, the instinct to seek Truth in truth. This natural instinct in man for Truth in truth, provides

---

[42] "It is necessary for man to accept by faith not only things which are above reason, but also those which can be known by reason: and this for three motives. First, in order that man may arrive more quickly at the knowledge of Divine Truth. Because the science to whose province it belongs to prove the existence of God is the last of all to offer itself to human research, since it presupposes many other sciences: so that it would not be until late in life that man would arrive at the knowledge of God. The second reason is, in order that the knowledge of God may be more general. For many are unable to make progress in the study of science, either through dullness of mind, or through having a number of occupations and temporal needs, or even through laziness in learning....The third reason is for the sake of certitude. For human reason is very deficient in things concerning God. A sign of this is that philosophers in their researches, by natural investigations, into human affairs, have fallen into many errors, and have disagreed among themselves." *Ibid.*, II-II, q. w, a. 4.

[43] *Metaphysica*, Bk. II, n. 276-7.

him with an initial openness and positive response to encounters with truth and the means of attaining it. Since man's most direct and ideal access to truth is found in communing with the minds of others, man by natural instinct seeks to enter into community with the minds of those surrounding him questioning, listening, probing, arguing, and using every means available to feed fully upon their possessed truth. Thus the child instinctively turns to the truth hopefully present in the minds of his parents to find the answers that he naturally longs to attain. This instinct for truth quickly extends beyond the family to every person who offers the promise of expanding his awareness of reality.

If a man's exercise of freedom is in harmony with this natural instinct he will consciously utilize whatever avenues are open to him for such communion with the minds of others. Study, reflection, reading and serious conversation with active, probing minds will form an essential part of his life—not idle communication which only satisfies curiosity or gives pleasure, but disciplined, programmed, persevering communication which ends in the attainment of new understanding. The urge for truth may take the form of a contemplative existence in which a man withdraws into solitude, not to close himself off from contact with others, but to enter more profoundly into community with the great ideas of great minds by a dedication to the pursuit of truth free of wasteful distractions. Thus the man living in studious solitude is often engaged in the listening, learning part of the dialogue of truth more intensely and profoundly than the person who passes the day in continuous conversation with others.

As actual truth evolves in the mind the other aspect of man's natural desire for perfection expresses itself in his instinct to communicate his acquired insights to others. The more godlike his possession of truth is, which is to say the more he gains of truth in depth whereby he knows Truth in truth, the stronger is his impulse to share this vision. Thus, as he realizes the contemplative perfection of image of God in his actual knowledge of God, he experiences the pull of the active perfection as image of God to impart his knowledge to other minds in order to move them to a similar perfection as images of God.

Here again if a man's exercise of freedom is in harmony with the natural tendencies that follow from this state of acquired perfection, he will consciously utilize whatever avenues of access to the minds of others are open to him in order to communicate his truth effectively. Thus the ecumenical character of man's instinct for the acquisition and dissemination of truth in depth will be developed in conscious dialogue as he enters into a community of truth with others.

Man's natural instinct for acquiring and sharing truth in community may never reach a significant level of conscious dialogue due to various obstacles such as the effects of uncontrolled passions that make his life more animal than human.[44] Where his desire for truth does attain a performance level of significant dialogue with others, it may evolve in one of two extreme directions, either of which will impede his development as the actual image of God in knowing divinity. The first extreme is represented by Pattern I in which we find the tendency to identify Uncreated Being and created being, and therefore, Truth and truth. Where this tendency holds, the communities of truth which form are inclined to arrest one in the conviction that the particular, mediate truths shared are in fact universal and ultimate truth. This impedes the movement to truth in depth where man achieves true knowledge of God and his perfection as the image of God through such knowledge.

The other direction is represented by the pattern that so opposes truth to Truth as to deny that truth is the positive means to knowledge of Truth. The result of this pattern is to discourage one from entering into serious dialogue with the great minds and mystics of the ages through whom alone one can on the natural level build the kind of insights into the mystery of God that permit him to achieve in any substantial degree his natural aptitude for becoming the actual image of God through knowledge.

The third approach to Uncreated Being is the pattern that asserts that truth has its origin in Truth and provides an imperfect revelation of Truth. This approach avoids the first two extremes and interprets man's natural evolution as the actual image of God in knowing divinity as one that demands that he enter into community with the collective thinking of all actual images of God by way of knowledge in whatever

---

[44] *Summa,* II-II, q. 179, a. 2, ad. 1.

time, place, culture, or human condition they may be found. Since this natural knowledge of God is normally not given, but must be discovered and earned by prolonged, disciplined, dedicated effort, such a community of actual images will be one which causes in itself its knowledge of God, or God-consciousness.

The experience of God's presence as Truth in the midst of such a community will be the experience of a group of men, often separated by cultures, continents, and centuries, in whom painfully, slowly, and with much obscurity and distortion, the knowledge of God continues to reappear according to different aspects and facets, and imperfectly evolves through the efforts of these seekers of ultimate truth. Man, according to Pattern III, by entering into dialogue and communion with the knowledge of God evolving in such a community of minds, will find in the natural order his most direct ideal access to union with God as Truth, and to the realization of himself as a being created ultimately to contemplate Truth's revealing presence in truth.

Image in Community of Love

Man's natural development as the actual image of God in love takes place through the evolution of his love for created good as the derivation and revelation of Uncreated Good. The more intensely and profoundly man loves the fullness of created good in *breadth* and in *depth*, as the expression of Divine Goodness, the more he evolves in the love of God Himself and becomes the actual image of God.

Love in Breadth

Since no individual creature can share fully in the infinite goodness of God, many creatures, sharing in complementary fashion diverse aspects of divine goodness, are required in order that the totality of created good may participate more fully in the goodness of God. Thus as man's love embraces more and more of the full sweep of created good as the expression of divine goodness, his love participates more fully in the love of God. Since love follows on knowledge of the good, in order that man may love created good in breadth, he must first in some way affectively experience the range of goodness of created being.[45]

As we have seen direct personal knowledge of the fullness of created truth is impossible for an individual man. He must depend upon communing with the minds of others in order to gain some comprehension of the sweep of created truth. So also direct, personal, affective experience of the variety of goodness of created being is outside the range of one man's possible contact with reality so that he must commune with the affective experience in the hearts of many men to achieve love for created good in breadth.

Therefore, just as the minds of other men offer the only access to the full breadth of created truth, so too it is the hearts of other men that provide access in love to the fullness of created good in breadth. It is the man who opens his heart fully to the collective heart of mankind and shares with all men their desires, hopes, fears, joys, ambitions, enthusiasm, and every other kind of affective response to the goodness of being in all of its variety, who can be said in some degree to love the full range of created good.

So, in order that a man may have some measure of access to the fullness of created good in breadth, he must live in continuous, intimate dialogue with the affective movements that go on in the hearts of men everywhere. It is by entering into community with their love that he can best expand his own love for created good as the revelation of divine goodness and thereby duplicate in his likeness to God's love the full sweep of divine love expressed in the multiple and diverse goods that He created.

The dialogue by which he enters into community with the hearts of other men must assume an affective and not merely speculative form. It must provide, not so much abstract knowledge of the love of others for good as, concrete stirrings of the very same affections in him which exist in others. Therefore he must be open to concrete example, inspiration, encouragement and every other form of expression and communication by which one man is able to awaken affections in others which correspond to the ones in himself.

---

[45] *Ibid.*, I-II, q. 27, a. 2.

IMAGE OF GOD BY NATURE

Love in Depth

Since created good comes from Uncreated Good, one cannot love good in depth without loving it in its relation to its source and in subordination to that source. Men love created good in depth when they love it explicitly as a participation in and revelation of divine goodness, and as a means to union with God. This implies that one love the particular good of created being in subordination to the whole of created good, and the whole in subordination to Divine Goodness as its source.

Since the particular good is visible, tangible, and immediately available in its capacity to fulfill desire, and since man tends to seek complete happiness in the here and now as quickly and effortlessly as possible, it is difficult for him to sacrifice the present, tangible fulfillment for a future, less tangible and less certain promise. It is difficult, therefore, for man to sacrifice the particular good for the whole, and the whole for its even less tangible and more remote source. This is to say that it is arduous for man to love virtuously and in depth; to love created good as a *means* to the Perfect Good instead of clinging to the particular, mutable good as though it were the Perfect, Immutable Good.

Few men, therefore, rise to the heights of human nature's capacity to love heroically. When the few do succeed in so rising to these heights, they find it impossible to sustain for long such intensity of love or to extend it beyond a narrow area of embrace. Thus together with the greatness of character they reveal, profound weakness will still be manifested in their makeup. Such greatness of love may be manifested in one man by way of his extraordinary commitment to God's will in relation to assisting another humans in need. In another person this commitment to God may express itself in his espousal of a principle of justice or truth. Still a third may reveal a heroic love of God in his loyalty to his country, and so on.

Since one person cannot express the full potential of human nature to love in depth, many persons are required, revealing in different ways and in visible and tangible form both the otherwise invisible, intangible dimensions of created good when related to Divine Goodness and the full scope of human nature's capacity to love God nobly and heroically in and through the love of created good in depth. It is the collective, concrete expressions of such extraordinary love of God in and through created good coming from many men that make known to the individual the potential of human nature to become the actual image of God in love.

If a man is to evolve in such likeness to God in love he must live in constant dialogue with the greatness of love in other men—being purified and inspired by the example of their lives so as to exercise the discipline necessary to be able to emulate their love. In the absence of continuous dialogue with such greatness in other men, which is to say in the absence of a community of love in depth, it is not possible for man on the natural level to develop in any substantial degree as the actual image of God in love.

Man's natural, necessary desire for the Perfect Good entails both the instinct to seek the Perfect Good in and through created good, and an initial openness and positive response to his encounter with good under any form as well as to the means of attaining good. Since his most direct and ideal access to full love of the good in breadth and depth is through the shared love of the good in the hearts of other men, by instinct man seeks to evolve in his capacity to love by entering into community with the love in the hearts of those about him—sharing their enthusiasm, desires, hopes, and other positive affective movements.

The child instinctively turns to the love in the hearts of his parents in order to learn both what to love and how to love. His instinct for growing in love through shared experiences quickly extends beyond the family to his contacts with every person who promises to expand his capacity to love the good in breadth and depth. If his exercise of freedom is in harmony with this instinct he will deliberately develop whatever avenues are open to him for such communion with the hearts of others.

When a man's instinct to love in depth leads to a situation where a price must be paid and sacrifice must be shouldered, then the moment of truth arrives. A conscious decision must be made either to pay the price of virtue and remain true to his nature or to refuse to pay the price demanded and live in conscious lack of harmony with his natural desire for perfection. It is in such moments of crisis that a man has indispensable need of a community of love by way of the inspiration and encouragement of others who have paid the price, to motivate him to be true to his nature.

As love in depth evolves in his heart and he becomes the actual image of God, he will experience the pull of this acquired perfection as image to impart his love to others, to move them to a similar perfection as images of God in love. Once again, if his exercise of freedom is in harmony with the natural tendency that follows on this acquired perfection, he will consciously develop whatever means are available to awaken effectively in others a similar love. Thus the ecumenical character of his instinct to grow in love of the Perfect Good, and to share that love with others, will develop into conscious dialogue in a community of shared love of the Perfect Good.

As in the case of man's growth in godliness through truth, if he is to develop as the actual image of God in love he must avoid both the extreme of Pattern I, which tends to identify created good and the Perfect Good, and the extreme of Pattern II which puts them in opposition to each other. Where the first tendency prevails, the communities of love that form will be inclined to deify the shared love of created good in breadth to the exclusion of that love in depth—wherein man finds Divine Good at the source of created good and his perfection as image of God by loving created good in subordination to Uncreated Good. Where Pattern II dominates there will be the tendency to downgrade the value of, for example, mutual support, and inspiration of others which is essential to man's evolution in actual love of God.

Lastly, as in the case of man's experience of God's presence as Truth in human nature, man's experience of God's presence as Love in this community will be the experience of an evolving, participated Love in which men will be causing their own development in love of God. Thus on the natural level man's ideal realization of himself as the actual image of God in his love of Divine Goodness will only occur in community with other men who are causing God's participated presence as Love in human nature.

Image in Community of Other Divine Perfections
An analysis similar to the one made with regards to truth and love can also be carried out with regards to the other simple perfections. Man's

special likeness to God can be examined in regard to life, beatitude, power, causality, justice, and mercy. Here too it must be said that man's natural aptitude for becoming the actual image of God through his evolution in each of these perfections can be ideally realized only in community with other men who have already achieved some degree of actual likeness to God through these perfections. Rather than pursue a separate analysis of each perfection I will treat them collectively for the sake of brevity, indicating the major points of traditional Catholic understanding concerning man's evolution in community as the actual image of God by way of these perfections. This traditional understanding affirms that:

1. Man's natural evolution as the actual image of God by participation in the Divine Life, Beatitude, Power, Causality, Justice, and Mercy takes place through the assimilation into his being of these perfections as they are found in their participated state in the created order.

2. Man's access to the fullness in breadth and depth of life, beatitude, power, causality, justice and mercy in the created order can take place only in community with men who already possess these perfections in varying and complementary degrees as actual images of God. Apart from such a community the individual, aside from other considerations, simply lacks the possibility of direct personal access to the multiple and diverse expressions of these perfections in the created order.

3. Man's natural thrust toward perfect happiness entails the instinct to seek contact with Life, Beatitude, Power, Causality, Justice and Mercy in life, beatitude, power, causality, justice and mercy in the created order. This instinct leaves him initially open and positively responsive to encounter with these perfections and to the means by which they may be encountered. Since it is only through other men that he can experience in some measure the fullness of the created expression of these perfections, man initially is instinctively open to the shared experience of these perfections in the community of men.

4. Man's exercise of freedom must be in harmony with this instinct to experience the fullness of these perfections in community. Therefore he should consciously, deliberately, utilize the means necessary to share completely in the fullness of life and beatitude present in human nature. He must develop means whereby he can act in community with all

IMAGE OF GOD BY NATURE

other images of God to impart collectively their shared perfection to the perfectible aspects of created being.

5. If he is to evolve as the actual image of God through these perfections, man must reject the interpretation of created being of Pattern I. It identifies life, beatitude, power, causality, justice, and mercy with Life, Beatitude, Power, Causality, Justice, and Mercy. Hence it leads to communities in which the members *substitute* their shared experience of created perfections for the shared experience of God that is to be achieved *in and through* created perfections. At the same time he must reject also the interpretation of created being espoused by Pattern II wherein created perfections are held to be in opposition to the Divine Perfections. He must reject the consequent negative judgment on the value of communities of life, justice, and mercy as means by which a man may evolve in actual godliness and gain union with God.

6. Lastly man must not seek a community of men in which he expects to find a mature, ideal, perfectly realized, created expression of life, beatitude, power, causality, justice and mercy as the revelation and point of contact with God. Rather he must seek a community of men who are struggling with great difficult, and often with little success, to evolve in life, beatitude, power, causality, justice, and mercy as a means of realizing their potential as images of God.

In Addition to these points there are several others that merit special attention. These concern man's development as the actual image of God when he unites in cooperative action with other men in exercising a perfecting role on created reality. As I previously noted, man becomes the image of God in the contemplative aspects of divinity by his assimilation to God in truth, love, life, and beatitude. As he participates more in these contemplative perfections of God, he acquires both the power and the impulse to imitate God's perfecting active role in the created order by participation in God's power, causality, justice, and mercy. The more fully he possesses these active perfections, the more he evolves as the actual image of God in activity. Here too man cannot evolve fully in such active likeness to God except in community.

Concerning this evolution in community of man as the image of God in activity, these further observations deserve mention:

1. The restrictions of the individual's participation in divinity is made particularly evident in his limited power as an efficient cause. Man's power to control himself and his surroundings is pitiably inadequate when he acts in isolation. His desire and need to control far outstrip his actual power to do so. This explains in part the individual's feelings of impotence before the demands of life. In the efficient power of many men one finds a fuller expression of divine power's participated presence in human nature than is to be found in an individual power. It is when a community of men act together in an orderly, unified manner, with the lower responding to the directions of the higher, that the power of human nature is enormously increased and the fullness of man's participation in divine power begins to be realized.

When these actions of men in community proceed under the motivation and direction of the knowledge and love of God, then there is expressed and experienced in such concerted action the fullness of God's active presence in human nature through participated power, causality, justice, and mercy. It is only when the individual enters into community with men acting in cooperation as actual images of God that he can fully realize his potential for becoming the image of God in action, and experience in his active participation in the creative activity of such a community his ideal contact with God's power, causality, justice, and mercy.

2. The natural desire in man for the Perfect Good entails his instinct to achieve mastery over his own being and his surroundings so as to be able to use reality for his special purposes.[46] Together with this instinct to master goes the impulse to unite in action with others in order to expand control when one encounters inadequacies in his isolated exercise of power. This instinct [47] to act in community is both one of the dynamics underlying the formation of societies and the expression of human nature's natural desire for godliness.

Freedom must build on this social instinct in man in such a way as to assure that the communities of power that are formed are directed to

---

[46] *Ibid.*, I, q. 26, a. 1.
[47] *Ethics*, Bk 1, lect. 1, n. 4.

ends truly perfective of human nature. Since the same instinct to expand power by acting in community is operative in sick individuals as well as healthy ones, communities for evil purposes are formed as quickly and act as effectively as do those formed for virtuous reasons, thereby enormously expanding man's power for evil. Recent history illustrates this. While the hatred of one man for the Jewish people was a sick and terrible phenomenon, its destructive power remained radically limited as long as he hated in isolation. However, when he succeeded in uniting around himself a community of men filled with a similar hatred, their expanded power in community proved adequate to the task of murdering six million Jews.

There undoubtedly were more men who opposed his hatred than the number of those who espoused it. However, since the former were not acting in a community of opposition, their divided, isolated opposition was rendered impotent by the combined action of the haters. The lesson of this is that ecumenical dialogue in action is necessary not only to allow the individual to develop as the actual image of God in perfecting activity, but also to assure that men who are the actual images of God in wisdom and love may prevail in human society over the destructive presence of communities of hate and godlessness.

3. Since no single age, culture or social grouping encompasses the full expression of human nature's participation in divine power, the individual's desire to act in community as a means of achieving full realization as the image of God must transcend time and place, and extend to identification with all men everywhere and at all times who strive to act in a godly way. To act in community then means to act in harmony not only with the good men of the present, but with those of the past also, as well as with openness to possible cooperation with good men in the future.

For Catholics a concrete expression of such action in community which transcends time is found in the building of the great medieval cathedrals when men of one generation laid the foundation of a work which they knew would not be completed for many generations to come, confident that others of a like mind and heart with them would carry on their efforts, and content to be part of such a community engaged in a transcendental undertaking

4. I have already noted that in the Catholic understanding of human nature, man finds himself involved not in the finished work of creation but in an ongoing work in which he is invited to cooperate with God in bringing creation to final perfection.[48] According to this tradition it is Divine Mercy which underlies the entire work of creation in which God, in a gratuitous act of love, brings created being into existence and continues to respond to its potentialities by moving it on toward final perfection. It is man's participation in Divine Mercy that inclines him to respond as an instrument of divine action to the deficiencies of created being that cry out for fulfillment. I have also noted that man's merciful response to the needs of created being provides the highest expression of human nature's participation in divinity in the practical order.[49]

Since the capacity of created being to be perfected is so vast and the active power of the individual to respond in mercy to these needs is so limited, it is only in a community of mercy that human nature can function as an adequate instrument of God in bringing creation to its full perfection. Further, it is only in such a community of mercy that human nature achieves its ultimate participation in and revelation of divinity in the practical order.

When the individual, therefore, freely joins with others in a community of merciful response to the deficiencies of created being and thereby experiences the divine quality of the gratuitous, perfecting love which motivates their combined action, he ideally realizes his own potential as the image of God in mercy, and encounters in the community and himself as an active part of it the highest expression of God's presence in the active workings of human nature. This understanding of Catholic tradition is dramatized in the Church's ideal of religious communities in which men unite in a lifelong espousal to works of mercy which respond to the deficiencies of created being.[50] Such communities in the Church's judgment provide the highest

---

[48] *Cf.* Chapter Five, Section III.
[49] *Summa*, II-II, q. 30, a. 4.
[50] *Ibid,.* II-II, qq. 187-188.

IMAGE OF GOD BY NATURE

revelation of God's presence in human nature in the practical order and offer men the most direct access to union with God in the same order.[51]

VI. FLAWED IMAGE

The Ideal

According to this analysis of traditional Catholic understanding of man as the image of God by reason of his natural aptitude for special participation in the divine life, the individual who has achieved such divine likeness may be described in the following manner. As the actual image of God he first and foremost participates in the contemplative aspects of divinity through a profound knowledge and intense love of God as the Author of nature, finding in his encounter with created truth and goodness in breadth and depth the revelation of and means of union with the Truth and Goodness of God. His state of contemplative perfection is attained principally by living in constant openness to, and dialogue with the truth and love in the minds and hearts of all men who have achieved in some degree likeness to God as image.

His encounter with these persons is not a fortuitous one, but results from deliberate cultivation of all the means available for such contact. Through community with other images of God he comes alive to the fullness of life in them as a revelation of Life, and experiences in their shared joy insight into the Beatitude of God. From his evolution in the participated Truth, Love, Life, and Beatitude of God the impulse is generated in him to join with others who share these perfections in imparting their godliness to the perfectible aspects of created being. Through this community of action he experiences the fullness of divine power, causality, justice and mercy working in and through human nature whereby he becomes the actual image of God in his perfecting activity. In each step and phase of his evolution as the actual image of God in contemplative and active perfection, the essential dynamics of his development is found in his participation in community with other actual images of God in a mutually perfecting, sustaining dialogue

---

[51] *Ibid,*. II-II, q. 186, a. 1.

through which God is not so much *found* as He is *created* in His participated presence as truth, love, and power in human nature.

This description of man as the actual image of God is not one that sets forth the reality of man's actual situation, but an idealization of it. Beginning with the raw potential for perfection in human nature and projecting this potential to its ideal realization, I have presented a picture of man's perfection and godliness as it would be if his natural aptitude for likeness to God were perfectly realized. Whether in fact such an ideal development has ever taken place can only be determined from the actual history of man and not from a priori speculations about human nature.

A Seeker

While man in theory may be the image of God in truth, love, life, beatitude, power, causality, justice, and mercy, in actual fact he presents himself more as the image of ignorance, confusion, lovelessness, paralysis, misery, impotence, sterility, exploitation, and self-love. Even in his more successful and noble moments he can be more aptly described as a searcher after truth, love, and power rather than the possessor of these perfections, much less the *creator* of them. Experience makes clear that in actuality man rarely achieves in any significant degree more than partial realization of his potential for godliness. And when he does in some notable degree achieve such perfection, his success is normally not sustained for any appreciable length of time.

The success of one generation often prepares the way for the mediocrity of the next. The fact of this relatively universal failure of human nature to realize its potential has been the object of reflection on the part of thoughtful men from the earliest times. This perplexity forms the significant half of the classic problem of evil. Interestingly enough this perennial speculation on man's failure and the problem of moral evil gives eloquent witness to the universal, though implicit, awareness of man as being the potential image of God. Since the very concept of evil (that is the absence of perfection in man's makeup and of action which *could* and *should* be present) is not possible except in the context of an awareness of an ideal state of perfection which man possesses the practical means of attaining.[52] This universal recognition

---

[52] *Ibid.*, I, q. 48, a. 1.

of man's failure stems from an equally universal conviction of man's natural aptitude for becoming the actual image of God.

Strangely enough often those philosophies of human nature which in theory would seem logically to exclude any concern about moral evil, for example atheistic materialism, in practice evince a most intense preoccupation with man's failure to achieve a level of perfection that answers his potential. At any rate, if man is the image of God he is at best a flawed image,[53] and the existence of these flaws in his makeup have obsessed, and continue to obsess, all serious students of human nature whatever be the philosophy of life they may embrace.

Interpretations
Each specifically distinct philosophy of human life provides an equally distinct explanation for the flaws that everyone encounters in the actual condition of man. Without going into the details of these different philosophies and their respective explanations of man's failure, in a general manner their interpretations of the problem of evil in the human context may be classified according to the three patterns proposed. in Chapter Three.

Pattern I tends to identify created and Uncreated Being and manifest a general response of optimism concerning human nature, attributing to man powers for evolving in self perfection that traditional Catholic thought ascribes more to the action of God on man. In consistency with this understanding, this pattern also tends to search for the explanation of man's failure outside of human nature itself. This may take the form of ascribing to environmental factors the prime responsibility for human failure so that with the proper readjustment of the environment the inner goodness of human nature automatically will express itself and man will become everything that ideally he should be. Salvation will come wholly from within, once the external obstacles to the redeeming forces in man have been removed.

Again this pattern may assume an evolutionary form according to which no real failure has occurred in human nature at all. We just happen to be experiencing human life at a lower, less perfect, stage of

---

[53] *Ibid.*, I, q. 93, a. 8 ad. 3.

development in the evolutionary process. Redemption will come in due time and from within as the irresistible wisdom and goodness of this mysterious inner force will inexorably move human nature to its realization.

In another expression of Pattern I's tendency to identify created and Uncreated Being, either the evolutionary process itself by which this advance takes place is adorned with attributes that Catholic thought traditionally ascribes uniquely to God, or the process and God are explicitly identified. When Pattern I is forced by evidence to attribute a significant degree of responsibility for man's failure to man himself, the endeavor to salvage an optimistic belief in the fundamental purity and goodness of human nature leads to the division of men into two groups—the good and the bad. In this case salvation for the good comes by way of suppressing the evil. In one form or another Pattern I tends to espouse an optimistic vision of the essential purity and goodness of man.

Pattern II tends to place created being and Uncreated Being in opposition, and denies or downgrades any positive relation between them whereby created being is the point of contact and union with Uncreated Being. This pattern also tends, in a pessimistic view of human nature, to ascribe the failure of man to radical flaws in that nature itself. In a Christian context man's failure is explained by an extreme view of original sin which interprets it as having resulted in the corruption of human nature itself. The flaw in man is an essential one, which leaves his inner reality incapable of being salvaged by intrinsic change or grace, so that salvation will come to man in no way from within his nature but totally from outside of him.

Among Catholics this concept of the intrinsic, essential corruption of human nature itself by original sin must be rejected in theory as opposed to the explicit teaching of the Church. However, some Catholics in practice tend to follow a course of action similar to Pattern II, as I have noted, and downgrade the capacity of human nature to be elevated and utilized by God as an active instrument in union with Christ in the work of redemption.[54]

---

[54] "As stated above (A.1) a sacrament in causing grace works after the manner of an instrument. Now an instrument is twofold; the one, separate, as a stick,

IMAGE OF GOD BY NATURE

Pattern III emphasizes both the distinction between Uncreated Being and created being and, at the same time, the positive relation between them as effect and cause so that created being is the means to union with Uncreated Being. This pattern also emphasizes that human nature is created positively in the image and likeness of God, and affirms that whatever is found in human nature that proceeds directly from the creative act of God and has not been altered or conditioned by man's abuse of his freedom, is necessarily good. Otherwise God would be the cause of evil in man. Pattern III, therefore, asserts that human nature remains essentially good and incorrupt even after original sin. Whatever defects are present in man as consequence of original sin derive uniquely from the failure of human nature and in no way from a failure of the part of God.[55] Aquinas described the loss of good in human nature as a result of original sin in the following manner:

> The good of human nature is threefold. First, there are the principles of which nature is constituted, and the properties that flow from them, such as the powers of the soul, and so forth. Secondly, since man has from nature an inclination to virtue, as stated above (Q.60, A.1; Q.63, A.1), this inclination to virtue is a good of nature. Thirdly, the gift of original just-

---

for instance; the other, united, as a hand. Moreover, the separate instrument is moved by means of the united instrument, as a stick by the hand. Now the principle efficient cause of grace is God Himself, in comparison with Whom Christ's humanity is as a united instrument, whereas the sacrament is as a separate instrument. Consequently, the saving power must needs be derived by the sacraments from Christ's Godhead through His humanity." *Ibid.* III, q. 62 a. 5.

[55] "The second kind of habit is the disposition of a complex nature, whereby that nature is well or ill disposed to something, chiefly when such a disposition has become like a second nature, as in the case of sickness or health. In this sense original sin is a habit. For it is an inordinate disposition, arising from the destruction of the harmony which was essential to original justice, even as bodily sickness is an inordinate disposition of the body, by reason of the destruction of that equilibrium which is essential to health. Hence it is that original sin is called the languor of nature." *Ibid.*, I-II q. 82, a. 1.

ice, conferred on the whole human nature in the person of the first man, may be called a good of nature.

Accordingly, the first-mentioned good of nature is neither destroyed nor diminished by sin. The third good of nature was entirely destroyed through the sin of our first parent. But the second good of nature, *viz,* the natural inclination to virtue, is diminished by sin. Because human acts produce an inclination to like acts, as stated above (Q.50,A.1). Now from the very fact that a thing becomes inclined to one of two contraries, its inclination to the other contrary must needs be diminished. Wherefore as sin is opposed to virtue, from the very fact that a man sins, there results a diminution of that good of nature, which is the inclination to virtue.[56]

Thus Pattern III combines something of the optimism of Pattern I with the pessimism of Pattern II. It is optimistic about the basic, essential goodness of human nature and the essentially positive inclination of nature toward virtue and the good. It is pessimistic about man's ideal use of his freedom and about the diminution of man's inclination toward virtue as a result of his defective behavior. But in acknowledging this diminution, Pattern III continues to affirm the essential goodness of human nature and the positive, though, weakened, inclination of man's nature toward virtue. Thus this pattern is able to espouse both the intrinsic redeemability and salvageability of human nature, and the presence of positive, though debilitated, tendencies toward the good, which God can utilize in effecting man's evolution as His image so as to permit man to be the proximate source of his own perfection (radical godliness). It is this conviction about the essential goodness of human nature and action, even after original sin, that underlies Catholic doctrine on man's redemption by intrinsic grace and God's utilization of man's dynamic forces as positive, active instruments through which his redemption is effected—for example, as in the sacraments, prayer, and good works.

Pattern III also affirms the unity of human nature as proceeding from God. It does this both in the sense that man is ordained to union with his Creator, and in the sense that as part of a unified whole he is

---

[56] *Ibid.,* I-II, q. 85, a. 1.

IMAGE OF GOD BY NATURE

ordained to a process of mutually perfecting behavior with all other men in which one person and one stage of human life is ordained to another—the lower to the higher, so that the parts find their perfection in and through the whole. Therefore, the unity of Divine Providence would never permit the failure of man's radical godliness in his groping toward becoming the actual image of God unless He intended in some way to incorporate man's failure into a relationship with the whole of human existence in which the failure would set the stage for man's ultimate success as image of God. That this is in fact the case is the teaching of Revelation as the Catholic tradition understands that teaching. In Scriptures we learn that God allowed man to fail on the natural level as a flawed image of Himself in order to incorporate this very failure into a plan which provides that man through his failure may succeed in a far more wonderful, higher way in becoming the image of God by Grace.

CHAPTER SEVEN

IMAGE OF GOD BY GRACE

I. THE MESSAGE OF CHRIST

According to Catholic doctrine the good news of Christ may be reduced to two basic truths:

1. God the Father intends not only that man achieve the perfection of actual image of God for which he possesses the natural aptitude, but also that he in a gratuitous act of divine love be elevated by grace to a level of extraordinary participation in the Divine Life. This new life as image of God by grace to which God calls man, lies completely beyond the power of human nature or any created nature to produce.

2 The life of grace will be initiated in man and will be brought to perfection through the proximate instrumentality of human nature itself acting in union with Christ.

In the present Chapter I will set forth the traditional Catholic understanding of the life of grace and then draw some of the ecumenical implications of this doctrine. In the concluding Chapter I will turn to the second part of Christ's message and present the traditional Catholic teaching on the human nature of Christ as man's primary, principal point of contact with God. I will then examine the role that human nature in general exercises in union with Christ in contributing to man's experience of God. My intention in both chapters, as before, will be to present the substance of traditional Catholic doctrine without critical evaluation so as to be able to draw from this doctrine the principal ecumenical implications inherent in it.

II. THE LIFE OF GRACE

The New Testament contains many passages in which Christ states that His mission is to initiate in man a radically new participation in the life of the Father. The Gospel of Saint John in particular is replete with this teaching:

> I tell you must solemnly unless a man is born from above,
> he cannot see the kingdom of God. Nicodemus said, "How

can a grown man be born? Can he go back into his mother's womb and be born again?" Jesus replied: "I tell you most solemnly, unless a man is born through water and the Spirit, he cannot enter the kingdom of God: what is born of the flesh is flesh; what is born of the Spirit is spirit."[1]

...everyone who believes in him (Christ) may have eternal life in him.[2]

But anyone who drinks the water I shall give will never be thirsty again: the water that I shall give will turn into a spring inside him, welling up to eternal life.[3]

Elsewhere in the New Testament we read:

We are offspring of God.[4]

...We are sons of God. But if we are sons, we are heirs also: heirs indeed of God and joint heirs with Christ.[5]

...and we, with our unveiled faces reflecting like mirrors the brightness of the Lord, all grow brighter and brighter as we are turned into the image that we reflect; this is the work of the Lord who is Spirit.[6]

In making these gifts, he has given us the guarantee of something very great and wonderful to come; through them you will be able to share the divine nature and to escape corruption in a world that is sunk in vice.[7]

According to Catholic tradition man's extraordinary participation in the Divine Life entails a vital transformation and elevation in both the

---

[1] *Jn.* 6.53-59.
[2] *Jn.* 3.14.
[3] *Jn.* 4.13.
[4] *Acts.* 7.29.
[5] *Rom.* 8.16-17.
[6] II. Cor. 3.18.
[7] II Pet. 1.4.

being and operation of human nature.[8] The principle effecting this transformation of man's being is called sanctifying grace. This entitative change is defined in Catholic doctrine as a supernatural quality inhering in the soul which effects in man a physical, formal participation in the very nature of God. By "quality inhering in the soul" this tradition understands that sanctifying grace is an accidental modification of man's living reality which adds a new, vital being to man's natural life somewhat in the manner in which man's soul actualizes and animates his body. Sanctifying grace then comes as a vital, entitative principle which fuses into a unity with man's natural being, transforming him into a new living reality.

Catholic tradition understands by *supernatural* that, the living physical reality communicated by grace so transcends the created order and so introduces one into the sphere of the divine and uncreated that no created being conceivable could possess by nature this level of perfection and participation in divinity. This reality exists either naturally in God or by accidental participation in an intellectual creature who has been elevated beyond the order of nature.

Catholic tradition understands by *physical, formal participation,* a real, objective, assimilation and expression in man of the living reality proper to the nature of God. This physical, formal participation in the divine nature is compared by Aquinas to the manner in which the moon participates objectively in the light of the sun, and an iron bar participates objectively in the being and activity of fire when brought into

---

[8] In my analysis of traditional Catholic understanding of sanctifying grace and the infused virtues and gifts I am essentially presenting Aquinas' theology of both. There are other acceptable interpretations of grace and the infused virtues and gifts within the Catholic community. (Cf. E. M. Burke, "Grace," *NCE*, Vol. 6, pp. 658-72).

As I stated in the Introduction, for practical reasons I am equating in this thesis traditional Catholic thought and the theology of Aquinas, on the basis that this thought is commonly accepted as the most authoritative expression of Catholic tradition. This is not to question or deny the liceity of other theological schools within the Catholic tradition. The substance of Aquinas' theology of grace is found in the *Summa,* I-II, qq.109-114.

proximity to that reality.⁹ Just as the iron is physically transformed and shares more intensely in the being and efficient causality of the heat proper to fire when it is brought into closer contact with it, so human nature, in the degree in which it is gratuitously brought into union with the infinite, creative, transforming Love of God, undergoes a transformation and elevation of its being and activity whereby it takes on in an accidental, created, and analogous manner an objective assimilation to the Divine Life. This assimilation transcends the power of its own nature and of any created nature to effect in it.

Together with the vital transformation of man's soul in the order of being by sanctifying grace, goes a corresponding elevation of his faculties of operation by supernatural, permanent, operative forms that permit him to give full expression in the order of operation to the divine life present in him in the order of being. These operative principles flow from sanctifying grace present in the soul in the manner in which man's natural faculties of operation are rooted in and flow from the natural life of his soul.¹⁰ Just as sanctifying grace provides man with a share in Divine Life, so these active forms permit him to share in the activity proper to God as God.

---

[9] The use of such comparison by medieval theologians is sometimes misleading. One should not make the mistake of considering such examples to be actual sources of doctrine or to have been offered as probative evidence in support of doctrine, no more than the common sense analogies of Christ should be considered sources of His teaching. Aquinas, having developed his theology of grace from sources which have nothing to do with the phenomena of light and fire, introduces a common sense understanding of these phenomena to illustrate by analogy his thought. The appeal to such analogies among theologians did, in fact, influence the scientific curiosity of their age. "A subject which was to see the most remarkable progress during the 13th and 14th centuries was optics. The study of light attracted the attention in particular of those who tended to Augustinian-Platonism in philosophy, and this was for two reasons: light had been for Saint Augustine and other Neo-Platonists the analogy of divine grace and of the illumination of the human intellect by divine truth, and it was amenable to mathematical treatment." A. C. Crombie, *Augustine to Galileo*, Vol. 1 (London: Mercury Books, 1964), pp. 99-100.

[10] *Summa*, I-II, q. 110, a. 4 ad.1.

IMAGE OF GOD BY GRACE

These permanent forms are called infused virtues and gifts of the Holy Spirit. Three of the infused virtues dispose man to participate in the divine activity by which God knows, loves, and possesses Himself. These are the theological virtues of Faith, Hope, and Charity. The other infused virtues endow human nature with a share in the activity of God by which He acts on the created order. Finally, the gifts of the Holy Spirit exist as permanent, infused forms which dispose man to respond vitally to the movements of the Spirit in him in an assimilation to the perfection by which within the divine unity the Spirit moves the Divine Essence.[11]

This doctrine can be stated in terms of our analysis of the relationship between the Uncreated Being, Truth, Love, Life, Beatitude, and Power of God and the created being, truth, love, life, beatitude and power of man:

1. By nature man possesses being, truth, love, life and power which is a created derivation and participation in the Being, Truth, Love, Life, and Power of God.

2. By the exercise of his natural aptitude for knowing and loving God man can evolve from a potential image of God to the actual image of God by nature.

3. This natural participation in divine life is radically inferior to the being and activity proper to God, and equips man to share only remotely in the existence and activity of the Divine Nature.

4. By the new life of grace God gratuitously bestows on man an extraordinary participation in His being and activity that introduces man into the inner life proper to the Divine Nature. Man thereby becomes a "partner in the Divine Nature"[12] a "son of God" and "heir"[13] to eternal life. This new participation in the divine Life while created, accidental, and analogous, so transcends the possibilities of nature and

---

[11] *Summa*, I-II, q. 68, a.1.

[12] II *Pet.* 1.4.

[13] *Rom.* 8.16-17.

is so proper to the Divine Essence that God could not create an entity which by nature possesses this level of perfection.

5. This life of grace can be described in terms of my analysis as the communication to man on the *level of being* (entitative) of a participation in the Being and Life of God, and on the *level of operation* of a participation in the uniqueness of Divine Truth (Faith), Beatitude (Hope), and Love (Charity) by which God knows, loves, and possesses Himself.[14] By the other infused virtues man participates in the Power, Causality, Justice, and Mercy of God by which He acts on created being.

6. Through the exercise of the theological virtues man becomes the actual image of God by grace in the contemplative aspects of the divine being. Through the exercise of the moral virtues he becomes the actual image of God by grace in the practical order.

III. EVOLUTION IN THE LIFE OF GRACE

As we have already seen the transition of man from potential to actual image of God in the natural order is not an instantaneous one.[15] Rather it is a gradual, lifelong process of growth in which man as a proximate, secondary cause actively develops in himself his natural aptitude for perfection. An analogous situation holds for man's development as the actual image of God in the order of grace.

The new life of grace does not effect an immediate transformation and elevation of human nature into actual divine likeness without man's exercising an active role in the process. God, providing for the workings of nature, ordinarily introduces sanctifying grace into man's soul in an initial stage of immaturity as a kind of seed of eternal life. He incorporates the maximum cooperation of human nature as an instrumental cause in a process of gradual evolution to maturity:

> Now it is evident that sanctifying grace bears the same relation to beatitude as the seed like form in nature does to

---

[14] *Summa*, II-II, q. 23, a2, ad1.
[15] Cf. p. 315 ff.

the natural effect; hence (*Jn.* 3.9) grace is called the *seed* of God.[16]

Every movement of the will towards God can be termed a conversion to God. And so there is a threefold turning to God. The first is by the perfect love of God; this belongs to the creature enjoying the possession of God; and for such conversion consummate grace is required. The next turning to God is that which merits beatitude; and for this grace is the principle of merit.

The third conversion is that whereby a man disposes himself so that he may have grace. For this no habitual grace is required, but the operation of God Who draws the soul toward Himself.[17]

Man was not intended to secure his ultimate perfection at once, like the angel. Hence a longer way was assigned to man than to the angel for securing beatitude.[18]

But if he [the angel] had not grace before entering upon beatitude, it would then have to be said that he had beatitude without merit, even as we have grace. This, however, is quite foreign to the idea of beatitude; which conveys the notion of an end, and is the reward of virtue.[19]

The charity of a wayfarer can increase. For we are called wayfarers by reason of our being on the way to God, Who is the last end of our happiness. In this way we advance as we get nigh to God, Who is approached "not by steps of the body but by the affections of the soul" and this approach is the result of charity, since it unites man's mind to God.

---

[16] *Summa*, I, q. 62, a. 3c.
[17] *Ibid.*, q. 62, a.2 ad. 3.
[18] *Ibid.*, q. 62, a.5 ad. 1.
[19] *Ibid.*, q. 62, a. 4c.

Consequently it is essential to the charity of a wayfarer that it can increase.[20]

The different stages of growth that the life of grace goes through in man have been a constant source of speculation for spiritual authors. Saint Theresa of Avila, for example, distinguishes seven stages or *mansions* in this evolution.[21] Aquinas, building his understanding of this evolution in grace primarily around the growth of charity in the soul, distinguishes three principal stages of development of grace in man in his movement from potential to actual image of God by grace:

> The spiritual increase of charity may be considered in respect of a certain likeness to the growth of the human body. For although this latter growth may be divided into many parts, yet it has certain fixed divisions according to those particular actions or pursuits to which man is brought by this same growth....
>
> In like manner the divers degrees of charity are distinguished according to the different pursuits to which man is brought by the increase of charity. For at first it is incumbent on man to occupy himself chiefly with avoiding sin and resisting his concupiscences, which move him in opposition to charity: this concerns beginners, in whom charity has to be fed or fostered lest it be destroyed; in the second place man's chief pursuit is to aim at progress in good, and this is the pursuit of the proficient, whose chief aim is to strengthen their charity by adding to it: while man's third pursuit is to aim chiefly at union with and enjoyment of God: this belongs to the perfect who desire to be dissolved and to be with Christ.[22]

God alone is the principal cause of the growth of sanctifying grace in the soul:

> Nothing can act beyond its species, since the cause must always be more powerful than its effect. Now the gift of

---

[20] *Ibid.*, II-II, q. 24, a. 4c.
[21] A. Royo, op. cit. pp. 217-219.
[22] *Summa* II-II, q. 24 a. 9c.

grace surpasses every capability of created nature, since it is nothing short of a partaking of the Divine Nature, which exceeds every other nature. And thus it is impossible that any creature should cause grace. For it is as necessary that God alone should deify, bestowing a partaking of the Divine Nature by a participated likeness, as it is impossible that anything save fire should enkindle.[23]

Man enjoys an active role in the evolution of grace in his soul when he acts in union with the instrumentality of the humanity of Christ. This activity of human nature in contributing in union with Christ to its own development in the life of grace takes place principally through the use of the Sacraments, the merits of good works, and the impetratory power of prayer:

> Christ's humanity is an "organ of His Godhead," as Damascene says (*De Fide Orthod* .3.19). Now an instrument does not bring forth the action of the principal agent by its own power, but in virtue of the principal agent. Hence Christ's humanity does not cause grace by its own power, but by virtue of the Divine Nature joined to it, whereby the actions of Christ's humanity are saving actions...as in the person of Christ the humanity causes our salvation by grace, the Divine power being the principal agent, so likewise in the sacraments of the New Law, which are derived from Christ, grace is instrumentally caused by the sacraments, and principally by the power of the Holy Spirit working in the sacraments....[24]

Likewise, neither can it be said that the Holy Spirit moves the will in such a way to the act of loving, as though the will were an instrument, for an instrument, though it be a principle of actions, nevertheless has not the power to act or not to act, for then again the act would cease to be voluntary and meritorious, whereas it has been stated above (I-II, q. 114, a. 14) that the love of Charity is the root of merit: and, given

---

[23] *Ibid.*, I-II, q.112, a. 1c.
[24] *Ibid.*, I-II, q. 112 a. 1 d. 1.

that the will is moved by the Holy Spirit to the act of love, it is necessary that the will also should be the efficient cause of that act.[25]

...prayer, besides causing spiritual consolation at the time of praying, has a twofold efficacy in respect of a future effect, namely, efficacy in meriting and efficacy in impetrating. Now prayer, like any other virtuous act; is efficacious in meriting, because it proceeds from charity as its root, the proper object of which is the eternal good that we merit to enjoy.... As to its efficacy in impetrating, prayer derives this from the grace of God to Whom we pray, and Who instigates us to pray.[26]

God bestows many things on us out of His liberality, even without our asking for them: but that He wishes to bestow certain things on us at our asking, is for the sake of our good, namely, that we may acquire confidence in having recourse to God, and that we may recognize in Him the Author of our goods.[27]

We have already seen how it pertains to the natural perfection of man that he be the secondary cause of his evolution to maturity, thereby participating in the divine self-sufficiency by possessing within himself the inner, secondary principles of his own fullness of being.[28] I have termed this participation of human nature in God's self sufficiency "radical godliness." Since grace perfects nature and operates according to the mode of nature, God provides in the order of grace for man's natural radical godliness by endowing him with supernatural inner principles of growth in grace, and by incorporating the maximum utilization of man's active and passive cooperation in His plan for man's evolution to actual image of God by grace.

It is principally through the sacraments, meritorious works, and the impetratory power of prayer that man in the order of grace expresses

---

[25] *Ibid.*, II-II, q. 23, a. 2c.

[26] *Ibid.*, II-II, q. 83, a.15c.

[27] *Ibid.*, II-II, q. 83, a. 2 ad. 3.

[28] *Cf.* Chapter Five, Section II.

his radical godliness and becomes under God and Christ a contributing cause to his own evolution as the image of God by grace.

IV. GRACE AND NATURE, THE NEW LIFE AND THE OLD

What happens to man's natural life and operation with the advent of grace? Sanctifying grace and the infused virtues do not suppress, eliminate, or by-pass the presence and necessity of man's natural life and operation. On the contrary, grace as an accidental modification of human nature presupposes the living reality of the rational soul as the subject of its modification Thus one does not baptize the corpse of a human, or an irrational living being. Grace, therefore, preserves, elevates, and perfects both the being and operation of human nature as a perfecting principle preserves and elevates the perfectible, and as the soul perfects the body or form perfects matter:

> So long as nature endures, its operation remains. But beatitude does not destroy nature, since it is its perfection. Therefore it does not take away natural knowledge and love.
>
> Natural knowledge and love remain in the angels. For as principles of operations are mutually related, so are the operations themselves. Now it is manifest that nature is to beatitude as first to second; because beatitude is superadded to nature. But the first must ever be preserved in the second. Consequently nature must be preserved in beatitude: and in like manner the act of nature must be preserved in the act of beatitude.
>
> The advent of a perfection removes the opposite imperfection. Now the imperfection of nature is not opposed to the perfection of beatitude, but underlies it; as the imperfection of the power underlies the perfection of the form, and the power is not taken away by the form, but the privation which is opposed to the form. In the same way the imperfection of natural knowledge is not opposed to the perfection of the knowledge in glory; for nothing hinders us from knowing a thing through various mediums, as a thing may be known at the one time through a probable medium and through a demonstrative one....

All things which make up beatitude are sufficient of themselves. But in order for them to exist, they presuppose the natural gifts; because no beatitude is self-subsisting, except uncreated beatitude.

There cannot be two operations of the one faculty at the one time, except the one be ordained to the other. But natural knowledge and love are ordained to the knowledge and love of glory. Accordingly there is nothing to hinder natural knowledge and love from existing in the angel conjointly with those of glory.[29]

...if either of them (that is angel or man) loved self more than God, it would follow that natural love would be perverse, and that it would not be perfected but destroyed by charity.[30]

Grace, as a quality, is said to act upon the soul, not after the manner of an efficient cause, but after the manner of a formal cause, as whiteness makes a thing white, and justice, just.[31]

Now in the manifestation of faith, God is the active cause, having perfect knowledge from all eternity; while man is likened to matter in receiving the influx of God's action.[32]

Grace is more perfect than nature, and, therefore, does not fail in those things wherein man can be perfected by nature.[33]

Nature is compared to charity which is the principle of merit, as matter to form.... Accordingly neither nature nor faith can, without charity, produce a meritorious act; but, when accompanied by charity the act of faith is made merit-

---

[29] *Summa*, I, q. 62, a. 7. Note replies to Objections 1, 2, and 3.
[30] *Summa*, I, q. 60, a. 5c.
[31] *Ibid.*, I-II, q. 110 a. 2, ad 1.
[32] *Ibid.*, II-II, q. 1, a. 7, ad 3.
[33] *Ibid.*, II-II, q. 9, a. 1c.

orious thereby, even as act of nature, and a natural act of the freewill.[34]

God is effectively the life both of the soul by charity, and of the body by the soul: but formally charity is the life of the soul even as the soul is the life of the body.[35]

This does not mean that human nature is proximately disposed for the elevating effect of grace. Since there is no proportion between natural human life and the life of grace, there is nothing present in human nature which demands this elevation by grace, or permits man to prepare himself through his own natural resources for the reception of grace.[36] However, even after having received grace through a gratuitous act of divine mercy, man still retains the power by sinful acts to destroy the life of grace present in him. There is an opposition of contradiction between sin and grace, between loving God above all things else and loving a created good over God:

I answer that one contrary is removed by the other contrary to charity by its very nature, which consists in man's loving God above all things, and subjecting himself to Him entirely, by referring all that is his to God. It is therefore essential to charity that man should so love God as to wish to submit to Him in all things, and always to follow the rule of His commandments; since whatever is contrary to His commandments is manifestly contrary to charity, and therefore by its very nature is capable of destroying charity.[37]

Since grace perfects nature the evolution of man as the actual image of God by grace builds upon and brings to ideal completion his evolution as the actual image of God by nature. While it is not essential to man that he possesses the acquired virtues in order that he be elevated by grace and the infused virtues, the presence of the acquired virtues makes the exercise of infused virtue easy and reduces the

---

[34] *Ibid.*, II-II, q. 2, a. 9, ad 1.
[35] *Ibid.*, II-II, q. 23, a. 2 ad. 2.
[36] *Ibid.*, I-II, q. 112, aa 2, 3.
[37] *Ibid.*, II-II , q. 24 a. 12 c.

danger of sinful movements destructive of grace and charity. Also the acquired virtues provide ideal instruments for the expression of grace. Charity as the form of all the virtues, acquired as well as infused, effectively commands the exercise of both.[38] As one grows in charity the exercise of the acquired and infused virtues becomes more frequent and intense, and the evolution of man as the actual image of God by nature and grace advances together. It is this development of the full range of man's natural aptitude for perfection as commanded by his supernatural growth in charity effecting his harmonious evolution as image of God by nature and grace that constitutes the form of Christian humanism which seems most congenial to the traditional Catholic doctrine concerning grace and nature. Implicit in Christian humanism understood in this manner, is a profound esteem and sympathy of the supernatural man for the values in breadth and depth of man's natural aptitude for perfection.

This analysis, brief as it is, presents the substance of traditional Thomistic understanding of the life of grace. It is an understanding that has been and is much criticized both outside the Church and within the Church. For example, the Church's teaching about man's intrinsic justification by grace is alien to the thought of Conservative Protestantism. Also its clear distinction between nature and grace, the natural and the supernatural order is rejected by many Liberal Protestants and by some contemporary Catholic theologians. Notwithstanding these and other reactions, this presentation of Aquinas' understanding of grace provides me with the basis for drawing some of the ecumenical implications of this doctrine.

V. IMAGE OF GRACE AND ECUMENISM

According to this doctrine the effects of sanctifying grace and the infused virtues and gifts in the soul are multiple. First and foremost, as we have seen grace effects in the just a formal, physical participation in the divine nature whereby the very kind of life proper to God now vivifies and animates man in an accidental, analogous, participated presence. The just man through grace, therefore, comes alive and pulsates with the kind of life uniquely proper in nature to God. By reason of this extraordinary participation in Divine Life, the just

---

[38] *Ibid.*, I-II, q. 65, a. 2; II-II, q. 23, a. 8.

becomes "sons of God" and by virtue of the Spirit now present in them cry out, "Abba, Father"[39] This effect is the foundation of the others which follow. According to Saint Paul because men by grace are "sons of God," they also become "heirs"[40] of eternal life with a valid, objective claim to this inheritance. Eternal Life consists primarily in the Beatific Vision with all that it implies by way of man's knowing, loving, and possessing God immediately and eternally by participation in God's knowledge, love and possession of Himself.[41] Now this is to become the image of God in the fullest sense.

Grace initiates this perfection as image of God in the present life in a less perfect degree and as the preparation for its consummation in the life to come. By reason of grace man also becomes a brother and co-heir with Christ, sharing with Him the life of the Father which He possesses in plenitude. "They are the ones (that is the just) He chose specially long ago and intended to become true images of His Son, so that His Son might be the eldest of many brothers. He called those He intended for this: those He called He justified, and with those He justified He shared His glory."[42]

From these effects others follow. Man by grace is made intrinsically just and pleasing to God.[43] He becomes capable of meritorious works by which he may earn eternal life.[44] He becomes the living temple of the Trinity and enters into intimate union with God.[45] This union brings man so close to the divine that it can be surpassed only by the grace of hypostatic or personal union which is the exclusive gift made to the humanity of Christ.

By reason of grace, therefore, man becomes the image of God in a manner that substantially transcends his perfection as image of God by

---

[39] *Rom.* 8.15.
[40] *Rom.* 8.16.
[41] *Summa*, I-II, q. 3, a. 8.
[42] *Rom.* 8.28-30.
[43] *Summa*, I-II, q. 113, a. 1.
[44] *Ibid.*, I-II, q. 114, aa. 1, 2, 3, 4.
[45] *Jn.* 14.23.

nature. He is transformed in being and operation with participated Divine Life. His contact with his humanity as image by grace becomes his point of most direct, immediate, and profound contact with God.

Since he becomes the image of God most properly through the act of knowing and loving God, the just man must be open to the possibilities of such knowledge and love which grace brings to him.[46] He must allow this part of his reality to exercise an increasing predominance in the order of operation over every other aspect of his being. This means that the just man must exercise a kind of ecumenism toward his own humanity and endeavor to relate more and more to that part of himself in which he encounters the potential and actual presence of grace and the potential for acts of knowing and loving God.

It means further, as we have seen, that he must approach his entire life, past as well as present, consciously open to the workings of grace on every level and in every aspect if his evolution as image of God is to progress ideally.[47] It is in the degree in which the just man is open and gives priority to the presence of grace in his own humanity that the actions proper to grace intensify and his union with God in actual knowledge and love is advanced. Teresa of Avila, John of the Cross, and Catherine of Siena all would exemplify such openness. Much of the spiritual discipline and counsel of the great mystics, in fact, expresses this ecumenical attitude toward themselves. They approach their humanity, conscious of the potential of grace there and by removing obstacles and disposing themselves in every way possible, endeavoring to cooperate with God as He causes the spring of living waters in them "to well up to eternal life."[48]

The just man's ecumenical approach to his own humanity as the image of God by nature and grace, controls the character of his ecumenical approach to all other men. To the extent that he is open to and experiences God's transforming presence within himself he will be open to and experience the potential and actual presence of God in others. If he is closed to that presence, potential and actual in his own humanity, he will be similarly closed to that presence in others:

---

[46] *Summa*, I. q. 93, a. 7.
[47] *Cf.* Chapter Three, Section IV.
[48] *Jn.* 4.14.

...properly speaking, a man is not a friend to himself, but something more than a friend, since friendship implies union, for Dionysius says (*Div. Nom.* iv) that "love is a unitive force," whereas a man is one with himself which is more than being united to another. Hence, just as unity is the principle of union, so the love with which a man loves himself is the form and root of friendship. For if we have friendship with others it is because we do unto them as we do unto ourselves, hence we read in *Ethics* ix. 4, 8, that "the origin of friendly relations with others lies in our relations to ourselves."[49]

Man finds his primary point of contact with God in his own humanity as transformed by grace into the image of God. In this encounter with himself as image by grace he also has his point of most direct immediate encounter with Christ. Since the grace in him is not only caused instrumentally by the humanity of Christ, but it belongs more to Christ than to himself, it effects the living presence of Christ in his soul. Lastly, in his contact with his own humanity as the image of God the just man finds his point of union with the potential and actual presence of God by grace and nature in the rest of mankind. It is this point that I now wish to consider.

VI. IMAGE BY GRACE IN COMMUNITY

Man's natural aptitude for becoming the image of God, as we have seen, cannot be realized except in community with other actual images of God.[50] According to our analysis it is in a community of truth, love, life, beatitude, and power with men who are in some degree actual images of God by their participation in Divine Truth, Love, Life, Beatitude, and Power that man evolves in his knowledge and love of God. Similarly in this community lies his power to impart this godly perfection to the rest of created reality.

An analogous situation holds in the order of grace. Man normally cannot become the actual image of God by grace except in community with other actual images of God. Such community is essential to the

---

[49] *Summa*, II-II, q. 25, a. 4c.
[50] *Cf.* Chapter Six, Section V.

initiation of supernatural life in man and to its evolution to perfection for three basic reasons:

First, community with other images of God is necessary because a man cannot receive the initial grace except through the instrumentality of other humans. And once grace is implanted in him, he still requires such community since grace cannot develop to maturity except through the nourishing, perfecting, sanctifying activity of other men as instruments of God's action on his soul.

God is the principal cause of grace, as we have seen, and He has no need of secondary causes in order to impart a participation in His Divine Life to the just. However, God has chosen to incorporate in the maximum degree the instrumental activities of men both in implanting grace and in developing it to maturity. He endows these instruments with the necessary gifts and graces to function in this ministerial way in union with Christ. Therefore a man must enter into community with such instruments and submit to their teaching, sanctifying and directing activities in order both to receive the initial gift of grace and to allow this gift to evolve to maturity:

> As the Apostle says (*Rom.* 13.1), "those things that are of God are well ordered." Now the order of things consists in this, that things are led to God by other things, as Dionysius says (*Coel. Hier.* iv). And hence since grace is ordained to lead men to God, this takes place in a certain order, so that some are led to God by others.
>
> And thus there is a twofold grace—one whereby man himself is united to God, and this is called *sanctifying grace:* the other is that whereby one man co-operates with another in leading him to God, and this gift is called *gratuitous grace*, and beyond the merit of the person. But whereas it is bestowed on a man, not to justify him, but rather that he may co-operate in the justification of another, it is not called *sanctifying grace*. And it is of this that the Apostle says (I *Cor.* 12.7): "And the manifestation of the Spirit is given to every man unto utility," i. e. of others.[51]

---

[51] *Summa*, I-II, q. 111, a. 1c.

IMAGE OF GOD BY GRACE

We are dealing here with a child/adult relationship in the order of grace which corresponds to the child/adult relation in the order of nature whereby the potential, child image of God in man must be nourished by the adult image of God in others in order to evolve to the maturity of an adult image itself.

Second, even after having achieved relative maturity as an adult image of God by grace, the individual still must continue in community with other adult images of God in order to fill out the limitations of his participation in the Divine Life by grace and attain the maximum knowledge, love, and possession of God possible. This necessity is made clear by the corresponding condition of man as the image of God in the natural level. No individual, family, community, nation, culture, age or particular social grouping of any size is adequate to express the full potential of human nature for godliness.

Thus, as we have noted,[52] a man must enter into the broadest and deepest experience of human nature as the image of God in a way that transcends the limited expressions of any particular age, culture, or social grouping if he is to attain the fullest possible encounter with God's participated presence in mankind.

Still less can an individual, community, nation, culture, age, or particular social grouping contain and express in the fullest manner possible the infinitely richer possibilities of God's presence in human nature through grace. Especially in the order of grace, therefore, a multiplicity and diversity of just men are required in order that an explicitly fuller presence of divine life may be realized in human nature. And the individual must enter into conscious community in breadth and depth with all expressions of grace in human nature if he is to fill out the limitations of his participation in the Divine Life by the grace in his own soul.

He must relate not only to the reality of grace present in men of his own time, but also to the expressions of grace in the past while being open to the possibilities of the future. He must be open to the experience of God's presence through grace in the people of the Old

---

[52] *Cf.* Chapter Six, Section V.

THE THEOLOGY OF ECUMENISM

Testament times as well as in those of the New Testament. He must commune with the expressions of Divine Wisdom and Love in all the centuries gone by as well as in our own. He must commune with the special workings of grace in the simple, weak, young, and ignoble as well as with workings of grace in the wise, strong, triumphant, mature, and admirable. He must unite his own experience of God's presence in himself with that presence in all others wherever, whenever, and however it may be found, so that in community with God's people and the fullness of grace, he may experience the miracle of God's extraordinary, gratuitous presence in mankind.

In this second form of community we are speaking of an adult/adult relationship in which adult images of God share with one another the reality of God's merciful action on their souls. This level of community represents the ideal of ecumenical dialogue in which adult images of God seek not so much to convert or to be converted, change or be changed, as to enter in to a mutually enriching relationship in which persons on a level of idealized equality share with each other whatever exists of positive value in their encounter with God.

Third, if a man is to become fully the image of God by grace he must not only receive the gift of divine life and allow it to mature in him, but he must also experience the inner movements of God's participated power, causality, justice and mercy by imparting to others as instruments of God a share in this life of grace which has been engendered in him. In this work of imparting grace to others in which the adult image in him enriches the potential and child-image of God in them, he experiences contact with the creating, sustaining, perfecting action of the power, justice, and mercy of God on the created order.

The just man cannot develop as the image of god in this aspect of God's action on created being without identifying and entering into intimate, daily community with the potential and child-image of God in other human beings. And just as in the natural order the limitations of man's ability to function as an efficient cause under God demand that he unite with other men in collective efficient causality, so also and with greater reason, in the order of grace the individual just man must join with other adult images of God in collective acts of efficient causality in order that the power of God may adequately act in and through their instrumentality. This phase of man's relation to the perfectible aspects of human nature is an adult/child relationship in which the just man in union with other adult images of God acts to implant grace in the potential image of God and to develop that grace already present in the child-images of God.

I don't intend to imply by this analysis that the relations of the just in such a community of faith are simple ones assuming only one of the three child/adult, adult/adult, or adult/child forms exclusively. Since the just in this life are always wayfarers and capable of further growth in grace, they combine in themselves elements of both the child and the adult. In their relations with each other one would normally expect to find all three levels at work so that in some aspects the child in them will be responding to the adult in others while in other aspects the adult will be either sharing with the adult in others or perfecting the child in them. In this mutually perfecting relationship in which the individual is both perfected and perfecting we have a dialogue in the order of nature by which men evolve in community as images of God.

When this dialogue is analyzed for the purpose of determining the proximate source of the impulse in the just to enter into such community, it seems to me that the source of this impulse is found to reside principally in the dynamics of the Theological Virtues of Faith, Hope, and Charity as understood in the Thomistic tradition. According to this doctrine the Theological Virtues have God as their principal object in the sense that He is both the reality attained by them as well as the means by which He is attained (*objectum formale quod et quo*). Since the virtues contact God as Truth, Goodness, and Beatitude, their acts constitute that exercise of knowledge, love and possession of God by which man is in the most proper sense the image of God by grace.

According to this same doctrine, moreover, while the Theological Virtues have God as their principal object, each of them encompasses within its dynamics a specific relation to human nature which demands a special openness and response to God's participated presence and activity in human instrumentalities as the condition for its existence and development. The openness to God in Himself and the openness to and community with his participated presence and activity in human nature are so inseparable that the growth in these virtues by which one comes closer to God entails a concomitant development by which one becomes more open and closer to God's participated presence in human nature. Because the dynamics of the Theological Virtues as it seems to me, entail this ecumenical component and give rise in the most fundamental manner to the ecumenical dialogue, it would be desirable to consider each of these virtues in detail.

VII. IMAGE IN A COMMUNITY OF FAITH

The object of the Theological Virtue of Faith is God as First Truth. Both the truth to which we assent by Faith and our motive for assenting is the Truth of God. By Faith we enter into union (community) with God as Truth, and it is our participation in this Truth of God which motivates our assent. Faith is the seed of and first step toward the Beatific Vision! It transforms man into the image of God in Truth by giving him his initial participation in the divine knowledge by which God knows Himself:

> Accordingly if we consider, in faith, the formal aspect of the object, it is nothing else than the First Truth. For the faith of which we are speaking, does not assent to anything, except because it is revealed by God. Hence the mean on which faith is based is the Divine Truth.
>
> If, however, we consider materially the things to which faith assents, they include not only god, but also many other things, which nevertheless, do not come under the assent of faith except as bearing some relation to God, in as much as, to wit, through certain effects of the Divine operation, man is held on his journey towards the enjoyment of God. Consequently from this point of view also the object of faith is, in a way, the First Truth, in as much as nothing comes under faith except in relation to God, even as the object of the medical art is health, for it considers nothing save in relation to health.[53]

Notwithstanding the fact that the First Truth is both the reality which is attained by Faith and the means of its attainment, God has chosen to utilize human instruments in proposing His Truth to man for belief. Therefore without contact (community) with these instruments Faith is not possible. For this reason one must be open to Truth's acti-

---

[53] *Summa*, II-II, q. 1, a. 1c.

vity in and through truth in human instruments as the condition for his encounter with Truth:

> As the Apostle says (*Heb*.11.6), "he that cometh to God, must believe that He is." now a man cannot believe, unless the truth be proposed to him that he may believe it. Hence the need for the truth of faith to be collected together, so that it might the more easily be proposed to all, lest anyone might stray from the truth through ignorance of the faith.[54]

> ...gratuitous grace is ordained to this, viz, that a man may help another to be led to God. Now no man can help in this by moving interiorly (for this belongs to God alone) but only exteriorly by teaching or persuading. Hence gratuitous grace embraces whatever a man needs in order to instruct another in Divine things which are above reason.[55]

> Now the knowledge a man receives from God cannot be turned to another's profit, except by means of speech. And since the Holy Spirit does not fail in anything that pertains to the profit of the Church, He provides also the members of the Church with speech; to the effect that a man not only speaks so as to be understood by different people, but also speaks with effect, and this pertains to the grace of the word.... In order to effect this the Holy Spirit makes use of the human tongue as of an instrument.[56]

This does not mean that one believes by Faith because of the authority of the human instruments. But it does mean that openness and community with the presence of the Spirit actively working in human instruments is a condition for Faith:

> If we say: (I believe) *in* the holy Catholic Church, this must be taken as verified in so far as our faith is directed to

---

[54] *Summa*, II-II, q. 1, a. 9c.

[55] *Ibid.*, I-II, q. 111, a. 4 c.

[56] *Summa*, II-II, q. 177, a. 1c.

the Holy Spirit Who sanctifies the Church; so that the sense is: I believe in the Holy Spirit sanctifying the Church.[57]

No single human instrument is adequate to express explicitly the fullness of the Infinite Wisdom of God. So the need of many witnesses for awareness of the contents of Christ's teaching is not due to a defect of the instruments. Witnesses operating in a complementary manner over a long period of time are required in order that human nature may instrumentally convey, with some fullness, the Truth of God. Due to the use of a community of instruments by the Holy Spirit over a period of time and in varying ways to convey the Truth of God, the Church must endeavor to propose a summary of the primary teaching of this community for the benefit of the faithful:

> The truth of faith is contained in Holy Writ diffusely, under various modes of expression and sometimes obscurely, so that, in order to gather the truth of faith from Holy Writ, one needs long study and practice, which are unattainable by all those who require to know the truth of faith, many of whom have no time for study, being busy with other affairs. And so it was necessary to gather together a clear summary from the sayings of Holy Writ, to be proposed to the belief of all. This indeed was no addition to Holy Writ, but something taken from it.[58]

With the advent of Christ and His teaching, the Truth of God receives its most perfect, authoritative, definitive statement. Christ's teaching contains the substance of Divine Truth in so far as it can be conveyed through the limitations of Christ's humanity operating as the instrument of His Divinity. However, man's ability to digest the richness of the Truth of Christ is limited and he continues to evolve in his explicit grasp of the unlimited implications of that teaching:

> ...as regards the substances of the article of faith they have not received any increase as time went on; since whatever those who lived later have believed, was contained, albeit

---

[57] *Ibid.*, II-II, q.1, a.9, ad. 5.
[58] *Summa* II-II, q. 1, a. 9, ad. 1.

implicitly in the faith of those Fathers who preceded them. But there was an increase in the number of articles believed explicitly, since to those who lived in later times some were known explicitly which were not known explicitly by those before them.[59]

This evolution in man's explicit awareness of the contents of Christ's teaching is not due to a defect on the part of the teacher or the message, but it exists by reason of limitations in the disciples.

> Progress in knowledge occurs in two ways. First, on the part of the teacher.... Secondly, on the part of the learner; thus the master, who has perfect knowledge of the art, does not deliver it all at once to his disciple from the very outset, for he would not be able to take it all in, but he condescends to the disciple's capacity and instructs him little by little. It is in this way that men made progress in the knowledge of faith as time went on.[60]

Therefore Faith demands not only an openness to the Spirit's activity in the instruments of revelation in the Old and New Testaments, but also an openness to the presence of the Spirit over the ages assisting the just man to understand the Truth of revelation and making explicit what is implicit in it. Since the Truth of God is infinite and the gift of Faith is a participation in that Truth, the evolution in explicit awareness of the contents of Faith, is, as in the case of growth in Charity, potentially infinite.

While Faith concerns primarily the Truth of God, it extends to all created things under the aspect of their ultimate relation to God. When radical shifts take place in the human situation and new conditions emerge that obscure the relation of man and created reality to God, a struggle must go on in which the just man focuses the light of Faith upon these areas to find answers and make explicit the illuminative powers of the teachings of faith. Such answers are implicit in revelation since they deal with ultimate truth and reality. However, the process of

---

[59] *Summa*, II-II, q. 1, a. 7c.
[60] *Summa*, II-II, q. 1 a.7 ad.2.

discovery by which they become explicit is a slow and difficult one. Often men must live for a long time with new situations, prayerfully and studiously evaluating them in the light of Christ's teaching before the clarifications come. And so in each age the just must be open not only to the Spirit's activity in the community of the past, but also to the Spirit's movements in the community of the just in the present as He assists men in their evolution as images of God in Truth.

When new shifts occur in the created order that bring about situations and problems significantly different from those of the past, the emerging wisdom of the present is indispensable if this evolution is to take place. In times of change it would be wrong to act purely with the wisdom of the past and uncritically embrace solutions to problems of a different age which fail to respond to the needs of the present. It would be wrong to ignore the warnings and insights of serious, thoughtful men who point out these differences. On the other hand, it would be equally wrong and presumptuous to ignore or reject the proven wisdom of the past—to affirm a unique presence of the Spirit in the contemporary age which permits men acting independently of the past order of the community to find the fullness of God's Truth in the present.

Rather the just are to act in community with the Spirit working in holy men both in the past and the present. They must build on the wisdom of the past by making explicit in the changing conditions of the present what was implicit in the wisdom of faith of that past. And since the Church, as the people of God, transcends the limitations of any particular age or culture—and most certainly individual persons—the criterion by which the Spirit's presence is deduced to be in an individual or particular community must remain the manner in which they act in community with the wisdom of the Church:

> The custom of the Church has very great authority and ought to be jealously observed in all things, since the very doctrine of catholic doctors derives its authority from the Church. Hence we ought to abide by the authority of the Church rather than by that of an Augustine or a Jerome or any doctor whatever.[61]

---

[61] *Summa*, II-II, q. 10, a. 12c.

IMAGE OF GOD BY GRACE

The evolution of Faith demands a community and dialogue of faith with mankind whereby we are open to persons as potential or actual images of God in Truth. Initially Faith involves a child/adult relation in which one receives the Truth of God from the community of adult images of that Truth of both the past and the present. As a person matures as image of God in Truth, he must fill out his possession of Truth in community on an adult/adult relation with other adult images. He must also, as circumstances permit, endeavor to impart that Truth in an adult/child relation to those who do not have it and yet seek it. This activity, moreover, should take place with due respect for persons and in a manner which avoids needless disturbance of others:

> The end of faith, even as of the other virtues must be referred to the end of charity, which is the love of God and our neighbor. Consequently when God's honor and our neighbor's good demand, man should not be contented with being united by faith to God's truth, but ought to confess his faith outwardly.... There is nothing commendable in making a public confession of one's faith, if it causes a disturbance among unbelievers, without any profit either to the faith or to the faithful.[62]

Faith as understood in Catholic tradition not only gives rise to community and dialogue with the just in the order of grace, but it also lays the basis for dialogue with persons on the purely natural level. Among other things Catholic doctrine affirms the natural perfection of man as the image of God. It teaches that man's natural hold on truth, love and goodness originates in the Truth, Love, and Goodness of God, and both reveals imperfectly these perfections in God and offers a point of union with Him.

All that we have seen about man's evolution in community as the image of God by nature falls within the traditional teaching of the Church and in substance is encompassed by Faith. Therefore, Faith demands of the Catholic that he approach the whole of created reality—and especially that he approach all manifestations of human life—as sacred, and points of contact with God. He must also affirm

---

[62] *Summa*, II-II, q.3 a.2 ad.1 and 3.

the intimate presence of God in the whole of the created order, and the qualitatively superior manifestation of that presence in human nature—notwithstanding error and personal defects that may be encountered in men.

Since Faith demands that a man be open to acknowledge and identify with the participated truth and goodness of God wherever he encounters it, it requires that the just be open to the possibility and fact of such truth and goodness in the breadth and depth of human nature. And whenever he encounters such a presence, he must be disposed to enter into a positive, personal relation with it.

At the same time Faith, together with the complementary activities of the gifts of knowledge and understanding, makes the just man acutely aware of the infinite difference between the created and the uncreated order—between God and his work.[63] Therefore, while Faith demands that the just enter into community with God's presence in the whole of the created order and especially, in human nature, it preserves the sense of the transcendence of God while affirming His immanence in created being.

Catholic Faith holds that while God is intimately present to every being, not every being equally participates in and reveals Him. God remains an infinite distance qualitatively from all created being. Thus according to Faith all truth participates in Truth, though not in the same degree, and Truth is present to truth and sometimes uses truth as an instrument to reveal itself in an extraordinary manner. But there remains an infinite qualitative difference between truth and Truth. In this understanding of Faith in the Catholic tradition, the tendency of Pattern I to identify truth and Truth is avoided. At the same time this understanding equally avoids the tendency of Pattern II to counter truth and Truth so that Truth is not reflected in truth and to hold that truth can serve neither as the instrument of Truth nor as a point of contact with Truth.

The effect of Catholic Faith is to make man approach human nature and the truth present in it as a reflection on the natural level of Truth; and as a potential instrument of Truth on the supernatural level; and as a point of extraordinary contact with Truth. Further, Faith demands that

---

[63] *Summa*, II-II, qq. 8-9.

a man enter into community with the truth in other men as the condition for entering into community with Truth. As Faith evolves in the just man his openness as image of God to Truth intensifies, together with his discerning, critical openness to Truth's potential and actual presence in the truth of human instruments. Thus the just man's movement toward God as Truth entails a concomitant movement toward the truth of human nature in depth and breadth as a participation in Truth by nature—and as the potential instrument of Truth through grace.

VIII. IMAGE IN A COMMUNITY OF HOPE

The object of the Theological Virtue of Hope is God as Eternal Happiness. The means by which one expects to achieve this object is that God in His infinite mercy and power makes this goal possible to man. Through Hope we enter into union (community) with God as Beatitude, and we participate in the certitude whereby God possesses His own goodness:

> As stated above, the hope of which we speak now, attains God by leaning on His help in order to obtain the hoped for good. Now an effect must be proportionate to its cause. Wherefore the good which we ought to Hope for from God properly and chiefly, is the infinite good, which is proportionate to the power of our divine helper, since it belongs to an infinite power to lead anyone to an infinite good. Such a good is eternal life, which consists in the enjoyment of God Himself. For we should hope from Him for nothing less than Himself, since His goodness, whereby he imparts good things to His creature, is no less than His Essence. Therefore the proper and principal object of hope is eternal happiness.[64]

The certitude of Hope is derived from the certitude of Faith:

> Hope does not trust chiefly in grace already received, but on God's omnipotence and mercy, whereby even he that has not grace, can obtain it, so as to come to eternal life. Now

---

[64] *Summa*, II-II, q. 17, a. 2c.

whoever has faith is certain of God's omnipotence and mercy.[65]

While God is both the object of Hope and the means of obtaining that object, Hope like Faith has its human component. It demands openness to God's mercy and power and that the condition for its existence and development is working through human instruments. In the first place Hope follows upon Faith and requires dialogue with the community of Faith for its existence. It is by Faith that the just have knowledge of the Eternal Beatitude of God and His will that men share in that Beatitude. Thus Hope depends upon Faith for knowledge of its object and the means of its attainment. Further, it is through the teaching of Faith that the just know that God intends to incorporate man's activity as the instrument through which divine mercy and power will principally operate to bring men to eternal happiness.

Thus, for example, Faith teaches with regards to the Sacraments that man must approach human nature with the certain expectation (Hope) of gaining perfect happiness. It teaches that he will find divine life communicated by a human act of religious washing; divine forgiveness in human forgiveness; divine strength and perseverance in human acts of anointing; contact with the Uncreated, Eternal, and Infinite in the mediating acts of a created, temporal, and finite human; Divine Love in human love; and the very person of God in the flesh of a man.

This does not mean that the just man must turn in Hope to human nature as the principal cause of eternal happiness It is only a secondary instrumental cause:

> Accordingly, just as it is not lawful to hope for any good save happiness, as one's last end, but only as something referred to final happiness, so too, it is unlawful to hope in any man, or any creature, as though it were the first cause of movement towards happiness. It is, however, lawful to hope in a man or a creature as being the secondary and instrumental agent, through whom one is helped to obtain any goods that are ordained to happiness. It is in this way that we turn to the saints, and that we ask men also for certain things;

---

[65] *Ibid.*, II-II, q. 18, a. 4, ad. 2.

and for this reason some are blamed in that they cannot be trusted to give help.[66]

Since no person or particular grouping of persons can be an adequate instrument of the omnipotence and infinite mercy of God, many persons operating in a variety of ways over a long period of time are required in order that a fuller expression may be given to divine mercy acting in and through human nature. Hope therefore will seek its encounter with God's mercy in community in His activity in a variety of persons and situations, and places and ways.

Since mercy involves a response to man's needs, the form in which mercy expresses itself is relative to the deficiencies that are to be relieved. As radical changes take place in the human situation which create new and different needs, corresponding changes in the manifestations of divine mercy and in the human instrumentalities of that mercy are to be expected. In such periods the man of Hope will be confidently open to community with these new modes of divine response to human needs and to the human instrumentalities of such response. He will also be in community with the expressions of divine mercy in the past in order to learn from and celebrate God's goodness in other times.

However, he will not make the mistake of slavishly continuing modes of merciful response to human deficiencies that were adapted to the needs of the past but which no longer answer the deficiencies of the present. From his community with the dynamics of God's mercy in the past, he will know how in times of radical change new instrumentalities invariably emerge under the movement of the Spirit. For example, new religious orders and reformed older orders emerging that provide a more relevant expression of divine mercy in the new situation and rekindle the sense of the divine presence and Hope in that presence when it has tended to die out.

Rather than bemoaning the changes taking place, or unjustly criticizing structures which worked effectively in other times but which were not designed to respond to contemporary situations, the man of

---

[66] *Summa*, II-II, q. 17, a. 4c.

Hope will take courage from his community with God's actions in the past. He will set about to initiate under the Spirit the new expressions of divine mercy which are required by the present.

The evolution of Hope like the evolution of Faith demands a developing community and dialogue with other men whereby one becomes more open and responsive to potential and actual movements of divine mercy in human nature. The initial stage of community in Hope is a child/adult one in which a person primarily looks to others for help by way of direction, encouragement, understanding, example, and love. As a man matures in Hope he enters into an adult/adult relation with others. In this, as adult images of God in Hope, they mutually share the positive results of their growth in the certain expectation of eternal happiness and their shared consciousness of the activity of divine mercy in their lives. Hope in this adult stage also engenders a growing desire that all others may participate in the good things of God.

The more a person matures in Hope the more broad and intense is his desire and expectation that others attain eternal happiness, and the more he is inclined to respond effectively to their deficiencies in this regard. Mature Hope, therefore, gives rise to an adult/child relation to other humans in their deficiencies in which the just man hopes and seeks for them the same happiness that he desires for himself. Such maturity presupposes charity by which he identifies with others and encompasses their potential for happiness under the same virtue of Hope with which he seeks eternal happiness for himself:

> ...if we presuppose the union of love with another, a man can hope for and desire something for another man, as for himself; and, accordingly, he can hope for another's eternal life, inasmuch as he is united to him by love, and just as it is the same virtue of charity whereby a man loves God, himself, and his neighbor, so too it is the same virtue of hope, whereby a man hopes for himself and for another.[67]

While the virtue of Hope has God for its object, it gives rise to the need for community and dialogue with other men as the condition for its existence and development. First, it requires community with adult

---

[67] *Summa*, II-II, q. 17, a. 4c.

images of God in grace through whom the just man may develop in grace and Hope as the image of God. Secondly, it requires community with adult images of God to fill out its experience of God's mercy and to have that experience sustained and intensified. Thirdly, adult Hope seeks a community with others in need that it may respond as an instrument of the Spirit to that need. In so responding Hope seeks to act in collective action with other persons of similar Hope to give more adequate expression to the mercy of God as the instruments of that mercy.

As in the case of Faith, Hope also lays the basis for community and dialogue not only with the just in the order of grace, but also with all men in the order of nature. Through his Faith the man of Hope knows that God uses truth, goodness, love, and all other perfections of the natural order as instruments of His mercy, and he approaches such perfections in whomsoever he finds them confident of their power to enrich his contact with eternal happiness. He also knows through Faith about the desire and potential of every man for eternal happiness as well as the desire of Christ for their salvation.

As man grows in likeness to Christ, he grows in the intensity of love by which he identifies with every man. He sees a potential or actual brother with him in Christ. Hope engenders confidence in the possibility of being both perfected and perfecting in contact with every human. In the order of nature as well as of grace, it motivates one to a true dialogue of mutually perfecting communication in which others are approached with respect and love.

As noted the Gifts of Knowledge and Understanding in union with Faith intensify the just man's insight into the infinite difference between the Creator and creature. They thereby deepen his sense of the transcendence of God while expanding his consciousness of the intimate presence of God to created being. So also the Gift of Fear operating in union with Hope leads to a heightened awareness of his total dependency upon the omnipotence and mercy of God as principal cause. This in turn confirms his certitude of encountering divine mercy in the instrumental workings of human nature.[68]

Hope, in this sense, while engendering the impulse to community in breadth and depth with human nature as the instrument of divine mercy, avoids the tendency of Pattern I to absorb divine mercy and power into human mercy and created power. It does not seek the principal cause in the instrumental cause. At the same time Hope explicitly rejects the opposite tendency of Pattern II, whereby in the expression of a kind of despair about human nature and created being, it minimizes or rejects the power of hope to function as an instrument of divine mercy. Or, as Aquinas would analyze this tendency, would deny to God the power to use human nature and created being in general as the instruments of His mercy.

Just as Faith demands that man approach human nature with confidence in its power as an instrument of the Spirit to contain and convey Divine Truth and become the condition for and point of contact with Truth, so Hope requires that man approach human nature with an equally firm certitude that in its activities as the instrument of the Spirit it contains and expresses the infinite mercy and power of God. As such, the activities of human nature become the condition and point of contact with the action of God whereby man is brought to eternal happiness.

As Hope matures in the just man, and the firm expectation of eternal happiness intensifies in him through God's mercy, he grows inseparably in his confidence in and openness to the presence of that mercy in the instrumental activities of human nature. His movement towards God as eternal happiness is at the same time a movement in depth into community with human nature as the instrumental means towards such happiness.

IX. IMAGE IN A COMMUNITY OF CHARITY

The object of the Theological Virtue of Charity is God as the Perfect Good. Through Charity man enters into community with God, loving Him immediately as He loves Himself and thereby becoming the image of God in Love:

---

[68] *Summa*, II-II, q. 19.

Now the proper object of love is the good, as stated above, so that wherever there is a special aspect of good, there is a special kind of love. But the Divine good, inasmuch as it is the object of happiness, has a special aspect of good, wherefore the love of charity, which is the love of that good, is a special kind of love.[69]

Accordingly, we must assert that to love which is an act of the appetitive power, even in this state of life, tends to God first, and flows on from Him to other things, and in this sense charity loves God immediately, and other things through God.[70]

But faith and hope attain God indeed in so far as we derive from Him the knowledge of truth or the acquisition of good, whereas charity attains God Himself that it may rest in Him, but not that something may accrue to us from Him.[71]

Charity involves true community and dialogue between God and man in which there is mutual love based upon communication after the manner of friendship:

According to the Philosopher not every love has the character of friendship, but that love which is together with benevolence, when, to wit, we love someone so as to wish good to him:

…Yet neither does well-wishing suffice for friendship, for a certain mutual love is requisite, since friendship is between friend and friend: and this well-wishing is founded on some kind of communication. Accordingly, since there is a communication between man and God, in as much as He communicates His happiness to us, some kind of friendship must needs be based on this same communication, of which it is written (I.*Cor*.1.9): "God is faithful: by Whom you are

---

[69] *Summa*, II-II, q. 23, a. 4c.
[70] *Summa*, II-II, q. 27 a. 4c.
[71] *Ibid.*, II-II, q. 23 a. 6c.

called unto the fellowship of His Son." The love which is based on this communication, is charity: wherefore it is evident that charity is the friendship of man for God.[72]

Not only is God the object which is immediately attained by Charity, (*objectum formale quod*), but He also is the means by which man is drawn in love toward His infinite goodness (*objectum formale quo*):

> Therefore charity can be in us neither naturally, nor through acquisition by the natural powers, but by the infusion of the Holy Spirit, Who is the love of the Father and the Son, and the participation of Whom in us is created charity....[73]

> The Divine Essence Itself is charity, even as It is wisdom, and goodness. Wherefore just as we are said to be good with the goodness which is God, and wise with the wisdom which is God (since the goodness whereby we are formally good is a participation of Divine goodness, and the wisdom whereby we are formally wise, is a share of Divine wisdom), so too the charity whereby formally we love our neighbor is a participation of Divine charity.[74]

While God is the immediate object of Charity, the community of love between God and man involves a human component whereby man is drawn into profound community with the rest of mankind as a condition of his community with God. The human element is so present in the workings of Charity that man can advance in his love of God only to the degree in which he enters into a corresponding community in breadth and depth with other men. The principal reasons that demand this evolution in community with men as the condition for man's evolution in a community of love with God are five:

First, In the order of generation Faith and Hope precede Charity which cannot exist and develop without them. Therefore, all that has been stated about the necessity of community with other men as the

---

[72] *Summa*, II-II, q. 23, a.1.
[73] *Ibid.*, II-II, q. 24, a.2.
[74] *Summa*, II-II, q. 23, a.2 ad.1.

condition for the existence and development of Faith and Hope, applies equally to Charity:

> By order of generation in respect of which matter precedes form, and the imperfect precedes the perfect, in one same subject faith precedes hope, and hope charity, as to their acts: because habits are all infused together. For the movement of the appetite cannot tend to anything, either by hoping or loving, unless that thing be apprehended by the sense or by the intellect. Now it is by faith that the intellect apprehends the object of hope and love. Hence in the order of generation, faith precedes hope and charity. In like manner a man loves a thing because he apprehends it as his good. now from the very fact that a man hopes to be able to obtain some good through someone, he looks on the man in whom he hopes as a good of his own. Hence for the very reason that a man hopes in someone, he proceeds to love him: so that in the order of generation, hope precedes charity as regards their respective acts.[75]

> Wherefore, just as friendship with a person would be impossible, if one disbelieved in, or despaired of, the possibility of their fellowship or familiar colloquy: so too, friendship with God, which is charity, is impossible without faith, so as to believe in this fellowship and colloquy with God, and to hope to attain this fellowship. Therefore charity is quite impossible without faith and hope.[76]

Second, charity exists in the soul together with sanctifying grace, and is inseparable from grace. As grace increases, so Charity is intensified. Now while God is the principal cause of grace, as we have seen, normally He incorporates human instruments in teaching, sanctifying, directing roles in the work of implanting grace in man's soul and developing it to maturity.

---

[75] *Summa*, I-II, q. 62 a. 4c.
[76] *Ibid.*, I-II, q.66, a.5c.

Therefore, Charity normally demands community with other men functioning as instruments of grace for its existence and development. And since God can use such instruments in an infinite variety of ways, community with such instruments involves a broad and profound openness to human nature as the potential conveyor of God's grace.

Third, since knowledge precedes love, in the genesis of Charity the just man must enter into community with the participated goodness of God present in other men as the means of acquiring and expanding his knowledge of the infinite goodness of God. The goodness of God cannot be adequately expressed in an individual, community, culture, age, or any particular social grouping, So a multiplicity and variety of men existing over a long expanse of time and in varied circumstances are necessary in order that the goodness of human nature may provide a fuller expression and revelation of the goodness of God. Community in breadth and depth with all manifestations of divine goodness in human nature is the condition for man's fuller knowledge of the infinite goodness of God, and for the perfection of Charity which depends on such knowledge:

> From the things it knows the soul learns to love what it knows not, not as though the things it knows were the reason for its loving things it knows not, through being the formal, final, or efficient cause of this love, but because this knowledge disposes man to love the unknown.[77]

> Since to love God is something greater than to know Him, especially in this state of life, it follows that love of God presupposes knowledge of God. And because this knowledge does not rest in creatures, but, through them, tends to something else, love begins there, and thence goes on to other things by a circular movement so to speak; for knowledge begins from creatures, tends to God, and love begins with God as the last end and passes on to creatures.[78]

Fourth, charity which has God for its direct object, does not stop with the love of God but encompasses in this very same love the whole of mankind in its potential and actual fellowship with God:

---

[77] *Summa*, II-II, q. 27, a. 3 ad. 1.
[78] *Summa*, II-II, q. 26; a.1.

IMAGE OF GOD BY GRACE

Now the aspect under which our neighbor is to be loved, is God, since what we ought to love in our neighbor is that he may be in God. Hence it is clear that it is specifically the same act whereby we love God, and whereby we love our neighbor. Consequently the habit of charity extends not only to the love of God, but also to the love of our neighbor.[79]

Friendship extends to a person in two ways: first in respect of himself, and in this way friendship never extends but to one's friends: secondly, it extends to someone in respect of another, as, when a man has friendship for a certain person, for his sake he loves all belonging to him, be they children, servants, or connected with him in any way. Indeed, so much we do love our friends, that for their sake we love all who belong to them, even if they hurt or hate us; so that, in this way the friendship of charity extends even to our enemies, whom we love out of charity in relation to God, to Whom the friendship of charity is chiefly directed.[80]

Thus the just man's community with God in Charity embraces within that friendship a very special community with all men. This impulse of Charity to commune in friendship and love with others extends to enemies as well as friends, sinners as well as the virtuous, and unbelievers as well as believers. In the minimum degree this impulse demands of the just a benevolence towards all men which entails his effective desire for their eternal happiness. Together with this general benevolence the just man must be prepared in soul to enter into specific relations of individual friendship and love as the circumstances require. As Charity intensifies in the soul, this impulse towards specific community with individuals also grows to the degree that in the case of the perfect they are prepared, even outside cases of urgency, to show particular signs of love to their enemies, seeking to overcome evil by good.

---

[79] *Summa*, II-II, q. 25; a.1.
[80] *Ibid.*, II-II, q. 23, a.1 ad. 2.

Since Charity is not only love between God and man, but friendship based on the communication of eternal happiness,[81] the love of Charity for other men entails a similar element of friendship in which the just seek to enter into relations of mutual love with others based on the fellowship of eternal happiness. When others already possess Charity, the resulting friendship is one of actual fellowship. In the case of those who are lacking in grace and Charity, the just must seek a mutual relation based upon their capacity for eternal happiness. It is this impulse of Charity to enter into community with all men on the basis of actual or potential fellowship in eternal happiness, which is the primary, proximate source of the ecumenical impulse in the soul of the just.

Fifth, in Catholic tradition Charity is considered to be the form of all other virtues, directing the acts of all virtues to the last end. Charity, therefore, commands and directs the exercise of the Theological Virtues as well as the acquired and infused moral virtues:

> Now it is charity which directs the acts of all other virtues to the last end, and which, consequently, also gives the form to all other acts of virtue.... Charity is called the form of the other virtues not as being their exemplar or their essential form, but rather by way of efficient cause, in so far as it sets the form on all, in the aforesaid manner.[82]

> In order that the act of a lower power be perfect, not only must there be perfection in the higher, but also in the lower power; for if the principal agent were all disposed, perfect action would not follow, if the instrument also were not well disposed. Consequently, in order that man work well in things referred to the end, he needs not only a virtue disposing him well to the end, but also those virtues which dispose him well to whatever is referred to the end: for the virtue which regards the end is the chief and moving principle in respect of those things that are referred to the end.[83]

---

[81] *Summa*, II-II, q. 23 a. 1.
[82] *Summa*, II-II, q. 23, a. 8c and ad.1.
[83] *Ibid.*, I-II, q. 65, ad. 1.

To the extent that these virtues motivate their subjects to acts which involve dialogue and community with other men, charity elicits and commands such acts of community in so far as they are related to man's ultimate happiness. From this point of view, also, charity entails a specific involvement in human community which affects a man's development towards union with God. Thus, for example, all acts of friendship among the virtuous are commanded and directed ultimately by charity. Therefore, to the extent that ecumenism involves forms of friendship other than that which is specifically proper to charity, they are motivated and directed by charity:

> Now since the good on which every other friendship of the virtuous is based, is directed, as to its end, to the good on which charity is based, it follows that charity commands each act of another friendship, even as the art which is about the end commands the art which is about the means. Consequently this very act of loving someone because he is akin or connected with us, or because he is a fellow-countryman or for any like reason that is referable to the end of charity, can be commanded by charity, so that, out of charity both eliciting and commanding, we love in more ways those who are more nearly connected with us.[84]

The evolution of the human communal aspects of charity involves three forms corresponding to the development of the virtues of faith and hope. The first development of charity is ordinarily a child/adult one in which the just man needs more to be loved than to love, and looks to others as instruments of grace to assist him in the struggle to keep grace alive in him. As Charity matures in him his communal rapport takes on an adult/adult form with those similarly mature in charity. In their rapport they share their actual fellowship in eternal happiness and fill out, support, and sustain their individual experience of God's love in a community of such love.

Towards those who are lacking in grace or who possess it on an immature level, charity in the just man gives rise to an adult/child relation in which he seeks to share with them the fellowship in divine

---

[84] *Summa*, II-II, q. 26, a. 7c.

life that has been communicated to him. Since charity extends to all men, this impulse in the just to enter into community with others allows of no exclusion. Since the perfection of charity expresses itself in mercy whereby the just man identifies in love with the deficiencies of others, the further removed a person is by reason of spiritual deficiencies, the more one perfect in charity is inclined in mercy to identify and seek friendship with him.

Charity, as perfected by the Gift of Wisdom, provides the just man with his most direct, immediate experience of God. Through charity one not only experiences love as derived from and revealing of Love, but also experiences Love's presence acting in and through love. The Gift of Wisdom in the charitable man reaches its highest point when God's transcendent being embraces man's created being allowing him to taste the infinite difference between Love and love so that the just man of mature charity comes to know in an affective, experiential, existential manner both the immanence and transcendence of Love. Charity, so perfected, assists the just to avoid the tendency of Pattern I to identify Love with love, absorbing Love into love. At the same time it shuns the opposite tendency of Pattern II to drive a wedge between love and Love by denying Love's presence acting in and through love.

X. SUMMARY

Through the Theological Virtues of Faith, Hope, and Charity the just man has the means of immediate contact with God as Truth, Beatitude, and the Perfect Good. He becomes the image of God in grace by knowing, loving, and possessing God as He knows, loves, and possesses Himself. Since the Theological Virtues can neither exist nor develop apart from God's participated presence and activity in human instruments, the just man must enter into community in breadth and depth with the divine presence in his fellow man if he is to evolve in community and friendship with God. Therefore, man's approach to God through the Theological Virtues and his approach to the potential and actual participated divine presence in human nature are inseparable. Just as Charity brings man into the most perfect contact and union with God, so also it brings man into the most profound community with God's presence in human nature.

If, as it seems to me, the ecumenical impulse in the image of God by grace proceeds primarily from the dynamics of charity, then no better description can be offered of the ideal qualities of soul with which one man should approach another in the ecumenical dialogue than a paraphrase of Saint Paul's description of Charity: *The ecumenist is always patient and kind; he is never jealous: the ecumenist is never boastful or conceited; he is never rude or selfish; he does not take offence, and is not resentful. The ecumenist takes no pleasure in other people's sins but delights in the truth; he is always ready to excuse, to trust, to hope, and to endure whatever comes.*[85]

---

[85] *See I Cor.* 13.4-7.

CHAPTER EIGHT

CHRIST AND HUMANITY

I. THE INCARNATION

Catholic tradition concerning the Incarnation includes the following points of doctrine:

1. *Christ is truly man*, possessing a human body[1] and rational soul[2] with vegetative, sensitive, and intellectual powers,[3] and everything else that goes to make up the reality of concrete human nature. He is like us, as Saint Paul states, in everything except sin. In terms of our analysis of created and Uncreated Being, this means to say that in His humanity Christ is a composite, imperfect, finite, changeable, localized, temporal, multiple entity Who possesses by participation but not by nature, being, truth, love, life, beatitude, power, justice, and mercy. All that constitute the negative and positive aspects of human nature that we have symbolized as A[4] are present in the humanity of Christ.

2. *Christ is truly God*, which is to say that Christ is Simple, Perfect, Infinite, Immutable, Omnipresent; Eternal, and One, possessing by essence Being, Truth, Love, Life, Beatitude, Power, Causality, Justice, and Mercy. In His divinity Christ is everything proper to Uncreated Being, that we have symbolized as B[5]

3. The two natures of Christ, human and divine, are distinct with the same infinite, qualitative difference that one finds between the created reality of every individual man and the uncreated reality of God, that is between the finite and infinite, the temporal and eternal, the created and uncreated, etc.[6] In no way, therefore, in the order of nature can the

---

[1] *Summa*, III, q. 5, aa. 1, 2.
[2] *Ibid.*, a. 3.
[3] *Ibid.*, a. 4; q. 18, a. 1.
[4] *Cf.* Chapter Four, Section I.
[5] *Cf.* Chapter Four, Section I.
[6] *Summa*, III, q.2, a.1; q.17, a.1.

humanity and divinity of Christ be conceived as one. At the same time, while preserving the infinite difference between both natures, the human nature of Christ as every created reality, is derived from, participates in, and reveals imperfectly the uncreated reality of His divinity.

4. For Aquinas, as for Catholic Faith in general, the incarnation cannot be understood except in the light of Catholic Faith's understanding of the Triune God. Catholic Faith radically affirms the revelation of the Old Testament that God is One God Who exists prior to and independently of the entire order of creation. What happens in the created order has no intrinsic effect on the Transcendent nature of God.

To this teaching of the Old Testament Jesus adds a new revelation, that he himself proceeds from the Father and shares the same divine nature with the Father. Jesus further adds that he will send the Holy Spirit Who proceeds from the Father and himself, to complete the work initiated by him and the Father. The Holy Spirit likewise, as with Jesus, is distinct from the Father and Jesus, while sharing the same divine nature with them.

This distinction of the Father, Son, and Holy Spirit without any compromise of the divine nature shared by each of them, is attributed to the perfection of personhood whereby each is distinct from the other while all three subsist in the same nature. It is the person of the Word who assumes the human nature of Jesus rendering his human nature unique and incommunicable with the uncreated perfection of His own personhood. The Word became flesh—not the Father or the Holy Spirit. Jesus is one in nature with all other humans. But, unlike other humans who possess the created perfection of personhood, Jesus is made unique by the uncreated perfection of the personhood of the Word of God. When Jesus acts he does so through his human nature, but the person acting is God.

This assumption of human nature by the Word involves no change in the Person of the Word[7] while effecting a radical change in the human nature assumed by passing from a state of potential existence into actual reality subsisting in the Word. By reason of subsisting in the Word contact with the humanity of Christ entails an immediate,

---

[7] *Ibid.*, q. 3, a.1 ad. 1.

personal encounter with the Person of God since the humanity of Christ has no existence of its own apart from the Word.[8]

In this traditional understanding of the Incarnation, Christ becomes the sign of the immanence and transcendence of God preserving and revealing both aspects of divinity. The radical distinction between the human and divine natures of Christ upholds the transcendence of God and His infinite difference from all created being, including that which is of the highest created level and intimately united to Him. At the same time the union of both natures in the Person of the Word, which is the most intimate of all possible unions, expresses the immediate personal immanence of the Transcendent God in the whole of created being.

In the context of our analysis, using A as the symbol of created rational being and B as the symbol of the uncreated reality of God,[9] the distinction of natures and the unity of Person in Christ, as traditionally understood in Catholic doctrine, may be expressed by the diagram 8-1.

This traditional understanding of Christ rejects the tendency of Pattern I to emphasize the humanity of Christ which is a principal cause of the denial or obscuring of His divinity. It also rejects the opposite tendency of Pattern II to affirm the divinity of Christ with a concomitant diminution of the reality or significance of His humanity and with the isolation of His humanity from the rest of human nature. Pattern II would deny to mankind the possibility of sharing in the role of Christ's humanity as the efficient, exemplary, final, and meritorious cause of man's salvation.

---

[8] *Ibid.*, q. 17, a.1.
[9] *Cf.* Chapter Four, Section III.

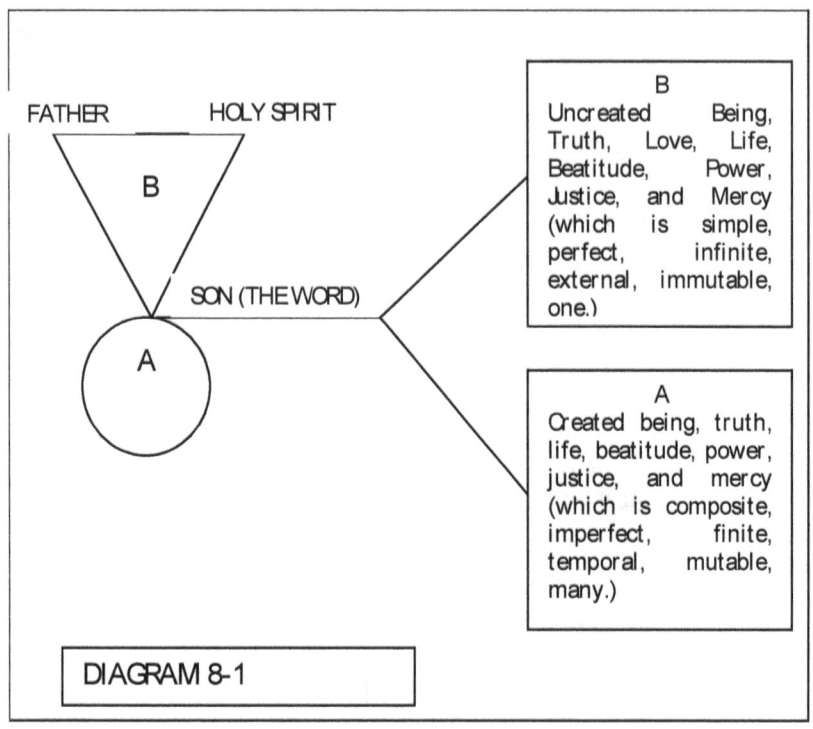

DIAGRAM 8-1

II. MISSION OF CHRIST

The mission of Christ, according to Catholic tradition, can be expressed by three statements:

1. Christ came to unite mankind to God.

2. Christ's humanity is the mediator of this union between God and man by being the efficient, exemplary, final, and meritorious cause of man's evolution as the image of God by nature and grace.

3. Christ wills to share with mankind the instrumental role of His humanity. In the work of redemption men in union with His humanity as the instrument of His divinity become the mediators and proximate efficient, exemplary, and meritorious causes of their evolution as images of God.

Each of these statements invites more detailed expression:

CHRIST AND HUMANITY

First, before all else Christ proclaims that His mission is to satisfy man's desire for union with God by operating as the unique, effective mediator of this union.[10] Man's natural, necessary desire for God involves his desire for the Simple, Perfect, Infinite, Omnipotent, Immutable, Eternal, One (See Chapter Three), who is by essence Being, Truth, Love, Life, Beatitude, Omnipotence, First Cause, Justice, and Mercy (See Chapter Four). Man's natural desire for godliness also entails the desire that his development in the knowledge and love of God and participation in divine causality, should in the fullest manner possible evolve proximately from his inner resources so that he may share in the self-sufficiency fundamental to God (See Chapter Five).

In the order of nature man's union with God consists in the development of his natural aptitude for knowing and loving God as the Author of nature, and in the exercise of such power as follows from this union, thereby becoming the image of God by nature (See Chapter Six). Christ presents Himself as the "living bread"[11] who has come down from Heaven to satisfy this natural hunger of man for God by effecting in him not only an evolution to perfection as the image of God by nature, but also by introducing him into an extraordinary participation in the inner life of God by grace.

The life of grace, in a way that transcends the natural order, provides man with a gratuitous participation in Divine Being, Truth, Love, Life, Beatitude, Omnipotence, Causality, Justice, and Mercy. By participation he knows God (Faith), possesses Him (Hope), and loves Him (Charity) as God knows, loves, and possesses Himself. He participates in the very power by which God acts on created being. In this evolution of New Life through Christ, man becomes the image of God by grace (Chapter 7).

Second, Christ presents Himself as the Mediator and efficient, exemplary, final and meritorious cause by which man's evolution in grace takes place. According to Catholic teaching Christ is the perfect Mediator of God and men through the reconciling effects of His death:

---

[10] *Summa*, III, q. 48.
[11] *Jn.* 6.51.

> Properly speaking, the office of a mediator is to join together and unite those between whom he mediates: for extremes are united in the mean. now to unite men to God perfectively belongs to Christ, through Whom men are reconciled to God, according to II *Cor.* 5.19: "God was in Christ reconciling the world to Himself." And, consequently, Christ alone is the perfect Mediator of God and men, in as much as by His death He reconciled the human race to God.[12]

It is by reason of His human nature that Christ is the Mediator of God and men:

> We may consider two things in a mediator: first, that he is a mean; secondly, that he unites others. Now it is of the nature of a mean to be distant from each extreme: while it unites by communicating to one that which belongs to the other. Now neither of these can be applied to Christ as God, but only as man. For as God, He does not differ from the Father and the Holy Spirit in nature and power of dominion; nor have the Father and the Holy Spirit anything that the Son has not, so that He be able to communicate to others something belonging to the Father or to the Holy Spirit, as though it were belonging to others than Himself. But both can be applied to Him as man. Because, as man, He is distant both from God by nature, and from man by dignity of both grace and glory. Again, it belongs to Him, as man, to unite men to god by communicating to men both precepts and gifts, and by offering satisfaction and prayers to God for them. And therefore He is most truly called Mediator as man.[13]

From the moment that the "Word was made flesh and lived among us,"[14] the plan of Providence for man's salvation is irrevocably fixed. Man is to find in the humanity of Christ as instrument of His divinity the efficient and meritorious source of the grace by which he may evolve in union with God. Whatever participation he attains in the inner life of God whereby he is transformed into the image of the

---

[12] *Summa*, III, q. 26, a.2c.

[13] *Ibid.* q. 26, a. 2c.

[14] *Jn.*1.14.

divinity, will be derived proximately from the humanity of Christ as Head of the Church.

>As the whole Church is termed one mystic body from its likeness to the natural body of a man, which in divers members has divers acts, as the Apostle teaches (*Rom.* 12, and I *Cor.*12), so likewise Christ is called the Head of the Church from a likeness with the human head, in which we may consider three things, *viz.* order, perfection, power.... Now these three things belong spiritually to Christ. First, on account of His nearness to God His grace is the highest and first, though not in time since all have received grace on account of His grace, according to Rom. 8.29: "For whom He foreknew, He also predestined to be made conformable to the image of His Son; that He might be the first-born amongst many brethren." Secondly, He had perfection as regards the fullness of all graces, according to John 1.14, "We say Him.... full of grace and truth." Thirdly, He has the power of bestowing grace on all the members of the Church, according to John 1.16: "Of His fullness we have all received." And thus it is plain that Christ is fittingly called the Head of the Church.[15]

The actions of Christ's humanity are the meritorious cause of man's union with God. And while every human act of Christ was meritorious, it was principally through His passion that Christ merited salvation for mankind:

>...grace was bestowed upon Christ, not only as an individual, but inasmuch as He is the Head of the Church, so that it might overflow into His members; and therefore Christ's works are referred to Himself and to His members in the same way as the works of any other man in a state of grace, merits his salvation thereby, according to Mt. 5.10: "Blessed are they that suffer persecution for justice's sake." Consequently Christ by His Passion merited salvation, not only for Himself, but likewise for all His members.

---

[15] *Summa*, III, q. 8 a. 2.

Christ's Passion has a special effect, which His preceding merits did not possess, not on account of greater charity, but because of the nature of the work, which was suitable for such an effect, as is clear from the arguments brought forward above on the fittingness of Christ's Passion.[16]

In the humanity of Christ man also finds the exemplary and final cause of his evolution as the image of God in the sense that on the created level man's goal must be to attain the likeness of image present in the humanity of Christ as his ultimate means to union with God:

> Secondly, predestination may be considered on the part of that to which anyone is predestinated, and this is the term and effect of predestination. In this sense Christ's predestination is the exemplar of ours, and this in two ways. First, in respect of the good to which we are predestinated: for He was predestinated to be the natural Son of God, whereas we are predestinated to the adoption of sons, which is a participated likeness of natural son-ship. Whence it is written (*Rom.* 8.29): "Whom He foreknew, He also predestinated to be made conformable to the image of His Son." Secondly, in respect of the manner of obtaining this good—that is, by grace. This is most manifest in Christ; because human nature in Him, without any antecedent merits, was united to the Son of God: and of the fullness of His grace we have all received, as it is written (*Jn.* 1.16).[17]

Therefore, it is by entering into community with the humanity of Christ, in breadth and depth as the Mediator and efficient, exemplary, final, and meritorious cause of grace, that man evolves as the image of God. The more profound and intimate that this union is with the humanity of Christ, the more complete will be man's evolution in grace and the more perfect will be his union with God. But the question remains as to how man can best enter into intimate community in breadth and depth with the humanity of Christ?

Third, according to Catholic tradition Christ teaches that He wills to share in a significant degree with mankind the power of His humanity

---

[16] *Ibid.*, q. 48, a. 2. Note Reply Objection 3.

[17] *Ibid.*, q. 24, a. 3c.

as the instrument of His divinity to function as mediator between God and men by being the efficient, exemplary, final, and meritorious cause of man's evolution as the image of God by grace. Here we again encounter a point of fundamental doctrinal difference with Patterns I and II. Also this involves the elevation of man's natural radical godliness to the supernatural order. As a consequence of Christ's intention, men find their means of intimate, profound community with the humanity of Christ in their intimate, profound community with human nature, in breadth and depth, when operating in union with and as the instrument of the human nature of Christ. Christ expresses this succinctly when He tells the Apostles, "As the Father sent me, so am I sending you."[18]

Thus Christ established Orders for the ministering of the Sacraments in which men primarily share with Christ's humanity the role of efficient, instrumental causes of grace:

> God wishes to produce His works in likeness to Himself, as far as possible, in order that they might be perfect, and that He be known through them. Hence, that He might be portrayed in His works, not only according to what He is in Himself, but also according as He acts on others. He laid this natural law on all things, that last things should be reduced and perfected by middle things, and middle things by the first, as Dionysius says. "Wherefore that this beauty might not be lacking to the Church, He established Order in her so that some should deliver the sacraments to others, being thus made like to God in their own way, as co-operating with God; even as in the natural body, some members act on others."[19]

As an effect of the gift of grace men are endowed with a share in the meritorious power of Christ's humanity whereby they too can merit eternal life and, in this sense, become the causes of their growth in grace as images of God as well as the meritorious causes of their salvation:

---

[18] *Jn.* 20.21.

[19] *Summa*, Suppl. Q. 24, a. 1c.

To have any good thing of oneself is more excellent than to have it from another, for "what is of itself a cause is always more excellent than what is a cause through another," as is said Phys. viii. 5. Now a thing is said to have, of itself, that of which it is to some extent the cause. But of whatever good we possess the first cause by authority is God; and in this way no creature has any good of itself, according to I Cor. 4.7: "What hast thou that thou has not received?" Nevertheless, in a secondary manner anyone may be a cause, to himself, of having certain good things, inasmuch as he co-operates with God in the matter, and this whoever has anything by his own merit, has it, in a manner, of himself. Hence it is better to have a thing by merit than without merit. now since all perfection and greatness must be attributed to Christ, consequently He must have by merit what others have by merit; unless it be of such a nature that its want would detract from Christ's dignity and perfection more than would accrue to Him by merit.[20]

Man's meritorious work may be considered in two ways: first as it proceeds from the grace of the Holy Spirit. If it is considered as regards the substance of the work, and inasmuch as it springs from freewill, there can be no condignity because of the very great inequality. But there is congruity, on account of an equality of proportion: for it would seem congruous that, if a man does what he can, God should reward him according to the excellence of his power.

If, however, we speak of meritorious work, inasmuch as it proceeds from the grace of the Holy Spirit moving us to life everlasting, it is meritorious of life everlasting condignly. For thus the value of its merit depends upon the power of the Holy Spirit moving us to life everlasting.... And the worth of the work depends on the dignity of grace, whereby a man, being made a partaker of the Divine Nature, is adopted as a

---

[20] *Summa*, III, q. 19, a. 3c.

CHRIST AND HUMANITY

son of God, to whom the inheritance is due by right of adoption, according to Rom. 8.17: "If sons, heirs also."[21].

In addition to sharing the efficient and meritorious powers of His humanity as the instrumental cause of grace, Christ also instructs mankind about the impetratory power of the human activity of prayer as a means of growth in grace.[22] He encourages the Apostles to ask the Father with confidence and in His name to respond to all their needs,[23] and leads them and mankind in general to participate in the prayer life of his human nature.

As men evolve into adult images of God they are to share in the exemplary and final causality of Christ's humanity by revealing the working of God's grace in them for the edification of others and the glory of God. And so Christ instructs the Apostles, "No one lights a lamp to put under a tub; they put it on the lamp-stand where it shines for everyone in the house. In the same way your light must shine in the sight of men, so that, seeing your good works, they may give the praise to your Father in heaven."[24] Lastly, men are called by Christ to share even His role as Mediator by acting in union with Him to unite men to God dispositively and ministerially.

And so it is in man's contact with other men functioning in union with Christ as mediators and efficient, exemplary, final, and meritorious causes, as well as impetrators of divine mercy, that he finds community with the humanity of Christ whereby he grows as the image of God by grace. Therefore in the degree in which a man is open to the potential and actual activity of Christ in the breadth and depth of humanity, he enters into community with the humanity of Christ as the instrument of divinity and thereby enters into community with God.

---

[21]*Summa*, I-II, q. 114, a. 3.
[22]*Ibid.*, III, q. 21.
[23]*Summa*, II-II, q. 83, a. 9.
[24]*Mt.* 5.14.

III. THE ENCOUNTER WITH GOD THROUGH THE HUMANITY OF CHRIST

In the light of Catholic teaching on the mystery of the Incarnation and the humanity of Christ three aspects that provided His Apostles with points of encounter with God can be distinguished—as the image of God by nature, as the image of God by grace, and as subsisting in the Person of the Word. Since these encounters with divinity in the humanity of Christ shed essential light on the ways in which man can encounter God in general, they demand further analysis.

Christ as the Image of God by Human Nature

The initial encounter of the Apostles with Christ took place through His concrete, sense perceptible reality as a man. He was someone Whom they could see, hear, touch, and be touched by. They experienced Christ walking, talking, eating, sleeping, rejoicing, and sorrowing. They witnessed Him when He was fatigued, hungry, and in pain. And so they know him as they knew each other and as they knew their selves. According to Catholic tradition, this humanity of Christ that the Apostles so experienced was perfect in knowledge and virtue on the level of nature as well as grace. No natural potentiality for knowledge and virtue went unrealized in Him.[25] Therefore, part of the perfection of the humanity of Christ entailed that of being the image of God by knowledge and love in the manner in which man has the natural aptitude for such perfection. Since created perfection is derived from, revealing of, and the point of contact with God, the Apostles' encounter with the perfection of Christ's humanity as the image of God by nature provided them with the highest revelation of divinity that the visible order can naturally offer. Hence this encounter with Christ's humanity was a point of special encounter with God as the Author of this natural perfection. For many persons who deny the divinity of Christ and reject the concept of grace and the supernatural order, the perfection of Christ is limited in their view to that of being the image of God in the natural order. This suffices to allow them to experience an encounter with God through the humanity of Christ—as God's image in His natural perfection.

---

[25] *Summa*, III, q. 9, aa. 1,3.

CHRIST AND HUMANITY

Christ as Image by Grace

In addition to His perfection in natural knowledge and virtue, Catholic tradition holds that in Christ's humanity is the fullness of habitual (sanctifying) grace. In virtue of this Christ possessed in the highest degree created participation in the Divine Life and is the perfect image of God by grace. The intensity and perfection of habitual grace in the humanity of Christ is attributed primarily to the intimacy of union between His humanity and divinity in the Person of the Word:

> It is necessary to suppose habitual grace in Christ for three reasons. First, on account of the union of His soul with the Word of God. For the nearer any recipient is to an inflowing cause, the more does it partake of its influence.... Secondly, on account of the dignity of this soul whose operations were to attain so closely to God by knowledge and love, to which it is necessary for human nature to be raised by grace. Thirdly, on account of the relation of Christ to the human race. For Christ, as man, is the Mediator of God and men, as is written, I *Tim.*2.5; and hence it behooved Him to have grace which would overflow upon others, according to Jn.1.16: "And of His fullness we have all received."[26]

Since grace is not a reality perceivable by the senses, it cannot be directly experienced by man, either internally in himself or in others.[27] Its presence may be known by revelation or, with varying degrees of certitude, from its effects. The Apostles' encounter with the humanity of Christ exposed them both to the effects of grace manifested in his external actions and the internally transforming effects of his actions on their souls. The external actions would include the sensible expressions of His love, wisdom, power, and mercy. In this encounter with the humanity of Christ as the perfect image of God by grace the Apostles' experienced the highest expression and point of contact with divinity that created reality can provide.

---

[26] *Summa*, q. 7, a. 1c.

[27] *Ibid.*, I-II, q. 112, a. 5.

THE THEOLOGY OF ECUMENISM

Theologians have long reflected on the interplay between the divinity and humanity, grace and nature, in Christ. They have endeavored to develop an understanding of these relations that would be faithful to the inspired Gospel account of His reality. From these reflections has emerged a doctrine that appears best to explain this interplay of the physical, instrumental causality of the human nature of Christ under the influence of both His uncreated divinity and the created fullness of grace in Him. Since this understanding of physical instrumental cause underlies traditional Catholic understanding of other primary doctrines that include, not only the human activities of Christ, but also, the Catholic understanding of the efficient causality of the Sacraments and the Church, Grace, and meritorious works, it would be desirable to review briefly this concept.

According to this understanding a physical, instrumental cause is an efficient agent that, acting under the elevating influence of a higher agent, produces in union with that higher agent effects that transcend its own natural operative powers. The instrument possesses its own physical reality and natural causative power. It becomes an instrument at the moment and in the degree in which the higher agent grafts onto its causative power qualities of operation that are not proper to its nature but to the nature of the higher cause. The result of this dynamic, cooperative union is that the instrument truly produces as an efficient cause effects that contain perfection of a being superior to its own.

A common example of such causality is the pen in the hand of the writer, producing by intelligently directed physical motion, intelligible effects (words) containing truth and perhaps beauty that totally transcend the perfection of being and natural powers of the inanimate, irrational pen. In an analogous manner the human nature of Christ is understood to operate as an animate instrument of His divinity and fullness of grace. Thus physically producing actions and effects that transcend the natural being and power of his humanity and belonging properly to Divine Life. Aquinas describes this interplay of divinity and humanity in Christ in the following manner:

> ...what is moved by another has a twofold action—one which it has from its own form—the other, which it has inasmuch as it is moved by another, thus the operation of an axe of itself is to cleave; but inasmuch as it is moved by the craftsman, its operation is to make benches. Hence the op-

eration which belongs to a thing by its form is proper to it, nor does it belong to the mover, except in so far as he makes use of this kind of thing for his work; thus to heat is the proper operation of fire, but not of a smith, except in so far as he makes use of fire for heating iron. But the operation which belongs to the thing, as moved by another, is not distinct from the operation of the mover; thus to make a bench is not the work of the axe independently of the workman. Hence, wheresoever the mover and the moved have different forms or operative faculties, there must the operation of the mover and the proper operation of the moved be distinct; although the moved shares in the operation of the moved, and, consequently, each acts in communion with the other.

Therefore, in Christ the human nature has its proper form and power whereby it acts; and so has the Divine. Hence the human nature has its proper operation distinct from the Divine, and conversely. Nevertheless, the Divine Nature makes use of the operation of its instrument; and in the same way the human nature shares in the operation of the Divine Nature, as an instrument shares in the operation of the principal agent. And this is what Pope Leo says (*Ep. ad. Flavian* 28): "Both forms (that is both the Divine and the human nature in Christ) do what is proper to each in union with the other, that is the Word operates what belongs to the Word, and the flesh carries out what belongs to the flesh."[28]

Without dwelling at length on this most important matter, I wish to emphasize five aspects of this understanding of physical, instrumental causality as applied to Christ that have immediate relevance to the question of the experience of God in humanity:

1. Christ's humanity, unlike our example of the pen, is the animate instrument of His divinity.[29] The human nature of Christ operated as a vital, rational instrumentality of His divinity in which divine action flows in, through, and from His human actions both internal and

---

[28] *Summa*, III, q. 19, a. 1c.

[29] *Ibid.*, q.7, a.1 ad.3.

external. Divinity's use of Christ's humanity does not suppress the natural activity of his human nature. Rather it amplifies and intensifies it. As we have noted concerning the interplay of grace and nature, the more perfect a nature is in its own level of being the more ideal an instrument of grace it makes.[30]

God can use human nature as an instrument without man being conscious of, or consenting to this use. In some instances man may even be consciously opposed to such instrumental use of his being without hindering God's action in areas of his person outside of his will. In cases of this kind when a man is not conscious of, or does not consent to God's use of him as an instrument, his entire nature is not the instrument of divine action, and our encounter with God as principal cause in him encompasses only part of his nature.

Since Christ's humanity is a voluntary instrument of His divinity His entire being is the vehicle of the divine action. Since this action is initiated in His intellect and will, from which it passes into the rest of His human nature and outwardly into external action, one must get to the truth and love (mind and heart) of the humanity of Christ in order to understand the external actions and to encounter the full presence of divinity in His human activity.

2. The perfection of operation of an instrument precisely as instrument depends on the quality and degree of its responsiveness to the movements of the principal cause. In the case of a voluntary instrument this quality and degree of response to the principal cause must be sought especially in the will which is the prime mover in human action. Conformity of wills between voluntary instrument and principal cause determines the quality of operation of the voluntary instrument as instrument. This submissiveness of will by which a rational being beomes a voluntary instrument is identified in Catholic tradition as obedience.

The condition for such obedience is knowledge of the will of the principal cause and its embrace. The humanity of Christ revealed this

---

[30] *Cf.* page. 426 ff.

perfection as instrument of His divinity most perfectly in His Passion—"He became obedient unto death, even the death of the cross."[31]

3. An instrument while functioning as an instrument, exercises its own proper causality as the vehicle of the action of the principal agent. Therefore one must experience the proper operation and effect of the instrument if he is to experience the operation and effect of the principal cause. The pen in the act of writing, leaves its mark on the page. One must see that mark in order to discern the intelligible signification of the words and experience the action and mind of the writer. Since the human actions of Christ as instruments of divine action contain and express that divine activity in and through the exercise of natural, human activity, one must first experience the presence and operation of Christ's humanity before he can experience the higher activity of divinity in them.

The Apostles had to see, hear, and experience the human presence and activity of Christ as the condition for their seeing, hearing, and experiencing divinity's presence and activity in Christ. Christ first had to be experienced as the image of God by nature before He could be encountered as the image of God by grace. And since the divine action comes through and from the full range of heightened, intense human activity, a profound, intimate experience of the humanity of Christ in breadth and depth was the condition for the profound, intimate experience of divinity and grace in Him.

4. Since the natural causality of the instrument is the vehicle of action of the principal cause, the instrument limits the manner in which it may be used by the principal agent. A pen can be used as an instrument for writing, and an axe may be used for making benches. But a principal cause, however talented, cannot use a pen to carve out benches, or an axe for writing poetry. Since the different actions of Christ's humanity possessed their own specific character and aptitude for use as instruments, God used different human acts of Christ as vehicles for different divine actions.

---

[31] *Phil.* 2.8.

Divinity used the human joy of Christ as the instrument of certain effects, and the human suffering of Christ as the apt instrument for other effects. We have already seen how Aquinas, while acknowledging the meritorious power of every human act of Christ, attributes the actual merit of mankind's redemption specifically to the Passion of Christ as the human work most suitable for such merit.[32] As another example of such specific instrumental use, consider the words of Christ. The truth and intelligibility naturally present in these words provided instruments for the utilization of Divine Truth. However Divine Truth was not expressed indiscriminately in these words. Certain statements of Christ served to convey some expressions of Truth. Other statements involving different expressions of truth served as vehicles for expressing different aspects of Truth. Thus one must study and reflect upon all the differing words and statements of Christ in order to fill out the encounter with the fullness of Truth's revelation in His truth.

It is not enough, however, to encounter the variety of human acts of Christ in breadth in order to experience the presence of divinity and grace operating in them. One must encounter these human acts in depth as instruments in order to find there the complementary manner in which divinity and grace can transform vital human actions and experiences into instruments of their presence and activity. Especially one must get to the human heart and mind of Christ at the moment of His different human experiences in order to discover what He saw of the divine will expressed in these situations and what He embraced in them to allow Him to become at such moments the instrument of divine action.

This understanding of the aptitude of natural causes to be used in specifically distinct and complementary ways by a principal agent is essential to the Catholic understanding of the Sacraments, and of the Church as a community. There are seven distinct Sacraments producing seven differing sacramental effects, and not just one Sacrament producing seven distinct effects. Christ acts through the specifically distinct aptitudes of seven different human acts to be used as instruments to produce these distinct effects.

---

[32] *Summa*, III, q. 48, a. 1 ad. 3.

CHRIST AND HUMANITY

So also we have a plurality of Apostles as instruments of divine presence and action. They differed in temperament and talents because each provided his own special aptitude to be used in a certain way different from the use of the others. Encounter with anyone of them provides an experience of divinity only according to that limited aspect in which he is the instrument of divinity. Therefore the encounter with all of them in community provides the fullest experience of divinity's presence and activity in them. And only in contact with the totality of all distinct human instruments through whom the Spirit operates in differing and complementary ways, does one have contact with the fullness of the principal cause's presence acting in and through such a community.

5. The action of an instrument, at the moment of instrumental use, by a principal cause, belongs more to and is more revealing of the principal agent than it belongs to and reveals the instrument. As I watch the pen moving purposefully across the page, leaving behind intelligible symbols conveying wisdom and beauty, I am experiencing in this movement and its effects what belongs more to and reveals more properly the writer than the pen. Suppose by mechanical means the writer removes his visible presence so that my only experience is one of seeing the pen moving on paper. Then in answering by written response my questions while proposing questions in turn for my consideration, I would know that I was not communicating with the pen as a principal agent, but with the invisible presence of a mind made visible and intelligible through the instrumentality of the pen.

When the Divine Nature acted in and through the humanity of Christ, endowing His human actions as instruments with a wisdom, love, power and life which lies completely beyond the natural capacity of human nature to express, the Apostles were experiencing in these actions more the reality of Christ's divinity than that of His humanity. When Christ reached out and touched the leper, the power of healing present in the human touch of Christ, belonged more to the Power of the divine touch than to the human touch. At that moment God touched the leper in and through the human touch of Christ. And the leper in his encounter with the human touch of Christ encountered the Divine Touch:

The proper work of the Divine operation is different from the proper work of the human operation. Thus to heal a leper is a proper work of the Divine operation, but to touch him is the proper work of the human operation. Now both these operations concur in one work inasmuch as one nature acts in union with the other.[33]

So it is with the other instrumental actions of Christ. In the instrumental use of the human truth, love, life, mercy, justice, and causality of Christ, the Apostles were experiencing Divine Truth, Love, Life, Justice, and Divine Causality more than the human actions of Christ. Through Christ's human actions the invisible, inaudible, intangible, impalpable reality of God became a visible, audible, tangible, palpable, sense perceptible presence. The Apostles were able to see God, hear God, touch God and be touched by God as they watched the humanity of Christ, listened to the words coming from his tongue, and touched Him and were touched by Him. This truth is brought out pointedly and touchingly by Christ's conversation with the Apostles at the last supper:

Thomas said, "Lord, we do not know where you are going, so how can we know the way?"

Jesus said, "I am the Way, the Truth, and the Life. No one can come to the Father except through me. If you know me, you know my Father too. From this moment you know him and have seen him."

Philip said, "Lord, let us see the Father and then we shall be satisfied."

"Have I been with you all this time, Philip," said Jesus to him "and you still do not know me? To have seen me is to have seen the Father, so how can you say, Let us see the Father? Do you not believe that I am in the Father, the Father is in me? It is the Father, living in me, who is doing this work. You must believe me, when I say that I am in the

---

[33] *Summa*, q. 19, a. 1 ad.5.

CHRIST AND HUMANITY

Father and the Father is in me; believe it on the evidence of this work, if for no other reason."[34]

This encounter with God through the humanity of Christ as the image of God by grace and as the instrument of His divinity, is still an encounter which does not transcend the created order. The Apostles were in contact with divinity through the medium of created humanity operating as the extraordinary instrument of divinity and grace. But the immediate, person to person encounter with God takes place through the encounter with the human nature of Christ.

Christ is the Person of the Word

According to Catholic doctrine since the humanity of Christ subsists in the Word, existing as complete, unique, incommunicable by the uncreated subsistence of the Word, the encounter with the humanity of Christ entailed an immediate encounter with the Person of God. Since human nature exists as part of the whole which is the suppositum or person, immediate contact with any part of a concrete human nature involves immediate contact with the person or subsisting whole. By virtue of the hypostatic union therefore, Christ's humanity provides men with an immediate personal encounter with God. Since actions belong to the person acting, whatever Christ said or did in His humanity was said and done by the Person of God. And whatever was said or done to Christ's human nature was likewise said and done to the Person of God:

> To operate belongs to a subsisting hypostasis; in accordance, however, with the form and nature form which the operation receives its species. Hence from the diversity of forms or natures spring the divers species of operations, but from the unity of hypostasis springs the numerical unity as regards the operations of the species: thus fire has two operations specifically different, namely, to illuminate and to heat, from the difference of light and heat, and yet the illumination of fire that heats and illuminates at one and the same time is numerically one. So, likewise, in Christ there are

---

[34] *Jn.* 14.5-11.

necessarily two specifically different operations by reason of His two natures; nevertheless, each of the operations at one and the same time is numerically one, as one walking and one healing.[35]

What I have said about the Apostles encountering the Person of God in the humanity of Christ holds true even if the human nature assumed were not the image of God by grace. Catholic theologians envision the possibility of a human nature having been assumed by the Person of the Word, that was not elevated by grace. In such a situation, while the humanity of Christ would not provide the Apostles with an encounter with God through the fullness of grace in Christ, their encounter with His humanity would still involve an immediate contact with the Person of God. However, since we know persons through their actions, unless Christ's humanity were in fact the image of God by grace, it could not serve to provide men with adequate insight into the mystery of His divinity.

For example, I could enjoy an immediate, personal relation with a man of extraordinary genius without knowing the identity and stature of his person. Imagine that I were to meet Beethoven in the compartment of a train in circumstances which required that we pass many hours together.[36] During which time, not knowing his identity, I engaged in lengthy, friendly, trivial exchange that revealed little of him to me. I would have been in personal contact with him without having really known his person. It would only be after he had expressed with some fullness by word or action the richness of his reality, that I would have begun to know the person with whom I enjoyed a personal contact.

So it was with Christ. The hypostatic union made contact with the humanity of Christ an encounter with the Person of God. However, it was only because His humanity possessed the fullness of grace that contact with that humanity provided a revelation of the identity of His person. In turn, since the experience of grace in Christ could only be attained through the instrumentality of His human nature, the encounter with Christ as the image of God by grace presupposed the encounter

---

[35] *Summa*, III, q. 7 ad 12 ad. 3.
[36] *Cf.* Chapter Three, Section III.

with Him as the image of God by nature. Thus the full, ideal encounter with the Person of Christ could not be separated from the encounter with Him as the image of God by nature and grace. Hence the surprise of the people of Nazareth who were familiar with Jesus, knowing him only as the carpenter's son.

It does not follow that an encounter with Christ in which He gives full expression to the divine life in Him would suffice to bring one to ideal union with the Person of God. Every individual who contacted Christ during his earthly life was encountering both the Person of God and the perfect image of God by nature and grace, but not everyone was thereby united to God. It was only as the Apostles and followers underwent an internal evolution as images of God by grace that they progressively grew in awareness of the objective reality of God's presence to them in Christ and they began to respond affectively to that consciousness.

My physical contact with the living, personal presence of Beethoven as he sits at the piano and gives full expression in music to the richness of his inner genius, is not sufficient to unite me fully to his reality if I lack the inner perception necessary to appreciate the beauty that he is imparting to his playing. It would be only to the degree that something of Beethoven's aesthetic qualities existed in me that I would recognize and respond to Beethoven's participated presence in his music and find in that music the revelation of the person of the composer and union with that person.

So also it was only as Christ the image of God by grace began to come alive within the Apostles, transforming them into images of God by grace, that they were able progressively to recognize and respond to God's participated presence in the humanity of Christ. They found in that humanity the revelation of the Person of God and ideal union with that Person. The evolution of the Apostles in their union with God in Christ involved no change in Him, but radical change in them. Christ as God had been present intimately to them from the first moment of their existence.

Christ as the perfect image of God by grace had been present to them from the first moment in which they encountered His humanity. It was only as the Apostles evolved as images of God within that they became fully alive to God's unchanging presence before them. The human actions of Christ were the physical instruments of the graces by which the Apostles evolved inwardly as images of God. Therefore, there was an evolution in Christ's external manifestation of His unchanging internal reality as He revealed this reality more clearly according to their evolving capacity to respond to it.[37]

This evolution in Christ's external manifestation of His inner reality became the source of the concomitant growth as images of God in those who opened themselves to the transforming effects of His love. It also became the occasion of a growing alienation from God in those who witnessed Christ's actions but internally closed themselves to the sanctifying effects of His work. Of these Christ would say at the last supper, "If I had not come, if I had not spoken to them, they would have been blameless; but as it is they have no excuse for their sin" (*Jn.* 15.22).

Since Charity involves a person-to-person relation between God and man based on the communication of eternal life,[38] the humanity of Christ serves as the perfect instrument of Divine Love. First, it allowed men to enter into immediate, personal contact with the Person of God. Secondly, Christ's humanity operated as the ideal instrument of His divinity in communicating eternal life to men's souls, transforming them into actual images of God by grace. The openness to community with the humanity of Christ, therefore, is openness to immediate community with the Person of God and an openness to community with Eternal Life. The conscious rejection of Christ is the conscious rejection of the Person of God and eternal life.

IV. THE SPECIAL WORK OF CHRIST

Part of the mission of Christ was to serve in His humanity as the instrument whereby His divinity became a palpable, sensible presence among men. The special part of that mission, moreover, was not merely to present this kind of sensible witness to His divinity, but as an instrument to cause the invisible life of the Divine Reality to become a visible, tangible, audible presence by grace. This is the meaning of

---

[37] *Summa*, III, q. 7; a. 12 ad 3.
[38] *Ibid.* II-II, q. 23, a. 2.

Christ's efficient and meritorious causality. This causality and, as an instrument, Christ's humanity causes God to be born and to grown among men as a vital, sensible presence through the effects of created grace.

> There is a twofold efficient agency—namely, the principal and the instrumental. Now the principal efficient cause of man's salvation is God. But since Christ's humanity is the instrument of the Godhead, as stated above (Q. 43, A. 2), therefore all Christ's actions and sufferings operate instrumentally in virtue of His Godhead for the salvation of men. Consequently, then, Christ's Passion accomplishes man's salvation efficiently.
>
> Christ's Passion, according as it is compared with His Godhead, operates in an efficient manner; but in so far as it is compared with the will of Christ's soul it acts in a meritorious manner: considered as being within Christ's flesh, it acts by way of satisfaction, inasmuch as we are liberated by it from the depth of punishment; while inasmuch as we are freed from the servitude of guilt, it acts by way of redemption; but in so far as we are reconciled with God it acts by way of sacrifice.[39]

In his Passion Christ presents the most explicit expression of the manner in which men must confront created reality—the reality of created being in general, the reality of mankind as a whole, and the reality of their individual humanity—if they are to attain union with God. Since Calvary sheds such direct light upon the question of man's encounter with God in the created reality of human nature, it would be desirable to set forth some of the aspects of Christ's Passion that are particularly illuminative of the encounter with Uncreated Being in created being:

1. Christ taught that all created being comes from the Father and is both totally dependent upon and revealing of Him. Creation in all its aspects obeys and reflects the divine will. Thus Christ can turn to any aspect of

---

[39] *Ibid.*, III, q. 48, a.6c; and ad.3. Note Reply ad. Objection 3.

the created universe, and find there both the revelation of the Truth of God and the expression of the divine will. This includes, for example, the water which men drink, fruitful and unproductive trees, games children play, and the number of hairs on a man's head.

2. Christ taught the Apostles that their encounter with the will of the Father must be sought in created reality as the expression of that will—not in reality as men might imagine it to be, or reality as men would like it to be, but reality as in fact it *is*. Which is to say, in reality as the Father has in His infinite wisdom willed it to be. Reality as it *is* encompasses both its actuality and perfections and its potentiality (both natural and as the instrument of God's power) and, therefore, its imperfections. Christ taught the Apostles to approach reality as the work of the Father so as to be able to approach the Creator in and through the creature.[40] They were to seek their conformity of will with the Father through the mediation of created being as the revelation of the divine will. It is by their wanting of life (their own and all others) what God wills of life that they are to become one in heart and mind with God.

3. Men, therefore, are neither to embrace created reality as though it were ultimate reality (the tendency of Pattern I) nor reject created being as opposed to the Ultimate reality (the tendency of Pattern II). Rather they are to recognize created being as coming from, revealing, and naturally seeking unity with the Ultimate Reality. They are to approach created being confident both of the intimate presence of God to it and His infinite love for it. So that by loving creatures primarily in terms of what they can become in participated godliness as instruments responsive to Divine Love, man can embrace in created entities that aspect of them whereby they are closest to God.

4. Christ preached this potentiality of created being for maximum godliness in his beatitudes of the Sermon on the Mount.[41] There Christ, in essence, tells men that in those aspects of their humanity where they seem furthest removed from God and eternal happiness, they will find the greatest potential for godliness. If a man can approach such states that provide the least happiness here and now and, therefore, the

---

[40] *Summa*, q.20, a.1.
[41] *Mt.* 5. 3-12.

CHRIST AND HUMANITY

minimal basis for creating an illusory substitute in the present for ultimate happiness in the future, and freely, positively embrace those states in obedience to God with confidence that they are the instruments of His wisdom and love, at that moment such a man's Faith is deepest, his Hope is strongest, and his Charity is purest.

The embrace of created reality in its harshest aspects in obedience to God, is in this life the most perfect embrace of God possible to man. Through such an embrace the most tragic human situations are transformed into instruments from which Beatitude proceeds. Out of poverty of spirit evolves possession of the kingdom of heaven. Out of mourning comes comfort. Out of hunger comes fulfillment. Out of mercy comes Mercy.

5. On Calvary Christ practiced what He had preached in the Sermon on the Mount. He embraced created being in its most impoverished, least godly aspects—the poverty of mankind as a whole, the godlessness of those crucifying Him, and the poverty of His own humanity. In Gethsemane He prayed "let the cup pass away from me" but He embraced created reality not as He humanly wanted it to be but reality as the Father here and now willed it to be. The cup that the Father held out to Him to drink—the cup over which He sweated blood, and then drained to the last drop—was reality in its least godly aspects.

Christ on Calvary embraced that reality and lived it to the end, teaching us that the only place one may encounter and embrace God, is in the embrace of created being as the expression of the wisdom and love of God.

6. The human *fiat* of Christ on Calvary is the counterpart in a spot in space and a moment in time of the omnipresent, eternal *Fiat* of God from which created being came into and is sustained in existence. On the surface the two acts of will appear related more by opposition than by conformity. God's *Fiat* is an act of the infinite goodness of the Divine Nature and brings into existence the universe. Christ's *fiat* is the anguished act of the impoverished being of a dying man, and terminates in death. The Divine *Fiat* is omnipotent. The human *fiat* is, to say the least, impotent. By God's *Fiat*, He masters the world. By Christ's *fiat*, He accepts the fact that apart from His divinity, He has little power even over Himself. Not being able to move even His hands

and feet, He must beg others for a drop to drink. The Divine *Fiat* is an act of a triumphant God. The human *fiat* is the acceptance of abject failure.

And yet, at the moment when Christ in his humanity accepts in the conditions of Calvary the infinite difference between that humanity and His divinity, and surrenders in obedience the life of His humanity into the hands of the Father, through this created, human act He comes closest to God. While various reasons for this perfection of union between created being and Uncreated Being on Calvary can be offered, one that proceeds from the dynamics of love is particularly relevant to our theme.

To love is to accept the reality and goodness of the person beloved, and to give ourselves in what we truly are to what the beloved truly is. To love God, therefore, means to love Him precisely as God. It means that we want God to be God, and we rejoice in the fact that He is God. It also means that we give ourselves for what we truly are to God as God.

For man to give himself to God as God, he must accept the fact that he is a creature, which is to say that he has no actuality apart from what has gratuitously been bestowed on him by God. It means, further, that the actual existence he enjoys belongs more to God than to himself, and that God as God can give such existence and take it away. Therefore, it is at the moment when a man knows that God demands life of him and freely, positively, confidently hands back his life as generously as God first gave it to him, at such moment he most completely accepts himself as a creature and therefore, most fully accepts God as God.

Christ on Calvary teaches us that by accepting His humanity in its totality as the Father willed it to be he was obediently submitting to God as God. It is the perfect meeting in the order of operation between Uncreated Being and created being in which man adores God through the medium of created reality by accepting life in all its aspects as the Father has willed life to be. In essence, in His humanity Christ on Calvary is saying to the Father, "You are God, I am not God. Therefore, I want what You want." In the conformity of wills in which Christ perfectly accepts the Father by perfectly accepting His human reality, the human *fiat* becomes the physical, instrumental cause of the Divine

Fiat. From that moment, according to Catholic tradition, whatever the Father wills by way of goodness for human nature, He wills through the proximate instrumentality of the human desire of Christ. The human *fiat* becomes an eternal act in union with the Divine *Fiat*, causing and sustaining throughout eternity whatever grace or perfection is bestowed on man.[42]

7. Therefore, on Calvary Christ reveals that the most meritorious, fruitful, and perfect act that man can perform in the present economy is the act of adoration—the act whereby he submits to the Father by embracing fully, confidently, and obediently in the way that the Father intends created reality as an expression of the divine will. This does not mean the passive acceptance of the *status quo*s since God gives ample evidence that He wills a substantial growth in the godliness of created being. Therefore the acceptance of created reality as the expression of the divine will demands a powerful, sustained, exhaustive utilization of every means available by which godliness can be advanced in oneself and in others.

Thus Christ for three years worked tirelessly and unceasingly to advance the kingdom of God among His people. But this obedient embrace of reality does mean that when existence allows of no immediate change or progress one must accept this also as an insight into the divine will and embrace with complete confidence and obedience the impotence of the present moment. Thus Christ hanging from the cross, helpless, unable to move, to act, can still accept fully that moment in obedience to the Father,[43] thereby transforming his failure and death into victory and life.

8. The Apostles' experience of God's presence and activity in the humanity of Christ was the experience of Christ's human nature. That human nature was an instrument causing God to come alive and grow among men through created grace. Over the years as they witnessed the growth of God's wisdom and love in quality and numbers among the Christian faithful, and experienced the inexhaustible power of Christ to transform individuals, communities, and nations, they realized more

---

[42] *Summa*, III, q. 22, a. 5.
[43] *Summa*, q. 48, a. 1 ad.1

and more clearly in thinking back to the dark moment of Calvary and the rigid body hanging from the cross, that they had been witnesses not to the death of a man so much as to the new birth of God's presence among men by grace through causative powers of that death.

V. CHRIST AND THE CHURCH

On the first evening of His resurrection Christ appeared among the Apostles and told them, "As the Father sent me, so am I sending you."[44] This mission that Christ gave to the Apostles has always been interpreted in Catholic tradition as extending through them to the Church. The mission of the Apostles and the mission of the Church are one since the Apostles and the Church are one. The presence and activity of Christ in the Apostles and in the Church are identical. And so it would be illuminating for our present purpose to examine some of the implications of this command of Christ in regards to the experience of God which is to be encountered in the Apostles and in the Church. How was Christ sent by the Father, and how does Christ send the Apostles and the Church?

1. Christ was sent by the Father to answer the natural, necessary hunger for God present in every man. He was to satisfy this hunger by making it possible for men to be united to God in and through his humanity. Christ was sent to enter into community with the actual and potential godliness of every man in a person-to-person relationship involving the mutual respect and love of brothers under the Fatherhood of God. He was to provide men with an immediate encounter with the Person of God in a relationship based on the communication of eternal life. He was to assist men as His brothers to evolve as images of God by nature and grace.

To relate as a brother to the actual and potential godliness of a man is to enter into a dialogue and community with him based on the sharing in depth of truth and love. It is to approach another man in love by explicitly relating to that which is the noblest and best in him. It is to be open to all that is present in him by way of actual participation in God's truth, love, beatitude, power, justice, and mercy, and to be open to the potential for godliness present in him both by nature and by the

---

[44] *Jn.* 20.21.

possibilities of grace. It is to approach him with a profound respect for what he is and an equally profound hope for what he can become under the infinite love of the Father.

This was the approach of Christ to every man without exception, and this is the approach that Christ implicitly obliges the Apostles and the Church to follow. Therefore, in obedience to Christ and as His instrument, the Church is commissioned to seek dialogue and community with every man as a potential or actual brother under the Fatherhood of God and on the basis of whatever there is present of potential or actual godliness in him.

2. Christ was sent by the Father as an exemplary cause, to make God's presence visible, tangible, and sensible through His humanity so as to reveal to men their vocation as images of God by grace. In their encounter with the humanity of Christ as elevated and perfected by grace, men were contemplating their own potential selves. Christ became for them their model and ideal, and fired in them the desire to imitate His perfection as the image of God by grace.

Christ sends the Apostles and the Church to perform a similar service for men. As instruments of the life of grace in them they are to allow God's invisible, intangible Being, Truth, Love, Life, Power, Justice, and Mercy to become a sensible living presence among men preparing the way for them to enter into community with God. They are to reveal in every age the potential for perfection in human nature when elevated by God's grace. And they are by concrete example to ignite in men the desire to share with them the divine life as images of God. The Church in every age must serve to permit the Word to become flesh in that age and walk once again among men.

3. Christ was sent by the Father as the efficient, instrumental cause of grace. By acting consciously as the voluntary, total living instrument of the Father His human actions were the vehicle of divine action imparting eternal life and transforming men into images of God by grace. Christ sends the Apostles and the Church to continue this work as instrumental, efficient causes of grace in union with Himself. In their acts of initiating life, forgiving, nourishing, strengthening, loving, empowering, and maturing, men in every age are to experience the divine action whereby they are brought alive, cleansed, nourished,

strengthened, and matured in their participation of Divine Life. In submitting to these instrumental acts of the Church men encounter action that belongs properly more to God than to the instrumentalities involved.

4. Christ was sent by the Father to merit eternal life for men. From the moment of His conception Christ's humanity possessed the fullness of the life of grace. But it was only through the Passion that He principally merited His sharing of this life with others.

In a similar manner Christ sends the Apostles and the Church, not only to give witness in a tangible manner to God's presence in them and to be the ministers of that presence, but also to earn the communication of divine life by which the men of their place and time are to be transformed into images of God.[45] They must merit this transformation by grace in the way that Christ merited. They must merit it by drinking with him the cup of reality which the Father handed to him; and which He passes on to the Apostles and the Church.

The Apostles and the Church must confront the reality of existence in the conditions in which they find it in their time and place. They must not run away from it but advance to confront its most disappointing, frustrating, confusing, destructive aspects. They, like Christ, must commune with the absence of God in human nature, their own and all others, and experience how the soul is ravaged in the absence of God's love. The Apostles and the Church must embrace the flawed image of God in man. They must be confident of God's love for all men and of His power to bring love out of hate, wisdom out of foolishness, strength out of weakness, order out of chaos, and life out of death.

Man's encounter with God in the Apostles and the Church must be one in which he sees the Church confront those aspects of reality that seem furthest removed from God. In these, by the Church's affirmation and embrace of God's invisible presence, to merit the emergence of the hidden God by bringing Him sensibly alive through the effects of grace in the souls of men.

---

[45] *Summa*, I-II, q. 114.

CHRIST AND HUMANITY

Thus Christ sends the Church of the Twenty-first Century not only to bear witness to Him but to merit His living tangible presence in this age. The experience of Christ as human and divine in the Church of the twentieth century must be an experience in which one encounters men acting in union with Christ who manifest a profound love of all that is best in this century together with a profound sensitivity and effective concern for all that is worst. And in this effective concern one must see the Church embrace in love the limitations within her and all around her as the means of earning (causing) the resurrection of the Word in living flesh in our times.

It is useless and insulting to offer an intensely suffering man abstract arguments to explain how such suffering is not incompatible with the Omnipotence and Mercy of God if one does not provide at the same time tangible expression of God's mercy in bringing transcending good out of such suffering. The Church cannot be satisfied with preaching the mercy of God. She must be the living proof and expression of His mercy by having confronted the suffering and limitations of each age, and having earned the triumph of grace in incarnational form over the evils of the time.

5. Christ was sent by the Father as a loving Son Who in his humanity lived in uninterrupted contemplation of the Father's presence and revelation in His created work. He sought, in constant communication with His Father, that the Divine Will be fulfilled in all things.

The Apostles witnessed in a variety of expressions this loving communication between Father and Son. They came to know the power in Christ's filial requests to obtain the desired response from the Father. Christ sends the Apostles and the Church, both as brothers with Him in His humanity and as loving Sons of the Father, to carry out their mission in constant filial communication with the Father. Others are to find in this habitual contemplation of the presence and revelation of the Father in created being, and in the power of their confident filial prayer to the Father, a manifestation of the actuality, love, and presence of God in their lives as a Father, and as a nearly irresistible invitation to enter into such filial community with God.

6. Christ was sent by the Father possessing the fullness of grace within his human nature in order to impart that life to his followers. In order

for the Apostles to share Christ's life with others they in turn had to experience Christ coming fully alive within. With reason, therefore, Christ did not send out the Apostles to carry out his mission until they had passed through their purification occasioned by Christ's death on the cross. Only then, having been emptied of their illusions and self love, were they opened to the coming of the Holy Spirit at Pentecost.

If Christ had sent Peter on this mission prior to Calvary he would have gone eagerly thinking that he was bringing God to others. But he would only have been bringing the pride, and the illusions of Peter. Having confronted the real Peter in his failure at Christ's Passion—the frightened, paralyzed, self-seeking Peter who denied with a curse that he even knew Christ—and having been emptied of this Peter, he was now open to the coming of the Spirit. It is only after this moment that Christ can tell Peter, "Feed my sheep."[46] And so it was with the other Apostles. Only with the coming of the Spirit could they go forth as adult images of God by grace and carry on the mission of Christ.

The coming of the Spirit to the Apostles presents its own problems concerning the encounter with God in human nature. Earlier Christ had promised the Apostles that He would never leave them. Later He tells them that he must leave; for if He does not leave the Spirit cannot come to them. In this later statement Christ appears to say that his presence is an obstacle to the coming of the Holy Spirit rather than the instrument of the Spirit's presence. How can Christ's presence obstruct the coming of the Spirit?

Aquinas points out that most men live in the senses, seeking their contact with reality, including God, in the sensible world around them. Thus, in an accommodation to this human condition, God sent an angel in visible form to the shepherds in order to lead them to Christ in the stable. He also led the wise men by a visible star to their meeting with Christ.[47] But the spiritual man, as Aquinas points out, is led primarily by the inner promptings of the Spirit. Simeon, a spiritual man, did not require an external sign to recognize Christ. As soon as he saw the child, he knew from the inner movement of the Spirit Christ's identity and he rejoiced. For Aquinas, Simeon is a symbol of the adult image of

---

[46] Jn. 21. 17.
[47] *Summa*, III, q. 36, a. 5.

CHRIST AND HUMANITY

God who is moved less by external signs and supports than by the inner presence and workings of the Spirit.

When Christ first came to the Apostles, they were still men of the senses, needing the tangible, sensible presence of Christ's humanity to bring them alive to the living presence of God. In the course of their formation under Christ, they developed inwardly as images of God to the point where they were disposed for the transition from a child image of God to an adult image, one moved primarily by grace within. However, as long as they continued to seek their primary encounter with God in the humanity of Christ sensibly present to them, the transition could not take place. Christ's sensible presence that initially was essential to the growth of grace in them, now became an obstacle since it encouraged them to continue seeking the experience of God in His humanity outside of them and not in their own, inner human reality.

Christ therefore withdrew His visible presence and the Apostles retired to the upper room—hovering between the emptiness of Christ's absence outside of them and the lack of awareness of His presence within them. With the coming of the Spirit the Apostles experienced within themselves a courage, wisdom, love, strength, and zeal that they had previously known only in the humanity of Christ outside of them. Now they understand that Christ has not left them, but that He has entered into and taken possession of them from within. They no longer needed Christ's external sensible presence—admonishing, encouraging, enlightening, and motivating them—since the fullness of His presence within and the promptings of the Spirit accomplish everything that previously was effected by His external presence.

With the growth in grace the Apostles open the doors of the upper room and issue forth as adult images of God to begin the mission that Christ had given to them. Their emergence from that room, according to one tradition, is the moment of birth of the Church when God became visibly, audibly, palpably, sensibly present in a community of men bound together as adult images of God by grace. In the collective, sensible presence of the Apostles men encounter the same contact with divinity acting in and through human nature that the Apostles encountered in the humanity of Christ.

This development of the Apostles—as images of God by grace in which they first experienced God's presence in the humanity of Christ outside of them and progress to the stage of having that same experience within their own humanity—exemplifies the pattern by which men normally grow in grace. Initially a man depends upon the presence and actions of adult images of God outside of him to implant and nourish grace in his soul. In the first, tenuous stage of development the new life in him demands that he be surrounded by external, sensible instruments of grace to support and sustain its frail existence.[48] When grace has developed in him to a level that requires the transition from the child to the adult stage, it is necessary that he be denied for a time the external instrumentalities of God's presence which heretofore were so essential to him, in order that he be forced to seek God's presence within.

The period of transition is normally a difficult and traumatic one since he no longer finds security and direction from God's visible presence outside and he has not yet experienced the workings of the Spirit within. But when the Spirit does move within, and he knows it as coming from within, and it awakens the confidence, certitude, love, and zeal which previously he found in adult images outside of him, the child image has become an adult image of God. He now seeks more to give than to receive, rather to help than to be helped. He then begins to radiate to others God's presence within him rather than seeking anxiously for reassurance from tangible signs of the presence of such grace in others.[49]

What is true of individual growth in grace is true in its own way of community growth in grace. It seems to me that this traditional insight into the dynamics of growth in grace has particular relevance in understanding the plight of the Church and the anxieties of its members in the present age. One generation functioning as a collective adult image of God will beget a collective child image of God in the next. In the tenuousness of grace in that new generation it will be essential that the child image can look back to its parent Church and find the supporting, encouraging, visible presence of a triumphant Church to sustain and motivate the life developing within it.

---

[48] *Summa*, q. 72, a. 5.
[49] *Ibid.* q. 72, a. 5.

CHRIST AND HUMANITY

For a time the new generation walks confidently and optimistically together with the old generation, sharing fully the benefits of its accomplishments without having earned or contributed anything to those accomplishments; just as the Apostles walked confidently with Christ sharing in the glory of his works, miracles, and successes without earning or contributing to his success. But if the new generation is to become collectively an adult image of God, it must experience the presence and workings of the Spirit not only outside and in the past, but within and in the present.

It is essential for its development that the new generation, for a time, be stripped of the supports and props of the past. Suddenly it finds itself seeking support in what is no longer the divine, triumphant Church, but a human, failing, confused, entity that is being torn apart by forces of the age that she neither understands not controls.

As the child image of the new generation witnesses the collapse of the old, it also experiences the inner collapse within itself of the confidence and faith of the past. These are replaced by anxiety and doubt. And the new generation discovers, as did the Apostles, the weakness of its faith, and its dependency upon outside support. In the humbling, purifying fire of this experience the way is opened for the coming of the Spirit as the illusions, pretentions, and pride of the age are burned away.

When the Spirit does stir, from the doubts, confusion, indecision, and torpor emerge certitude, insight, decisiveness, and zeal. And when the new generation with confidence and understanding of the potential for godliness of its time takes up the work of transforming that age into a collective image of God, the child image becomes the adult image of God and the Church in that generation comes of age. This has been the pattern of grace in the past. It seems to me that our community with that past demands a similar interpretation of the events of the present and a firm confidence for the Church in the future.

7. Christ was sent by the Father as an individual possessing the fullness of grace in His humanity. Christ sends the Apostles to continue His mission as a collective instrument acting in community. Since no individual Apostle could possess the fullness of grace in Christ, many Apostles of diverse temperament and talents were necessary in order to

accomplish the work of Christ through a multiplicity and diversity of instruments acting in community. Since the Apostles were sent as true instrumental causes, their individual persons were totally involved as animate, rational instrumentalities in their work. Each had to be known and experienced profoundly in his individual humanity in order for the experience of God's grace working in him as an instrument to be encountered.

In each case one had to know and experience what was proper to him as a person in order to know and experience him as an instrument of divine action. Peter had to be known as Peter and John as John in order to experience the special operations of God's grace in each. If I went to Peter to obtain what God intended to give me through the instrumentality of John I would neither receive what I was looking for nor gain what Peter as an instrument was able to give me. The same holds true for my approach to John. In a similar manner God acts through different cultures, nationalities, and ages as collective instruments of His grace. Each age, culture, and nationality can be a partial instrument of divine action. But no single human grouping can be the total, adequate instrumental source of that action.

In using different human communities as instruments of His presence, God will be true to each so that one must first know and appreciate its natural participation in godliness before he can know and experience the divine presence and activity in it. Just as one must know Peter as Peter, and John as John, in order to experience the divine presence in each, so one must know the natural godliness of the East as the East, and the West as the West, before one can experience the special workings of God's grace in these instrumentalities. Just as I must not see an experience of God in John that is to be found in Peter, nor in Peter what must be found in John, neither should I approach the East for an experience of god's grace that is to be found in the West, nor approach the West for what is to be experience of the divine presence in the East.

At the same time, one knows that whatever he experiences of the various manifestations of grace in human nature, will be complementary to, and in harmony with every other valid experience of the divine's presence in humanity. He knows, further, that whatever he experiences of God's presence in any culture or age, will be revealed as having its origin in the fullness of grace in the humanity of Christ.

8. Christ was the Word sent by the Father to provide men with an immediate encounter with the Person of God. Christ as the Person of God walked among men, eating and conversing with them, offering men in that daily human commerce not only the encounter with the image of God by grace but also with the Person of God himself.

How did Christ send the Apostles and the Church in such a way as to allow them to fulfill the mission given to him of providing men with a personal encounter with God? It seems to me that in the transcendent unity of the Church as a community, that according to Saint Paul is achieved by the immediate presence of the Holy Spirit, one can best explain the encounter with the Person of God that men have in their encounter with the community of images of God by grace which is the Church.

According to Aquinas, *person* is that substantial perfection whereby an intellectual entity subsists as unique, complete, existing in and of its own right, and is incommunicable. The effect of such subsistence is an encompassing existential unity whereby the parts exist inseparably from the whole and the whole is present to every part. In my encounter with a man, for example, I confront a complex rational being possessing many distinct physical parts. His hand is one part, his head is another, and his foot is a third. While each of these parts is significantly distinct from the others, all exist in a subsisting whole so that when I touch either the hand, head or foot, I am in immediate contact with the subsisting whole. It is my consciousness of the radical unity encompassing these significantly differing parts that makes me recognize that they belong to one and the same whole entity. In touching any part of him I am in direct contact with the whole person.

So also in the Church, when I experience the complexity of parts, which Saint Paul compares to the complexity of the human body,[50] and experience the transcending unity that binds vastly different persons, nations, cultures, and ages extending over a period of two thousand years, it seems to me that in this encounter with the unity in this diversity of the human community which is the Church, one is encountering the Spirit, the Person of God. It would follow from this that

---

[50] *I Cor.* 12.12-30.

openness to the actual and potential presence and activity of the Spirit in every individual, community, nation, culture, and age is the condition for openness to the Person of the Spirit, and to personal union with God.

VI. CHRIST AND THE SACRAMENTS

According to Catholic tradition the Sacraments are man's principal contact with the efficient and meritorious causality of the humanity of Christ.[51] In one's encounter with men ministering the sacraments in union with Christ he finds his point of special extraordinary encounter with God's activity in and through human nature. The different approaches and interpretation of the sacraments illustrate with particular clarity the different attitudes toward the encounter with God in human nature. It would be illuminating for our understanding of the experience of God in man to examine briefly these diverse approaches and interpretations. Just as there are three basic interpretations of the encounter with God in created being, there are similarly three general attitudes towards the sacraments.

Pattern I tends to see the sacraments as it sees all reality in a natural setting.[52] Since the existence of the transcendent God, the supernatural order, and grace are either denied or obscured in this pattern, sacraments that are instruments of such a God and supernatural grace can scarcely be acknowledged. Where sacraments are acknowledged and used, they tend to be seen more as principal causes possessing a natural religious value and a purely natural effectiveness.

For example, confession may be practiced as a salutary religious exercise since value is attributed to it somewhat in the manner of psychiatric counseling. The Eucharist tends to be a celebration of human life and the immanence of God in humanity. The priest is accepted not as an instrument of a transcendent God and a channel of grace, but as one who should symbolize the best in human nature (the image of God by nature), and assist others as a father or elder brother figure to be true to the best of their natural religious and humanistic instincts.

---

[51] *Summa*, III, q. 62, a.5.

[52] For the attitude of mind represented by Pattern I see Chapter Three, Section III.

Pattern II tends either to deny the existence of sacraments altogether or to accept them as unique, isolated points of contact with divinity in human action. They not only fail to dramatize the broader possibilities of encounter with God in human nature, but confirm that such possibilities do not exist.[53] When the existence of sacraments is denied, the reason for the denial are opposite to those of Pattern I. The reality of God as transcendent is such that no human activity could serve as the vehicle of divine action, not even in an instrumental manner, to say nothing of functioning as secondary principal causes of participated divine action.

Where the sacraments are admitted, this pattern tends to see them as the only means whereby God acts through human activity. The only place where man encounters God's presence in human nature is in the Eucharist. God's forgiveness cannot be found in human forgiveness in a broad level, but solely in the forgiveness of Penance. No man can serve as mediator between God and men except the anointed priest. He in turn, tends to be an other-world figure, not like the rest of men, who serves to remind men at large that salvation comes from outside humanity and in no way from within their humanity. The sacraments according to this pattern, therefore, tend to be not so much human acts as somewhat disembodied religious rituals whose power operates independently of the human activity involved.

Pattern III considers the sacraments to be true human acts that instrumentally *as human acts* contain and convey sanctifying grace so as to serve as the vehicles of divine action. Unlike Pattern I, this approach conceives the sacraments to be instrumental causes and not principal causes, so that their effects belong more to the action of the transcendent God than to the natural causality present in their exercise.[54] Unlike Pattern II, this approach affirms that the sacraments are true instrumental causes that exercise their own proper (natural) causality as

---

[53] For the approach to created reality of Pattern II see Chapter Three, Section III.

[54] *Summa*, III, q. 62, a. 1.

the instrumentality of divine action.[55] Just as the instrumental role of Christ's humanity did not mean the suppression of human activity in him, but rather its heightening and intensification as a vital, conscious instrumentality, so the instrumental role of human activity in the sacraments heightens and intensifies this human component as the carrier of grace.

Not only are the sacraments human acts, they represent the most profoundly human of human activity, expressing the deepest aspects of man's hunger for perfect happiness, his need to forgive and be forgiven, his desire to love and be loved in the most profound manner, and his yearning for life in its purest form. Part of the universal character of the sacraments, which permits them to transcend in their signification the shifts and changes in cultures and ages, rests in this radically human quality.

They represent elementary kinds of human activity which take place daily wherever human communities are found, for example, acts of forgiving, loving, nourishing, empowering, maturing and begetting life. Thus the sacraments function not only as instruments of the efficient causality of Christ, but they also share in his exemplary causality by dramatizing before men the potential in all human activity to exercise a sanctifying role as an instrument of God's grace.

Christ claimed that his humanity possessed extraordinary power as the instrument of divine action. However, Christ did not jealously keep this power to himself. On the contrary, his long years of forming the Apostles were devoted in great part to awakening in them the awareness that their humanity potentially possessed a similar power to act as the sanctifying instruments of His divinity; and that the Father willed to use them in union with him as vehicles of his action among men.[56] In this way Christ as the perfect image of God by grace, revealed the potential in the whole of mankind to operate in union with him as sanctifying agents. Thus Christ for the first time revealed fully to men the sanctifying power potentially present in the capacity of human

---

[55] For the human dimensions of the sacramental act see the whole of *Summa*, III, q. 60, and q. 64, aa.1,3,5,8,9,10.

[56] *Ibid.* q. 64, a. 4.

nature to love, forgive, mature, beget life, and embrace reality as the work of the Father.

Just as Christ dramatized the potential power of human activity to exercise a sanctifying role in man's development as the image of God, so the sacraments may be seen as constant, living reminders in daily life of the universal power of all human activity to contribute to man's union with God.[57] This is not to say that the sanctifying power of human activity is potentially the same as the power operating in the sacraments. In the sacraments, according to Catholic tradition, one encounters the efficient causality of Christ's Passion in a way that is not duplicated in any other channel of grace.

So intimate and primary is this efficient causality of Christ, that the power of the sacraments to produce grace operates independently of the state of soul of the minister.[58] Even should the minister be in a state of serious sin so that his motive in administering the sacrament could not be Charity—as long as he acts in conscious conformity to the intention of Christ, the sacrament is valid and effective. The power of human action in general to function as a sanctifying agent in union with Christ is not the efficient power proper to the sacraments. Rather it is the power of all such activity to operate as meritorious exemplary causes that have a dispositive effect on souls. Thus preparing them for the reception of grace, and as possessing impetratory power in the case of prayerful human desires.

For example, the Sacrament of Penance may be approached as man's unique encounter with the forgiveness of God operating through the human act of forgiveness of Christ in such a way as to be in no manner duplicated in other human acts of forgiveness (Pattern II). Or, on the contrary, Penance can be seen as providing not only an extraordinary encounter with divine forgiveness efficiently acting through the instrumentality of Christ's human forgiveness, but also as exemplifying a meritorious and dispositive power present in every act of human forgiveness when offered in union with Christ (Pattern III). When seen in this latter way the sacrament serves to illustrate to all

---

[57] *Ibid.* q. 60, a. 3.

[58] *Ibid.* q. 64, a. 5.

men the divinely healing, purifying, transforming, elevating, sanctifying power present in the universal human capacity to forgive.

In this approach the penitent is obliged to relate the divine forgiveness he seeks in Penance to the potential for forgiveness present in the entirety of his life and in all human life, so that his approach to divine forgiveness encompasses and qualifies his approach to the entire phenomenon of human forgiveness as a sanctifying force ("Forgive, and you will be forgiven").[59] "Forgive us our debts, as we have forgiven those who are in debt to us."[60]

The penitent finds the benefits of divine forgiveness only when he has confronted the divine presence in all aspects of human forgiveness in breadth and in depth. He fully encounters divine forgiveness when he has related his own acts of forgiving and seeking pardon as parts to a whole, to the ultimate, perfecting, finalizing forgiveness of Christ that encompasses and unites all human forgiveness in its source in divine forgiveness.

Again, the Eucharist can be regarded as providing a unique encounter with God in and through the humanity of Christ which is *in no manner* duplicated in the rest of mankind. So God's presence in Christ is a symbol and reminder of His absence from mankind at large (Pattern II). Or, on the contrary, the Eucharist can be understood as both a unique presence of divinity in the humanity of Christ, and also as the symbol of God's actual and potential extraordinary presence by grace in all men as adopted sons after the image of Christ. In this way the adoration of God's presence in the humanity of Christ cannot be separated from the reverential acknowledgement of God's participated presence by grace in all men (Pattern III).

According to this latter understanding, one cannot truly go on his knees before the Eucharist without going on his knees before God's presence in all men. One cannot feed upon God's nourishing presence in the Eucharist unless he daily feeds upon the nourishing aspects of that presence as it may be found in every person and human situation. One cannot embrace the humanity of Christ as his brother under the Fatherhood of God without encompassing in that embrace the whole of

---

[59] *Mt.* 6.14.
[60] *Mt.* 6.12.

CHRIST AND HUMANITY

mankind as actual and potential brothers under the Father by fellowship in eternal life.

The symbol of approach to the Eucharist of Pattern II is the solitary contemplator. Kneeling alone with Christ in the Eucharist in isolation from the rest of mankind he considers that the further he withdraws from the community of man the closer he comes to the community with the humanity of Christ and with divinity in Christ.

The symbol of Pattern III's approach to the Eucharist is the man who is impelled to relate in breadth and depth to the community of man as the condition for approaching in breadth and depth the humanity of Christ. This is the means to contact with His divinity. He may, in fact, spend many solitary hours before the Eucharist. But his motivation will not be to shed his identity with the community of man as the means of identifying with the humanity of Christ. Rather, it will be to free himself from a superficial distracting involvement with the secondary aspects of his own humanity and that of others. In his freedom he may go to the depths of human existence as the condition for communing with the fullness of divinity's presence in the depths of the humanity of Christ.

The sacrificial character of the Eucharist[61] will remind him that he must confront and embrace in union with all suffering mankind aspects of human existence. He must confront those aspects where God's presence is least apparent and where man seems furthest removed from God. This is the condition for encountering the humanity of the Christ of Calvary where His divinity is at the same time least apparent and most effectively working.

According to Pattern II the priest tends to be the disembodied symbol of another world and another life. He performs equally disembodied religious rituals that support man's flight from created reality and human life rather than forcing a movement into human life in depth as the point of principal contact with divinity. In the approach to the Sacraments of Pattern III, the priest must relate the sacramental action to the whole of human life and assist men to confront God's presence

---

[61] *Summa*, q. 73, a. 6.

in the breadth and depth of humanity. Certainly, he must not support the natural tendency of man to flee from the crucifying aspects of reality which cannot be avoided without a flight from reality itself.

In the Catholic tradition the priest is a mediator under Christ between God and men. If man's primary encounter with God is found in the humanity of Christ and in all humanity operating in union with Christ as instrumental efficient, exemplary, and meritorious causes of grace, the priest must mediate by bringing men to a confrontation with human life in breadth and depth as the instrument of God's presence and activity. He must lead others especially to the depths of human experiences, searching there for community with the heart and mind of Christ whereby all human experience is transformed into a vital instrument of divine action.

As the multiplicity and diversity of the human experiences of Christ provided different instrumentalities for divine action in Him, so the priest must assist others in their diverse human experiences to become voluntary instruments of the specific effects which God intends to achieve through these experiences. The priest, for example, must assist the man who is dying to see his approaching death through the eyes of Christ on Calvary. He must assist the dying so that they may discern God's wisdom and love present in the moment of death, and with Christ embrace Life in death so as to change death into Life. In order to perform this mediating role the priest must first become the voluntary instrument of God's grace. Acting in and through his own life he must learn and experience how divinity transforms the diversity of human experiences into complementary participations in divine life as man is being formed into the image of God by grace. This is to say that the priest as mediator like Christ, in a primary manner must be an ecumenist, open to dialogue and community with the special presence and activity of divinity in the full range of human experience—in himself first and then in others.[62]

VII. CHRIST AND HUMANITY—CONCLUSION

As stated in the Introduction the aim of my study has been to analyze, in the light of Catholic tradition, the experience of God to be found in

---

[62] *Ibid.*, Suppl. Q. 36, a. 1.

the community of man. The occasion for this study was the expressed desire of the Church in Vatican II to enter into discourse with all men as brothers. To dialogue with them under the Fatherhood of God who share a common destiny that is both human and divine. My intention has been to evaluate this thrust of Vatican II to dialogue with all men in the light of traditional Catholic theology to determine how it can be reconciled with that tradition.

Accepting the judgment of Vatican II that this impulse originates in the workings of the Holy Spirit in the Church, I set out to determine where in the dynamics of grace and spiritual growth such an impulse should be located. My intention has been to establish that this impulse of the Spirit should be recognized as an essential aspect of the normal development of grace in the soul and that it should be accepted as proceeding proximately from the activity of the Theological Virtues, with particular emphasis on the primary role of Charity. I will now summarize my interpretation of the place to which this impulse should be assigned in Catholic tradition and add some final conclusions under three headings; humanity's need of Christ, Christ's need of humanity, Man's need of humanity.

Humanity's need of Christ.
Mankind at large needs Christ as the perfectible needs its perfecting principle. In this case it is man as the potential image of God who in order to become the actual image of God requires the humanity of Christ as the perfect, actual image of God by nature and Grace. Specifically mankind needs the exemplary, efficient, and meritorious causality of the human nature of Christ and the impetratory power of His prayer to evolve fully to maturity as images of God by nature and grace.

Exemplary causality of Christ
Humanity requires the revelation of the humanity of Christ both to know God and to know itself. The human nature of Christ as the instrument of his divinity was able to make the invisible reality of God a visible, tangible, audible, palpable presence, so that men find in the sensible words and actions of Christ their most revealing insight into the mystery of God.

At the same time mankind depends upon the revealing presence of Christ in order to know its own reality. Since only the actual is intelligible, man's potential to be the image of God remains hidden and unintelligible until human nature develops into the actuality of the image of God.[63] In the encounter with the humanity of Christ as the image of his divinity, men find the revelation of the perfection to which they have been called, and encounter their own true reality.

Efficient causality of Christ

It is not enough for man to find in Christ the revelation of God and himself. He requires also the interior grace of Christ by which he progresses as the image of God toward union with the Divine Nature. The efficient causality of Christ's humanity as the proximate source of grace is so unique and extraordinary that other human instruments exercise a similar causality only by way of immediate participation in the power of Christ and when they act in conscious union with Him. In the created level the human nature of Christ remains the ultimate source of every grace and blessing that contributes to man's evolution as the image of God by nature.

Meritorious causality of Christ

Christ by reason of the hypostatic union was able to merit salvation for mankind with the merit of strict justice. Mankind needs the humanity of Christ in order that it may possess within its inner reality the means by which it can, through the presence of Christ, earn its evolution in divine likeness.[64] Through the Incarnation and the Passion Christ elevated the natural radical godliness of human nature to the supernatural level and brought it about that men in union with Him could become causes, in the sense that merit implies such causality, of their evolution as images of God.

---

[63] *Summa*, I, q. 87, a.1.

[64] The power of man to earn eternal life is one of the effects of grace in him. In meriting grace for man, Christ merited also that men now have the power in union with Him to earn. (that is cause, in the sense of meritorious causality) their salvation.

Cf. *Summa*, I-II, q. 114, aa. 1, 2 , 8.

CHRIST AND HUMANITY

Impetratory power of Christ's prayer

Man needs the prayer of Christ on his behalf. Christ's intersession enables him to efficaciously articulate his needs and call down as a loving son from a beloved and loving Father the graces necessary for his ideal development as the image of the Father.

Christ's need of humanity

Christ needs the community of man as a perfecting principle requires perfectible being in order to give full expression to its power to impart goodness to others. Specifically, Christ as the perfect image of God requires the community of man so that by reason of his grace as Head of the Church he may impart to humanity the fullness of the life of grace that he possesses.[65] One aspect of the perfection of God, as we have seen,[66] is his power to act outside of his Divine Nature by creating, sustaining, and bringing to perfection beings made by him in his image and likeness. If Christ's humanity is to participate in this aspect of his divinity, Christ needs the community of man to act upon as the Head, initiating, sustaining, and bringing to perfection in men their participation in his perfection as the perfect image of God.

In exercising this perfecting power, Christ does not increase internally in grace and evolve further as the image of God,[67] but he does add extrinsically to his inner perfection by his action on others. Since the richness of Christ's inner created grace is so great and the merit of his Passion is infinite, a vast multiplicity and diversity of humans reflecting every aspect of human life is required in order that Christ may give full expression of his grace in the community of man. Thus Saint Paul says that "the saints together make a unity in the work of service, building up the body of Christ."[68]

Humanity, therefore, is the extrinsic occasion by which Christ adds to his inner perfection:

---

[65] *Summa*, III, q.8, aa. 1, 2, 3, 5, 6.
[66] *Cf.* pp. 152 ff.
[67] *Summa*, III, q. 7, a. 12.
[68] *Eph.* 4.12.

1. *Christ as an exemplary cause needs humanity.* Since the created participation in God's Being, Truth, Love, Life, Beatitude, Power, Justice, and Mercy is present by grace in Christ with fullness, an extensive multiplicity and diversity of men is required if Christ is to give full expression in the community of man to the richness of grace in Him. No single person, community, nation, culture, or age, for example, can possess and give explicit expression to the Wisdom of Christ. The Truth in Christ requires a community of minds existing over a long period of time in widely differing circumstances and constantly reflecting upon His words and actions, in order that man may be able in some small degree to become aware explicitly of the implications of the teaching of Christ.

The collective wisdom of the Christian community of men who have dedicated their lives to contemplating and living the Truth of Christ over a period of two thousand years has not yet been adequate to make fully explicit His Truth. So also two thousand years of generous and even heroic cooperation of countless thousands of Christians have not been sufficient to manifest the full power and richness of the love of Christ.

This is likewise true of the other divine perfections present in the plentitude of created grace in the humanity of Christ. A two thousand year community of a vast multitude and diversity of images of the Love, Beatitude, Life, Power, Justice and Mercy of God have not succeeded in giving expression in their collective perfection as images of God to the fullness of grace in Christ. In each age the mustard seed continues to grow to greater perfection as it transubstantiates the men of that age into other, complementary expressions of the fullness of vitality in it. Thus Christ continues to need other men of different circumstances, facing different aspects of life outside and manifesting different potentials of human life within, to unite under His vital influence as Head in order to fill out His body in love:

> If we live by the truth and in love, we shall grow in all ways into Christ, who is the head by whom the whole body is fitted and joined together, every joint adding its own strength,

for each separate part to work according to its function. So the body grows until it has built itself up, in love.[69]

2. *Christ as an efficient cause needs humanity.* Just as it was fitting that God communicate to Christ as His image the power to perfect others in grace, so it is fitting that Christ in a godly manner share with other men the power of his humanity as a teaching, ruling, and sanctifying instrument of Divine Love.[70] But in order to share this perfection as efficient cause of grace, Christ stands in need of men who are capable of such elevation in power. Once again, such is the power of Christ's efficient causality that a vast community of human instrumentalities are required if he is to duplicate with fullness in the community of man the sanctifying power that the Father has bestowed upon Him.

Since that power is sufficient for the salvation of all mankind, Christ needs human instruments in every place and in every age in order to give explicit expression to this instrumental power of his humanity. Since the limitations of the instruments render them less apt in varying degrees for such instrumental operation, Christ will act in one age through one community of instruments and in another age through a different community of cooperators. Christ will use nineteenth century men as the proximate instruments of his sanctifying action whereby he changes that period into the actual image of God. He will use twentieth century men in that era to do the sanctifying work of that time. Since single persons and particular groupings of men are not adequate to the full expression of Christ's power to sanctify a specific age. He will use collective instruments acting in unity in every age so that men in community will make explicit in every age the sanctifying power of Christ.

3. *Christ as a meritorious cause needs humanity.* As the Father provided that Christ in his humanity would possess the power to merit salvation for mankind, so Christ needs other men with whom he can share his meritorious power in order to do for them what the Father had done for him. Through the merits of Christ, the whole of mankind

---

[69] *Eph.* 4.15-16.
[70] *Summa*, Suppl. Q. 34, a.1.

potentially has, in union with Him, the power of causing (in the causal modality of merit) its own salvation.[71]

Christ's work of merit took place principally through his Passion wherein he confronted the godlessness in human life and, in obedience to the Father, embraced and fully lived the reality of the long hours of the Passion in obedience to the Father's will. In that confrontation Christ implicitly faced the total phenomenon of godlessness in human nature and his *fiat* embraced not only the painful reality of those hours but also every aspect of the absence of God from the collective human experience of life.[72] In order that the actuality of Christ's *fiat* may find explicit expression among men, he needs many persons over many years confronting every aspect of godlessness in human life, uniting their *fiats* with his in conformity to the Divine *Fiat*, so as to transform those periods of failure, sorrow, and death into victory, joy, and life. In every age Christ needs men to face the deficiencies of that age and to make an act of faith in the Father's wisdom and love controlling those Calvaries so that by the embrace of those aspects of reality they may in a visible, tangible form, repeat the miracle of Calvary.[73]

4. *Christ's power of prayer needs humanity*. In Christ's uninterrupted prayer life he constantly articulated as a loving Son to his Father the needs of all men in their hunger for God. Christ's prayer was not the plea of one man, but the plea of all men in the one man. If Christ is to share with other men this privilege of daily loving commerce that the Father had bestowed on his humanity, he needs a multiplicity and diversity of men in every age who, in union with him, articulate the specific spiritual needs of the men of their place and time in order for them to evolve as images of God by grace.

Man's need of Humanity.

Man needs the encounter with Christ's humanity in breadth and depth. in order to evolve as the image of God by grace. By the dispositions of divine providence such an encounter normally takes place *only* in community. In order to achieve ideal union with Christ the encounter

---

[71] *Cf.* note 208 of this chapter.
[72] *Summa*, III, q. 49, a.5.
[73] *Col.* 1.24.

needs to be with a community of men, in breadth and depth, where they are functioning in union with Christ as instrumentalities of grace. All that has been outlined about Christ's acting in and through a vast community of human instruments in every age, endowing them with a participation in his exemplary, efficient, meritorious causality and united them to him in the exercise of his prayer life, points up this necessity.

Without developing this matter further, I will point out two aspects of our contact with Christ through the community of man. These illustrate the role of community with human nature in broad terms.

The fullness of grace in Christ is such that the human intellect cannot fathom its richness by direct contemplation of Truth of Christ independently of his effect upon others. Many have sensibly reflected in words and actions on the implications of that Truth. It is only as we enter into community with the many minds that we begin to grasp something of the inexhaustible contents. Just as Christ needs a multiplicity and diversity of human instrumentalities to give more explicit expression to his Truth in a human context, so we need that explicit manifestations of this community of instruments of Truth to provide in a more tangible, digestible, simple form of the richness of the Truth of Christ.

The same hold true with regards to the expression in the community of believers of the other divine perfections present in a created fullness and mystery in the humanity of Christ. Consider the person, for example, who ignores the effects of Christ's Wisdom and Love upon generous souls over the two thousand years of Christianity, and endeavors to leap-frog over the visible, sensible signs of the interior effects of Christ's action upon the community of Christians. He who ignores these things as though they were an obstacle to his encounter with Christ and attempts to penetrate directly into the inner reality of Christ, has abandoned the one means of adequate encounter and revelation of that inner mystery.

Community with the unfolding effects of Christ's love transforming men over the two thousand year span of Christianity provides one with his best access into the inner life of Christ. Rather than a wall separating modern man from the reality of Christ, the community of the faithful serves as a kind of microscope that permits one to enlarge and delineate aspects which otherwise would not even be visible. Like all human instrumentalities it is flawed and imperfect, even with the action of grace. So that a constant struggle must be sustained to discern the actions of grace in that community and separate them from the imperfect workings of nature. But the only alternative to this flawed instrumentality is the substitution of another human instrumentality which, when operating out of community with the proven effects of Christ's action upon others, provides an immeasurably inferior basis of approach to Christ.

Since Christ presents Himself as the "living bread"[74] Who has come to answer man's deepest hunger for the experience of God, one must live close to the community of man in depth in order to know and keep fresh in mind the fundamental desires and needs of human nature. Such human desires must exercise their proper, illuminating role as a component in the hermeneutics by which the Truth of Christ can be better discerned. Any interpretation of the reality of Christ and his message that results in one handing a stone to the starving person who comes seeking bread, is irreconcilable with Christ's revelation of himself.

Just what that true hunger is in man that Christ came to satisfy may be best known on Calvary. It is the profoundly suffering man who lives closest to this hunger. Contact with the kerygma of Christ, therefore, demands intimate, continuous community with suffering mankind where the encounter with the deepest desires of human nature normally is to be found.

One's insight into the true meaning of the resurrection, for example, would promise to evolve in a sounder, more valid manner when reflected upon in a cancer ward than when investigated in the security of a university surrounded by healthy persons who have had little or no personal experience of death.

When one witnesses the constant, rapid shifts of interest and emphasis in the theological world today, where new interpretations of the Christian message and new concepts of the relevance of Christ constantly emerge, hold the stage briefly and as quickly disappear, one fears that the relevance in all this has more to do with the latest pre-

---

[74] *Jn.* 6.51.

occupations of an intellectual elite than with the profound, universal hunger of man for God. This is not to ignore the indispensable role of the scholarly approach to the study of Christ, nor is it to assert that contact with human suffering is a substitute for the illuminating teaching of the Gospel, but it is to affirm that one of the conditions of understanding the message of Christ and, therefore, Christ himself, is that one experiences them in the context of encounter with the genuine depth of human nature and desire.

The encounter with the community of men sharing with Christ as His instrument the exemplary, efficient, and meritorious causality of His human nature as well as His prayer life, is the means of contact in breadth and depth with Christ Himself. The question remains as to what the proximate forces are in the just person that impel him to enter into such community.

As we have seen,[75] it is the virtue of Faith that makes man assent to the revelations of God concerning his presence by the fullness of grace in the humanity of Christ. Similarly it is Faith that gives insight into His utilization of the community of the faithful as the instrumentality by which Christ continues his effective presence among men. It is the virtue of Hope which, under the guidance of Faith, inclines one to approach the community of the faithful acting as the instruments of Christ—with confidence that the encounter with the merciful acts of this community is the encounter with Mercy. Lastly, it is the virtue of Charity by which man is drawn in love to God by sharing in the very love with which God loves Himself, and that man encompasses in that same love all men as actual or potential sharers with him in the fellowship of God and eternal life.

According to this interpretation the impulse that led the Church in Vatican II to open her arms to all men was inseparable from the impulse of grace by which the Church opens her arms to God. The approach, at least in preparedness of soul, to all men as brothers under the common Fatherhood of God, is inseparable from the approach to the Father.

---

[75] *Cf.* pp. 442 ff.

THE THEOLOGY OF ECUMENISM

In line with this interpretation, then, ecumenism may be said to have been formally promulgated by Christ when He was asked the question concerning the greatest commandment of the Law and he responded:

> You must love the Lord your God with all your heart, with all your soul, and with all your mind. This is the greatest and the first commandment. The second resembles it: You must love your neighbor as yourself. On these two commandments stand the whole Law and the Prophets also.[76]

In commenting as to whether the precept of the love of neighbor was fittingly expressed, Aquinas set forth both the reason for loving one's neighbor, and the mode of this love. Since his response, which provides for ecumenical friendship on both the natural level and the level of grace, sets forth beautifully the qualities which ideally should bind men to each other and to God in community, I will conclude by offering his statement as a possible model for ecumenism:

> This precept is fittingly expressed for it indicates both the reason for loving and the mode of love.
>
> The reason for loving is indicated in the word *neighbor*, because the reason why we ought to love others out of charity is because they are nigh to us, both as to the natural image of God, and as to the capacity for glory. Nor does it matter whether we say neighbor, or *brother* according to I *Jn.* 4.21, or friend, according to *Levit.* 19.18, because all these words express the same affinity.
>
> The mode of love is indicated in the words as thyself. This does not mean that a man must love his neighbor equally as himself, but in like manner as himself, and this in three ways. First, as regards the end, namely, that he should love his neighbor for God's sake, even as he loves himself for God's sake, so that his love for his neighbor is a *holy* love. Secondly, as regards the rule of love, namely, that a man should not give way to his neighbor in evil, but only in good things, even as he ought to gratify his will in good things alone, so that his

---

[76] *Mt.* 22.36-40.

love for his neighbor may be a *righteous* love. Thirdly, as regards the reason for loving, namely, that a man should love his neighbor, not for his own profit, or pleasure, but in the sense of wishing his neighbor well, even as he wishes himself well, so that his love be a *true* love: since when a man loves his neighbor for his own profit or pleasure, he does not love his neighbor truly, but loves himself.[77]

---

[77] *Summa,* II-II, q. 44, a. 7.

BIBLIOGRAPHY

The bibliography is arranged in three sections. The first lists the works of Aquinas from which the substance of my presentation of traditional Catholic theology was drawn. The second lists the primary books and the third lists the primary articles which have contributed to the evolution of ideas in the study. Since the thesis covers broad areas of theology, I have limited my selection of texts to those only which have proximately influenced the development of the thesis.

Works of Thomas Aquinas

Commentarium on the Nicomadaean Ethics, 2 volumes, translated by C.I. Litzinger (Chicago: Henry Regnery Co., 1964).

Compendium of Theology, tr. by Cyril Vollert (St. Louis: B. Herder Co.,1952).

In Aristotelis Librum De Anima Commentarium, ed. P. Angelus Pirotta (Roma: Marietti, 1936).

In Metaphysican Aristotelis Commentaria, ed. M.R. Cathala (Roma: Marietti, 1935).

Summa Contra Gentiles (Rome: Desclees and Co. Herder, 1952).

Summa Theologica, tr by Fathers of the English Dominican Province (New York: Benzinger Brothers, 1947).

Books

Abbott, W. M., S.J., (ed.) *The Documents of Vatican II*, tr. and ed. by Joseph Gallagher (New York: Guild Press, America Press, Association Press, 1966).

Alitzer, Th., *The Gospel of Christian Atheism* (The Westminster Press, 1966).

Alitzer, Th. and Hamilton, W., Radical Theology and the Death of God (The Bobbs Merrill Company, 1966).

Arintero, J., *The Mystical Evolution in the Development and Vitality othe Church*, 2 volumes, (St. Louis: B. Herder, 1950).

Augustine, Saint, *Confessions*, tr. by Vernon Bourke (New York: Fathers of the Church Inc., 1953).

Barth, K., *Church Dogmatics: A Selection*, tr. by G.W. Bromly (New York: Harper Torchbook, 1961).

------ *The Epistle to the Romans*, tr. by Edwyn Hoskyns (Oxford University Press, 1968).

------ *The Faith of the Church A Commentary on the Apostles' Creed* (Collins, Fontana Book, 1958).

------ *The Humanity of Christ*, tr. by John Newton Thomas (Richmond: John Knox Press, 1963).

Bea, A. Cardinal, *The Unity of Christians*, ed. by Bernard Leeming (London: Geoffrey Chapman, 1963).

------ *Unity in Freedom* (New York: Harper and Row, 1964).

Borne, E., "Atheism" *20th Century Encyclopedia of Catholicism*, volume 91, tr. by S.J. Tester (New York: Hawthorne Books, 1961).

Bouyer, L., *The Spirit and Forms of Protestantism*, tr. by A.W. Littledale (Westminster: The Newman Press, 1956).

Brown, R. McAfee, *The Spirit of Protestantism* (Oxford University Press, 1965).

Callahan, D., (ed.) *The Secular City Debate* (New York: The Macmillan Co., 1966).

Colllins, J., *The Existentialists* (Chicago: Henry Regnery Co., 1964), pp. 40-87, 211-251.

Congar, Y., *Ecumenism and the Future of the Church* (Dubuque: Priory Press, 1964), pp. 97-312.

------ *A History of Theology* (New York: Doubleday, 1968).

Coomaraswamy, A. R., *The Transformation of Nature in Art* (Dover: Constable, 1937).

Cooper, J. C., *The Roots of the Radical Theology* (The Westminster Press, 1967).

Cox, H., *The Secular City* (New York: The Macmillan Co., 1966).

Cunnigham, F. L., *The Christian Life* (Dubuque: Priory Press, 1959).

de Guibert, J., *The Theology of the Spiritual Life* tr. by Paul Barnett (New York: Sheed and Ward, 1956).

Del Prado, N., *De Veritate Fundamentali Philosophiae Christianae* (Friburgi: Ex typis Con. S. Pauli, 1911), pp. 217-254.

Dewart, L., *The Future of Belief* (London: Burns and Oates, 1966).

Dillenberger, J. and Welch, C., *Protestant Christianity. Interpreted Through Its Development* (New York: Chas. Scribner's Sons, 1954).

Edwards, D., *The Honest To God Debate*, ed. by David Edwards (The Westminster Press, 1963).

Eckhart, M., *Meister Eckhart: A Modern Translation*, tr. by B.Blakney (Torch Books, Harper and Rox, 1957), pp. 2-23.

Garrigou-Lagrange, R., *Christian Perfection and Contemplation*, tr. by Sr. Timothea Doyle (St. Louis: B. Herder, 1949).

------ *God-His Existence and His Nature* (St. Louis: B. Herder, 1934).

------ *Grace* (St. Louis: B. Herder, 1952).

------ *The One God* (St. Louis: B. Herder, 1934).

------ *Three Ages of the Spiritual Life*, tr. by Sr. Timothea Doyle (St. Louis: B. Herder, 1954).

------ *The Trinity and God and Creation*, tr. by Frederick Eckhoff (St. Louis: B. Herder, 1952), pp. 340-661.

Giardioni, F., *Alla Presenza Di Dio* (Milano: Ancona, 1965).

Gleason, R., *The Search for God* (New York: Sheed and Ward, 1964).

Groff, W. F. and Metle, D. E., *The Shaping of Modern Christian Thought* (The World Publishing Co., 1968).

Hammer, J., *Karl Barth* (Westminster: The Newman Press, 1962).

Hessert, P., *Christian Life: New Directions in Theology Today* (The Westminster Press, 1967).

John of Saint Thomas, *The Gifts of the Holy Spirit*, tr. by Dominic Hughes (New York: Sheed and Ward, 1957).

Journet, Ch., *The Meaning of Evil* (London: Geoffrey Chapman, 1963).

Lee, A. D., *Vatican II - The Theological Dimension* (Thomist Press, 1963), pp. 551-618.

Leeming, B., *The Churches and the Church* (Westminster: The Newman Press, 1960).

MacQuarrie, J., *God and Secularity*, New Directions in Theology Today, volume III (Philadelphia: The Westminster Press, 1967).

Maritain, J., *Approaches to God* (Harper, 1954).

Mondin, B., *The Principle of Analogy in Protestant and Catholic Theology* (Hague: Martinus Nizhoff, 1963).

Mouroux, J., *The Meaning of Man* (New York: Sheed and Ward, 1948).

O'Meara, Th. and Weisser, C., (eds) *Paul Tillich in Catholic Thought* (Dubuque: Priory Press, 1964), pp. 97-312.

Rahner, K., *Nature and Grace* (New York: Sheed and Ward, 1963), pp. 3-46.

------ "God, Christ, Mary, and Grace," *Theological Investigations*, Vol. I., tr. by Cornelius Ernst (Baltimore: Helicon Press, 1961).

------ "Man in the Church," *Theological Investigations*, Vol. II., tr. by Karl Kruger (Baltimore: Helicon Press, 1963).

------ *Theological Investigations*, Vol. V., (Baltimore: Helicon Press, 1966), pp. 3-22.

------ "Concerning Vatican II: The Man of Today and Religion," *Theological Investigations*, Vol. VI. (Baltimore: Helicon Press, 1969).

Robinson, J., *Honest to God*, (London: SCM Press, 1963).

Royo, A. and Aumann, J., *The Theology of Christian Perfection*, (Dubuque: Priory Press, 1962).

Schillebeeckx, E., *Christ the Sacrament of the Encounter With God*, (New York: Sheed and Ward, 1963).

------ *God and Man* (New York: Sheed and Ward, 1969).

------ *God and the Future of Man*, tr. by N.D. Smith (New York: Sheed and Ward, 1968).

------- *Secularization and Christian Belief in God* (New York: Sheed and Ward, 1968).

Shinn, R. L., *Man: The New Humanism, New Directions in Theology Today* (Philadelphia: The Westminster Press, 1968).

Tavard, G., *Paul Tillich and the Christian Message* (New York: Chas. Scribners, 1962).

Tillich, P., *Systematic Theology*, Vol. I, (London: James Nisbet and Co., 1964).

Weigel, G., *The Modern God: Faith in a Secular Culture* (New York: The Macmillan Co., 1963).

Willems, B., *Karl Barth: An Ecumenical Approach to His Theology*, tr. by Matt. van Velzer (New York: Deus Book, Paulist Press, 1965).

Williams, D. D., *What Present Day Theologians Are Thinking* (Harper, 1967).

ARTICLES

Adwickle, R. F., "Did Christ Believe in God, Some Reflections on Christian Atheism," *New Theology* No. 5, ed. by Martin Marty and Dean G. Peerman (New York: The Macmillan Co., 1969), pp. 62-68.

Baltazar, E., "God in An Evolving World," *Catholic World*, 211, June 1970, pp. 103-106.

Baum, G., "The Ecclesial Reality of the Other Churches," *Concilium*, Vol. IV (New York: Paulist Press, 1965), pp. 62-86.

Bouillard, H., "Human Experience as the Starting Point of a Fundamental Theology," *Concilium*, Vol. VI, tr. by Eileen O'Gorman (New York: Paulist Press, 1965), pp. 79-93.

Bouyer, L., "Gnosticism," *Dictionary of Theology*, tr. by Chas. Underhill Quinn (Tournai: Desclee and Co., 1965), pp. 180-182.

Burke, E. M., "Grace," *New Catholic Encyclopedia*, Vol. 6, (New York: McGraw and Hill Co., 1966), pp. 658-672.

Cognet, L. J., "Jansenism," *New Catholic Encyclopedia*, Vol. 7, (New York: McGraw and Hill Co., 1966), pp. 81-88.

Collins, J., "God and Contemporary Theology," *Commonweal*, Vol. 85, no. 18, June 1970, pp. 528-534.

Congar, Y., "The People of God," *Concilium*, Dogma Vol. 1, tr. by Kathryn Sullivan (New York: Paulist Press, 1964), pp. 11-38.

Connolly, Th. K., "Quietism," New Catholic Encyclopedia, *Vol. 12*, (New York: McGraw and Hill Co., 1966), pp. 26-28.

Cox, H., "Evolutionary Progress and Christian Promise," *Concilium*, Vol. 26, (New York: Paulist Press, 1967), pp. 35-48.

Cunningham, R. L., "Positivism," *New Catholic Encyclopedia*, Vol. 11, (New York: McGraw and Hill Co., 1966), pp. 621-623.

de Guilou, M. J., "Mission: Obstacle Or Stimulus to Ecumenism?," *Concilium*, Vol. 4, tr. by Kathryn Sullivan (New York: Paulist Press, 1965), pp. 5-18.

de Letter, P., "Justification in Protestant Theology," *New Catholic Encyclopedia*, Vol 8, (New York: McGraw and Hill Co., 1966), pp. 88-92.

de Vaux, R., "The Presence and Absence of God in History According to the Old Testament, *Concilium*, Vol. 50, tr. by Theodore Westow (New York: Paulist Press, 1969), pp. 7-20.

Dewart, L., "God and the Supernatural," *New Theology*, No. 5, ed. by Martin Marty and Dean G. Peerman (New York: The Macmillan Co., 1969), pp. 62-68.

Dubarle, D., "Does Man's Manner of Determining His Own Destiny Constitute a Threat to His Humanity," *Concilium*, Vol. 26 (New York: Paulist Press, 1967), pp. 85-96.

Fessard, G., "The Theological Structure of Marxist Atheism," *Concilium*, Vol. 16 (New York: Paulist Press, 1966), pp. t-24.

Fontinell, E., "Transcendent Divinity and Process Philosophy," *New Theology* No. 7, ed. by Martin Marty an Dean G. Peerman (New York: The Macmillan Co., 1970), pp. 172-189.

Klubertanz, G. P., "Analogy," *New Catholic Encyclopedia*, Vol. 1 (New York: McGraw and Hill Co., 1966), pp. 456-458.

Kung, H., "The Charismatic Structure of the Church," *Concilium*, Vol. 4, tr. by Theodore Westow (New York: Paulist Press, 1965), pp. 41-67.

Larcher, Ch., "Divine Transcendence as Another Reason for God's Absence," *Concilium*, Vol. 50, tr. by John Drury (New York: Paulist Press, 1969), pp. 49-64.

Lawler, J. G., "The Future of Belief Debate," *New Theology* No. 5, ed. by Martin Marty and Dean G. Peerman (New York: The Macmillan Co., 1969), pp. 178-190.

Lauer, R. Z., "Deism," *New Catholic Encyclopedia*, Vol. 4 (New York: McGraw and Hill Co., 1966), pp. 721-724.

Lonergan, B. J. F., "The Dehellenization of Dogma," *New Theology*, No.5, ed. by Martin Marty and Dean G. Peerman (New York: The Macmillan Co., 1969), pp. 156-177.

Lyonnet, Saint, "The Presence of Christ in the Spirit of Man," *Concilium*, Vol. 50, tr. by Theodore Westow (New York: Paulist Press, 1969), pp. 93-106.

Macrae, G., "Gnosticism," *New Catholic Encyclopedia*, Vol. 6, (New York: McGraw and Hill Co., 1966), pp. 523-528.

Mascall, E., "The Scientific Outlook on the Christian Message," *Concilium*, Vol. 26 (New York: Paulist Press, 1967), pp. 125-134.

Matteucci, B., Jansenistic Piety," *New Catholic Encyclopedia*, Vol. 7, (New York: McGraw and Hill Co., 1966), pp. 88-92.

Mesthene, E., "Religious Values in the Age of Technology," *Concilium*, Vol. 26, (New York: Paulist Press, 1967), pp. 109-124.

Metz, J., "Unbelief as a Theological Problem," *Concilium*, Vol. 6, tr. by Tarisius Ratter (New York: Paulist Press, 1965), pp. 59-79.

Moltman, J., "Hope Without Faith: an Eschatological Humanism Without God," *Concilium*, Vol. 16, tr. by John Cummings (New York: Paulist Press; 1966), pp. 25-41.

Mondin, B., "Analogy, Theological Use of," *New Catholic Encyclopedia*, Vol. 1 (New York: McGraw and Hill Co., 1966), pp. 465-468.

Murphy, J. L., "Analogy of Faith," *New Catholic Encyclopedia*, Vol. 1, (New York: McGraw and Hill Co., 1966), pp. 468-469.

Murphy-O'Connor, J., "The Presence of God Through Christ in the World," *Concilium*, Vol. 50 (New York: Paulist Press, 1969), pp. 107-120.

Naughton, E. R., "Pantheism," *New Catholic Encyclopedia*, Vol. 10 (New York: Paulist Press, 1966), pp. 947-950.

Nogar, R., "Evolutionary Humanism and the Faith," *Concilium*, Vol. 16 (New York: Paulist Press, 1966), pp. 49-58.

Ogden, Sch., "The Christian Proclamation of God to the So-Called 'Atheistic Age,' " *Concilium*, Vol. 16 (New York: Paulist Press, 1966), pp. 87-98.

Rahner, K., "Christianity and Ideology," *Concilium*, Vol. 6, tr. by Bernard Scott (New York: Paulist Press, 1968), pp. 59-79.

------ "Evolution and Original Sin," *Concilium*, Vol. 26, tr. by Theodore Westow (New York: Paulist Press, 1967), pp. 61-74.

Reis, J., "Manichaeanism," *New Catholic Encyclopedia*, Vol. 9, (New York: McGraw and Hill Co., 1966), pp. 153-160.

Reid, P. J., "Atheism," *New Catholic Encyclopedia*, Vol. 1 (New York: McGraw and Hill Co.), pp. 1000-1003.

Schillebeeckx, E., "The Church and Mankind," *Concilium*, Dogma Vol. 1, tr. by James Byrne (New York: Paulist Press, 1964), pp. 69-102.

Schreiner, J., "Sin As the Cause of Man's Turning Away From God," *Concilium*, Vol. 50, tr. by John Drury (New York: Paulist Press, 1969), pp. 34-48.

Taylor, J. C., "Essence and Existence," *New Catholic Encyclopedia*, Vol. 5 (New York: McGraw and Hill Co., 1966), pp. 548-552.

Vahanian, G., "Theology and the 'End of the Age of Religion,' " *Concilium*, Vol. 16, tr. by Kathryn Sullivan (New York: Paulist Press, 1966), pp. 99-110.

Van Kets, R., "The Dialogue Between The Church and Contemporary Cultures," *Concilium*, Vol. 1 (New York: Paulist Press, 1964), pp. 169-177.

von Balthasar, H. U., "Meeting God in Today's World," tr. by James F. McCue *Concilium*, Vol. VI, (New York: Paulist Press, 1965), pp. 23-41.

Welte, B., "The Philosophical Knowledge of God and the Possibility of Atheism," *Concilium*, Vol. 16, tr. by Eileen O'Gorman (New York: Paulist Press, 1966), pp. 111-130.

Williams, B., "Who Belongs to the Church," *Concilium*, Dogma Vol. 1, tr. by Theodore Westow (New York: McGraw and Hill Co., 1964), pp. 131-152.

www.ingramcontent.com/pod-product-compliance
Lightning Source LLC
Chambersburg PA
CBHW030109240426
43661CB00031B/1344/J